D0786815

World Order, Multipolarism and Terrorism

The Indian Approach

World Order, Multipolarism and Terrorism

The Indian Approach

Debidatta Aurobinda Mahapatra

New Century Publications
New Delhi, India

NEW CENTURY PUBLICATIONS
4800/24, Bharat Ram Road,
Ansari Road, Daryaganj,
New Delhi – 110 002 (India)

Tel.: 011-2324 7798, 4358 7398, 6539 6605
Fax: 011-4101 7798
E-mail: indiatax@vsnl.com • info@newcenturypublications.com
www.newcenturypublications.com

Editorial office:
LG–7, Aakarshan Bhawan,
4754-57/23, Ansari Road, Daryaganj,
New Delhi – 110 002

Tel.: 011-4356 0919

First Published: **2011**

ISBN: **978-81-7708-260-9**

Published by New Century Publications and printed at Salasar
Imaging Systems, New Delhi.

Designs: Patch Creative Unit, New Delhi.

PRINTED IN INDIA

To my mother

Foreword

The reader has in the hands a very important book on world politics, the world as a system, not as the sum of foreign policies of states, nations, regions and civilizations. It is written from an Indian perspective. There should be many, many books like this, written from various perspectives, adding up to what the German physicist and peace researcher Carl Friedrich von Weizsdcker called *Weltinnenpolitik*, global domestic politics.

This is an old Indian perspective, the world as one family, *vasudhaiva kuttumbakam* I refer to in my Peace By Peaceful Means. Beautiful, even if not all families are beautiful, there is the idea of mutual relevance, interdependence. A limit to absolute egoism, a call for solidarity if not altruism. Actually, beyond the Golden Rule the author quotes from the World Parliament of Religions in 1993, with everything ending up to one's own benefit, there is the daoist notion of harmony, to suffer the suffering of others, and enjoy the joy of others. As the author so rightly points out, "any evolving world order must in its core have an eclectic approach", combining world views, picking the best (like I try in my Globalizing God) "according states, big or small, developed or developing equal voice in the global decision making process". And, one might add, giving the peoples equal voice through a UN Peoples Parliament. Thinking global.

And that, of course, leads us beyond terrorism to state terrorism so much more lethal than small needle pricks from non-state terrorism; like in Vietnam, Iraq, Afghanistan. And like in India--who kills more children, aged and women, the Naxalites, or the Indian police-military? May be there is soft and hard power in all four fields of power, political and military, economic and cultural, and caste is very hard economic power, legitimized by very hard aspects of the cultural power of Hinduism?

Thus, there were certainly a Bangladesh mutiny, a Maoist crisis in Nepal, the rise of Taliban in Afghanistan and Pakistan--and there were West Pakistan exploiting East Pakistan grotesquely, a permanent crisis of exploitation of lower castes and casteless, non-Nepali speaking, women, illiterates for ages in Nepal, and five invasions of Afghanistan in modern times for the colonial, military, imperial benefits of the UK, the Soviet Union and the USA and their "chess game". A global perspective is so important in making us see the world from above, all sides to the issues, all aspects, all angles.

We are led into all these problems contemplating what the author calls the Ideal Human Unity, so important to Gandhi. It is there all the time. Today we witness the decline and fall of one more empire, the American one, the decline of the state system in favor of regions (except for the bigger states, the BRIC and the USA), we see the search for unity in the emerging force of local communities and NGOs, in a certain sense also in the transnational corporations who one day will become much more progressive in the struggle against climate change. We see regions taking shape, and the beginning of globalizations with no single civilization dominating.

In short, we need more books like this one and in the meantime, express our gratitude to the author for focusing on such problems!

Versonnex, France   Johan Galtung
September 2010   Professor of Peace Studies
                                                          Founder,
Transcend: A Peace Development Environment Network

About the Book

The book is an attempt in chronicling and analyzing international developments from a non-western perspective. It scrutinizes the prevailing discourse in international politics in the light of recent developments. The analysis adopts a descriptive format while factoring India in the entire gamut of national, regional and international politics and arguing that the developments indicate both challenges and opportunities. The challenges from climate change to confronting and managing troubled regions in the world have become daunting tasks and India's role has become prominent in meeting these challenges. Opportunities too are varied and range from collective shaping of the international dynamics to widening international peace and development discourse in the framework of ideal human unity. India with its non-antagonistic foreign policy projections has a significant role towards the realization of this framework.

Coverage of a wide range of issues including the regional dynamics of Central Eurasia and South Asia, the happenings in Afghanistan-Pakistan and the issue of terrorism have made the book timely. The book is an important reading for all those interested in contemporary international developments and their implications.

About the Author

Debidatta Aurobinda Mahapatra is currently working at the Centre for Central Eurasian Studies, University of Mumbai, Mumbai. He holds Ph.D. degree from Jawaharlal Nehru University (JNU), New Delhi. In 2010, he was a Charles Wallace Fellow at Queen's University, Belfast, UK. He was a Visiting Fellow at Institute for Conflict Research, Belfast in November 2008.

He is the author of several books including *India-Russia Partnership: Kashmir, Chechnya and Issues of Convergence* (2006) and *Central Eurasia: Geopolitics, Compulsions and Connections* (2008). Dr. Mahapatra has published more than 100 articles in journals and magazines including *Peace and Conflict Review* (San Jose), *Central Eurasian Studies Review* (Ohio), *Conflict Trends* (Durban), *International Studies* (New Delhi) and *India Quarterly* (New Delhi).

Contents

Preface

Contemporary international relations have evolved with developments transcending national and regional frontiers. The developments indicate shaping of politics of nations with the changes in the earlier paradigms and notions about state system, interstate relations and their implications. In the last decade international politics has witnessed developments with wider strategic, political and socio-economic ramifications. Developments in Central Eurasia, Balkans, Trans-Caucasus, and South Asia particularly the Afghanistan-Pakistan region have significantly shaped international political discourse. The locus of international political discourse has certainly shifted from west to east, with the world becoming increasingly multipolar in the post-cold war world.

In the changing world, India has potential to emerge as a responsible global power. It can play a vital role in shaping the evolving contours of international politics towards a friendly world, which recognizes diversities and reconciles differences. On the eve of independence in 1947, one of India's leading philosophers of 20th century Sri Aurobindo in his message had envisaged five dreams for free Indian republic, the fourth of which emphasized on India's role in promoting the ideal human unity. In the emerging world order, India is poised to free itself from the fixed coordinates and adopt a pragmatic approach to its surroundings and its relations with the nations of the world. Its management of relations with troubled neighbourhood and confrontation with issues like extremism pose challenges as well as opportunities.

The book is divided into seven chapters excluding conclusion. The first chapter analyzes the ideal human unity framework to set a barometer for conduct of states. The second chapter elaborates one of the crucial trends in the post-cold war politics—multipolarism. The third and fourth chapters focus on the reigning international debates involving multiple players while analyzing international developments in various regions of the world including the Balkans, Trans-Caucasus and AfPak region. The fifth chapter focuses on terrorism, one of the most complex issues of the post-cold war world. The sixth chapter particularly focuses on South Asia and turmoil it passed through in the past decade. The last chapter reflects on India's foreign policy and relations to analyze how in the post-cold war world Indian policy makers have endeavoured to adopt a multi-vector foreign policy approach while pursuing national interests in a non-antagonistic fashion.

I am thankful to all those who made the idea of this book possible. I am thankful to Johan Galtung for sparing his precious time to write foreword for the book. Special mention must be made of Vladimir Maximenko, Director of Strategic Culture Foundation, who published some of my initial thoughts on international developments in his magazine. I must also thank Andrei Volodin who is always helpful as a senior colleague. My thanks are also due to Emanuela del Re and Antonio Rosa for their cooperation. I am indebted to my wife Seema who went through all the chapters and made useful comments and suggestions. Finally, I thank Sandeep Sury, Chief Executive, New Century Publications, New Delhi for publishing the book on time. However, the inadequacies of the book, if any, are mine.

Mumbai   **Debidatta Aurobinda Mahapatra**
June 2010

Abbreviations

AELM	APEC Economic Leaders' Meeting
ANSF	Afghan National Security Forces
APEC	Asia Pacific Economic Cooperation
ASEAN	Association of South East Asian Nations
AVM	Advanced Technology Vessel
BASIC	Brazil, South Africa, India and China
BDR	Bangladesh Rifles
BRIC	Brazil, Russia, India and China
CBMs	Confidence Building Measures
CIS	Commonwealth of Independent States
CPN-UML	Communist Party of Nepal (Unified Marxist Leninist)
CTBT	Comprehensive Test Ban Treaty
ECO	Economic Cooperation Organization
EU	European Union
FATA	Federally Administered Tribal Areas
HM	Hizbul Mujahideen
HUJI	Harkat ul Jihadi Islami
IAEA	International Atomic Energy Agency
IDPs	Internally Displaced Persons
IMF	International Monetary Fund
IMU	Islamic Movement of Uzbekistan
ISAF	International Security Assistance Force
ISRO	Indian Space Research Organization
JeM	Jaish-e-Mohammad
LeT	Lashkar-e-Toiba
LOC	Line of Control
LTTE	Liberation Tigers of Tamil Elam
NAM	Non-aligned Movement
NATO	North Atlantic Treaty Organization
NDA	National Democratic Alliance
NPT	Non Proliferation Treaty
NWFP	North West Frontier Province

NSG	Nuclear Suppliers Group
OCHA	Office for the Coordination on Humanitarian Affairs
OIC	Organization of the Islamic Conference
OPEC	Organization of Petroleum Exporting Countries
RTC	Round Table Conference
SAARC	South Asian Association for Regional Cooperation
SCO	Shanghai Cooperation Organization
SEATO	South East Atlantic Treaty Organization
SU	Soviet Union
TTP	Tehrik-e-Taliban Pakistan
UCPN-M	Unified Communist Party of Nepal (Maoist)
ULFA	United Liberation Front of Assam
UN	United Nations
UNESCO	United Nations Educational, Scientific and Cultural Organization
UNFCCC	United Nations Framework Convention on Climate Change
UNICEF	United Nations Children's Fund
UNSC	United Nations Security Council
UPA	United Progressive Alliance
WB	World Bank
WHO	World Health Organization
WTO	World Trade Organization

1

From Nation-State to
Ideal Human Unity

This chapter makes the case for the evolution of the
current state system towards ideal human unity as it argues that
the current nation-state system and the bodies created at its
behest have not been able enough to create and sustain a stable
world order and provide peace and harmony. Whether the
situations like Afghanistan or the poverty in developing
countries or estrangement in social life or differences over
global commons or the menace of terrorism the reigning global
order has been unable to confront and mitigate manifold
challenges. Drawing substantially from the Indian thinker Sri
Aurobindo's concept of ideal human unity [1], this chapter
argues international peace and stability can not be achieved by
mere mechanical coming together of nation-states but by some
kind of psychological understanding and feeling of the
necessity of the world union. Following this line the chapter
argues the evolution of human society cannot stop at the
formulations like state and nation rather the evolutionary urge
points towards its culmination in ideal human unity. The
widest possible common framework for the human society in
which three supreme values: liberty, equality and fraternity can
coexist in harmony can be materialized when the nation states
come out of their narrow confinements reflected in aggressive
ideologies and practices.

Nation-State, Nationalism and World Order
Sri Aurobindo makes a distinction between the concepts of
state and nation – the state represents the transition of society
from the infrarational organic stage to the rational stage and it
attempts to bring about an organic unity of the aggregate
people's political, social and economic life through centralized

administration. The need for compactness, single-mindedness and uniformity to promote security and strengthen national defence is sought to be fulfilled by the state-idea. According to him, "The state has been most successful and efficient means of unification and has been best able to meet the various needs which the progressive aggregate life of societies has created for itself and is still creating." [2] The state is only an outward form, a convenient machinery to enforce unity and uniformity, while the nation idea implies the living unity of the aspirations and powers of its peoples. A common race-origin, a common language, a common culture and geographical unity may be its elements but it is basically a psychological unit with a distinct personality or 'soul' of its own. The evolution of the state follow this order: man by nature seeks the association of his fellow beings, and this seeking of association of individuals begins within the family followed by the tribe, then the clan, the community and subsequently the nation. But the progression does not end at the nation idea because there is a drive in Nature towards larger agglomerations and this drive can lead to the final establishment of the largest of all and the ultimate union of the world's people. [3]

Though the concept of nationalism emerged in the 18th century Europe, it emerged not as a concept embodying evolutionary consciousness but proceeded from some kind of expediency, mainly geographical and historical. In the beginning, it surfaced as a secondary or even tertiary necessity which resulted not from anything inherent in the vital nature of human society but from circumstances. [4] It lacked the idea of larger human unity in its core. Though Sri Aurobindo did not reject the role of external factors, i.e. geography, language, and common objectives, or the internal factors like common sentiment and culture in the emergence of the nation-state idea, he applied a more nuanced approach. He argues, "nationalism is not a mere political programme; nationalism is a religion ...

If you are going to be a nationalist, if you are giving assent to this religion of nationalism, you must do it in the religion spirit." [5] On the surface this approach may give a sense for the advocacy of crude revivalism, but a deeper analysis does not hold this viewpoint true. Karan Singh argues, "Sri Aurobindo's nationalism never descended into chauvinism or obscurantist revivalism. He always placed it in a broader, international context." [6] In his *Open Letter to Countrymen,* written in 1909, Sri Aurobindo emphasized, "our ideal of patriotism proceeds on the basis of love and brotherhood and it looks beyond the unity of the nations and envisages the ultimate unity of mankind. But it is a unity of brothers, equals and freemen that we seek" [7] But, the evolutionary principle which Sri Aurobindo emphasized in his analysis of nationalism does not find place in the works of other scholars on nationalism. E. J. Hobsbawm (quoting Stalin) writes, "a nation is a historically evolved, stable community of language, territory, economic life and psychological make-up manifested in a community of culture." Benedict Anderson emphasizes on the psychological aspect and writes, "it (nation) is an imagined political community- and imagined as both inherently limited and sovereign." [8] Among other differences, Anderson's nationalism does not take into account the evolutionary and ideal nature that forms an integral part of Sri Aurobindo's nationalism.

The psychological feeling of being in nation brings unity among people of different shades of opinion as it makes the principle of unity in diversity possible. It has the following utilities: first, it brings the sense of unison among people; second, it helps in developing a collective consciousness leading to collective goals in national affairs; and third, it transcending national divides bears the seed of a larger formation, towards a greater unity of human beings. Nationalism is evolutionary in nature and its evolution towards a higher form of synthesis of mankind is mandated in its very nature. There is always an urge in nation idea even in a way to 'destroy it' in the larger synthesis of mankind. In the growth of human civilization nationalism is an intermediary stage towards higher forms of union, transcending narrow national boundaries because the nation idea finds its consummation in the development of ideal human unity. But, the nation idea must be developed to its full before any possibility of formation of world union arises.

In *The ideal of Human Unity* Sri Aurobindo explicates the possibility of emergence of world union. For him, the exact name does not matter, whether it is called world union or federation of states, what matters is the highest possible achievement of human civilization in which different nations and different cultures live in peace and harmony, as in one family. The characteristic feature of Sri Aurobindo's concept of nationalism is the development of a crucial tool to explicate the instability in the world order and the crises that afflict it by making a distinction between 'national ego' and 'nation-soul'. While national ego, i.e. a vague sense of group subjectivity is reflected in national idiosyncrasies, habits, prejudices and marked mental tendencies, nation-soul embodies a deeper awareness of group subjectivity. [9]

While national ego is a barrier towards larger unity of mankind, nation-soul has in itself a tendency towards larger agglomerations of mankind. Wherever there is domination of national ego, there is a tendency on part of national leaders to profess supremacy of their nation and to proclaim their right to expand into other territories, thus leading to imperialism. Whether it is British or French or German imperialism, an inherent urge was prominent on part of those nations to assert supremacy and domination over other nations and cultures. This tendency of national ego and domination persists even now as the recent developments in the international politics indicate. These developments are dealt in detail in the later chapters.

For Sri Aurobindo nation-state system is not the culmination of the formations of human civilization, rather it is an intermediary phase for the ultimate ideal human unity. Nationalism is neither aggressive nor imperialistic rather it is a significant phase towards the evolution of ideal human unity. While Sri Aurobindo argued for moderation of aggressive nationalism towards evolution of larger human unity in the wake of the First World War, almost same line of argument was followed by two worth mentioning scholars on the eve of the Second World War. Clarence Streit's *Union Now* and W. B. Curry's *The Case for Federal Union* were full of insightful arguments with roadmaps for moderation of the concept of aggressive nationalism, especially practiced in Germany under the leadership of Hitler. Curry appealed nations to come out of their narrow grooves to make the idea of federal union possible. For the survival of the civilization, Curry argued, "the groups which we call nations should become like other groups, less fierce, less exclusive, less aggressive, less dominating, admitting allegiance to, and submitting to some measure of control by the community consisting of mankind as a whole." [10]

Ideal Human Unity

Nationalism in its true spirit leads to internationalism as it cannot provide the anchor for the final solution to the problems emerging out of the nation-state mechanism. When nation-states do not mature and transform themselves to a larger possible human unity, they become subject to evils of aggressive and imperialist impulses. Only when the spirit of nationalism is developed to its full, it graduates to the higher goal of human unity. The nature which embodies the world is basically a 'pluriverse' not a universe, which contains in its core an inherent urge towards multiple poles of interaction which negotiates and reconciles diverse forms of expression as is the case with the nation-idea embodying plurality and diversity.

Attempts were made in the past to establish some kind of world order, howsoever limited in scale, but these failed mainly because these were not based on intrinsic values of the ideal human unity but purely on mechanical and superficial means. Empires like the Roman and the Persian adopted absolutist and monarchical means to bring some kind of unity and order among divergent units but those attempts failed because they were not addressed to the basic values of humanity in its genuine form. Sri Aurobindo developed the idea of religion of humanity to make his scheme of ideal human unity a feasible initiative. The underlying basis of this religion is not any kind of dogma or exclusivist tenets or ideas, rather three supreme values- liberty, equality and fraternity. This supreme social trinity or 'three godheads of soul,' as he names it, can provide a stable basis for a new world order based on peace and harmony.

However, these three supreme values cannot develop and transform the world until the nation states rise to the occasion and cultivate them in habit, thinking and ways of life. In fact none of these values has really been realized in true spirit in spite of all the progress that has been achieved by the human society. Sri Aurobindo writes: "The liberty that has been so loudly proclaimed as an essential of modern progress is an outward and mechanical and unreal liberty. The equality that has been so much sought after and battled for is equally an outward and mechanical and will turn out to be an unreal equality. Fraternity is not even claimed to be a practicable principle of the ordering of life and what is put forward as its substitute is the outward and mechanical principle of equal association or at best a comradeship of labour." [11]

Liberty, equality and fraternity are largely in conflict with each other, unless transformed and reconciled in a balanced framework. Liberty on its own emphasizes on human freedom, some kind of laissez faire, thus neglecting the principle of equality. Similarly, the principle of equality on its own contradicts the principle of liberty as it emphasizes on parity - at the cost of individual freedom, hence the never-ending debate in political theory concerning the principles of liberty and equality. Sri Aurobindo argues these two apparently contradictory principles can be reconciled with the higher principle of fraternity. But this reconciliation appears unworkable in the present scheme of things which put emphasis on mere perfunctory order because fraternity as it is implied in its present working means mere formal coming of nations together or just some kind of formal unity without change in character and motives.

The religion of humanity is the true embodiment of the three supreme values in proper harmony. Liberty in its true sense is not exclusive. Freedom not only implies 'freedom to' but also 'freedom from'. Similarly, equality in its true sense not only implies equitable rights but also equitable duties. This harmonious working of the principles of liberty and equality is possible only when the spirit of brotherhood encompasses all the human minds including the minds that govern the nation states. Only then the ideal for human unity will emerge not as a distant possibility but as an imperative for the mankind because, as Sri Aurobindo argues, with the passing of time nations have come closer to each other. The major contributions made by 'science, commerce and rapid communication' [12] in this regard cannot be ignored. His allusion in the early decades of the 20th Century to these three important vehicles of globalization brings forth the seminal character of this approach of ideal human unity and its relevance in the 21st century. As the achievements of commerce, science and technology transcend national boundaries, similarly the religion of humanity transcends all narrow national mentalities and all those forces that confine national mentality to rigidities.

The basic underlying motive behind the ideal of human unity is not the establishment of any particular kind of formation like world state or world federation or confederation. The objective is the achievement of the highest possible world unity among nations and their peoples. It may take the shape of a world state or federation or confederation, that is not more important but what is more important is that the nations must come out of the confinements of the collective ego to participate in the widest possible human unity. Hence, the world union will neither be rigid nor dogmatic nor subject to dictates of a particular nation or group of nations. It will not succumb to hegemonic ambitions of any particular nation because a true world union will be based on the 'principle of equality in which considerations of size and strength will not enter.' [13] It will give equal respect to diverse cultures and patterns of life. It will, in the language of *Crossing the Divide: Dialogue among Civilizations* [14], recognize the principles of equality and distinction, not domination and disintegration. It will not allow big, powerful nations to usurp the rights of other nations in violation of the basic principles of the world body.

This world order will be akin to a rich tapestry in which different shades of colour are beautifully placed in their own places or like an ornament in which different precious stones are placed in their requisite order. *Crossing the Divide* written under the auspices of the UN and forwarded by then UN Secretary General, Kofi Annan challenges the theories of 'Clash of Civilizations' and 'End of History' and posits hope on the UN for the resolution of the global problems. It envisages the emergence of the UN as a kind of 'global social contract,' which recognizes the principle of equality and distinction among the nations and rejects the old paradigm of international relations and advocates for a new paradigm governing the relations between nations on the following bases: equal footing, reassessment of 'enemy', dispersion of power, stake holding, individual responsibility, and issue-driven alignments. [15]

International Bodies and Ideal Human Unity
Did the League of Nations and the United Nations Organization live up to the expectations with which they were established? Did they make in any sense the world better for the progress of nations and for the humanity at large? Both these mechanisms were not free from defects in their origin

and conception. Sri Aurobindo writes, "the League (the League of Nations, established after the end of the First World War) was eventually formed with America outside it as an instrument of European diplomacy, which was a bad omen for its future." [16] He warned about the danger of assigning 'preponderant place to the five great powers in the Security Council' of the UN, thus ensuring a 'strong surviving element of oligarchy' in the international body. [17] He further warned that its defects might lead to pessimism and doubt regarding its final success.

The League of Nations failed because it was not truly representative of the nations and the member nations frequently violated its principles. Many members of the League gave the impression that they joined the League not for universal peace and harmony but the fulfilment of their narrow interests. This was reflected in frequent violation of the League principles and agreements like Kellog-Briand Pact and Nine-Power treaty and many others. The key player in the formation of the League, the US did not join it because of opposition from its Senate. The humiliation of Germany at the Versailles treaty in 1919 opened up the possibilities of the rise of aggressive nationalism. Instead of resolving the problem it gave vent to the suppressed anger and frustration on part of Germany to come out in open two decades later. These developments finally led to the Second World War, shattering the hopes for the building of a new world order.

In the emerging post-cold war scenario the UN could have provided avenues for divergent nations to display their diversities in a harmonious way under one roof, where the differences among them could be resolved under the framework of international law applicable equally to all nations. But the sanctioning of veto power to the five permanent members of the UN Security Council marred the prospects of the rise of an egalitarian world structure. As the past records show, this veto power has been exercised arbitrarily by the big powers for the fulfilment of their interests. Ostrom J. Moller, an advocate of world governance, argued, "The five victorious nations decided that they should govern the world. Is that the best solution? Whether the world should be governed by the Security Council is itself an interesting question, but if so should it then be these five nations who should do it?" [18] Moller also pointed that a new international system cannot be built upon sovereign nation-states as participant but has to be built on the transfer of sovereignty from the nation-state to international institutions. He does not reject nation-states as participants in international mechanism but they have to partially transfer their sovereignty. [19] For this to happen some kind of 'creative destruction' on part of the nation-states need to take place.

The UN, which emerged as a 'global social contract', appeared to be more representative in comparison to its predecessor the League of Nations. The General Assembly, comprise almost all nations of the world (at present the number of the members is 192; in 1945, the year it was established, the number was 51). The Assembly has been working on the principle of one nation, one vote, thus giving equal voice to all nations, big or small, powerful or marginal. Through its various bodies like UNESCO, UNICEF and WHO the UN has done a commendable work in adopting and organizing welfare activities throughout the world. This supreme international body was expected to provide the ground for the emergence of the ideal human unity but as its functions later showed the powerful nations in the Security Council used their special powers arbitrarily.

The defects in the working of the UN and in its structure can be summarized in the following points. First, the system built up more than fifty years ago has not developed suitable mechanisms to adapt itself to the changing circumstances. The menace of terrorism, the challenges emerging out of market economy and globalization, the accentuating north-south divide, the problems related to human rights and democracy have not been tackled by the world body appropriately.

Though the theories of Clash of Civilization and End of History have been challenged by the proponents of the UN system, no grand alternative or any kind of mechanism to address these emerging problems have been devised. Second, the decision-making power has been concentrated in few powerful centres. The Permanent-5 countries by the means of veto power have weakened the real motive behind the establishment of the UN. Third, the UN lacks the effective means to enforce its rules and regulations. It lacks adequate financial means to implement its plans and programmes. [20] What Curry said about seventy years ago seemed to be true now: "There still remains the idea that nationalism somehow is defensible in terms of freedom and must there be resisted. This obsession is very deeply rooted". [21] Fourth, in many cases the effectiveness of the UN has been challenged or dominated by other international bodies like International Monetary Fund and World Bank, controlled by the developed nations.

The weakness of the UN machinery as mentioned above does not nullify its validity. Further improvements can be made on this system by gradual reforms. In this context two simultaneous developments need to be undertaken. First, nations must shun narrow considerations and participate in the international process towards peace and development in an egalitarian framework. The organizations like European Union, Association of South-East Asian Nations, Asia-Pacific Economic Cooperation, G-8 and G-20 have already shown the ways to success, when working in unison. This collective spirit should be imparted in the working of the UN. [22] Second, the structure of the UN and its decision-making process needs reforms. Measures like the enlargement of the membership of the Security Council, providing financial autonomy, and giving wider recognition to the leadership of the Secretary General can be undertaken to this effect.

There have been attempts to impart greater visibility and dynamism to multilateral organizations like the G-20 towards bringing regional centres of economic power in playing an important role in global economic management. The rising clout of the G-20 and coming together of developed and developing countries shows a clear inclination on part of crucial players in international politics to promote the path of multilateralism to manage global economic crisis. Since 1999 the grouping has played an effective role to set common principles for sound economic management, broaden the Washington consensus on economic development, devise strong measures to curb terror finance. It has also adopted the Accord for Sustained Growth outlining policies to promote monetary and financial stability, enhance domestic and international competition, and empower people to participate successfully in markets. The G-20 may appear small but the grouping represents about 90 percent of the world's economic output with 67 percent of world population and its success in meeting global crisis show that this body with diverse countries with diverse levels of growth and societal make up have struck a right balance between legitimacy and effectiveness and met the challenge better than any similar effort. [23]

The Canadian leader Paul Martin, who chaired the first G-20 meeting, argued that the G-20 model which is primarily a multilateral economic instrument in international politics can be replicated in the form L-20 (Leaders-20) to meet the global challenges. The lessons drawn from working of the G-20, i.e. crucial decisions are taken at political level, commonality despite differences and focus on larger issues of stability and predictability can be further extended in creating another organization L-20 which can focus on political issues confronting nations of the world. The globalized world where borders seldom work as barriers in the spread of ideas, commerce or devious forces like terrorism or diseases or weapons of mass destruction or environmental concerns justify the creation of an L-20.

The complex international relations of the 21st century appear to be fraught with same old problems as in past towards creating a multilateral body to solve the global crises. For instance, in case of the proposed L-20 who will be the members? Who will set the agenda for the body to deliberate upon? Whether the body will meet the issues of common concern such as terrorism (which is much contested), or environmental degradation (too much divergence as the Copenhagen summit of 2009 shows), or pandemics (politics about vaccines, etc.) with effective mechanism to enforce its decisions, or it will just impart guidelines leaving to nation-states to follow at their will? The post-cold war (still it is cold war with the prefix post) so far lacks the needed momentum to evolve a global egalitarian architecture. Attempts or ideas such as L-20 will be fraught with the similar problems as that of the UN. The structural and conceptual reform of the UN including inclusion of new permanent members such as the rising nations of India, Brazil and South Africa in the Security Council has been marred by disagreements. The reluctance on part of some of the big powers to come out of their national egos and accommodate the rising aspirations in the council has delayed the reform process. The same kind of 'confinement' and 'exclusion' mentality will likely continue for the near future, thus obstructing any attempt towards ideal human unity.

Unless the UN is transformed into a genuine representative of divergent nations, it will not be to cater the divergent aspirations of nation states in a global framework in a harmonious blending. The concern expressed by Sri Aurobindo regarding the future of the UN has also been echoed by the noted scientist Albert Einstein, "The United Nations is an extremely important and useful institution provided the peoples and governments of the world realize that it is merely a transitional system towards the final goal, which is the establishment of supranational authority vested with sufficient legislative and executive powers to keep the peace." [24] Similarly, Emery Reves in his *The Anatomy of Peace* writes, "World government is not an 'ultimate goal' but an

immediate necessity. It has been overdue since 1914". [25]
Likewise, the Parliament of World Religions in 1993
advocated for the adoption of the Golden Rule [26] by the
nations for the evolution of a world union.

Golden Rule has both positive and negative dimensions: in
its positive dimension it embodies the principle: do unto others
what you would want others to do unto you; and in its negative
dimension it embodies the principle: do not do unto others
what you would not want others to do unto you. If nations
could adopt this rule shared by all great religious traditions the
authors of the *Crossing the Divide* argue, it will help in the
evolution of a global ethic to be equally observed and
respected by different nations towards emergence of a
multipolar world without compromising national interests
rather elevating them to a higher pedestal in which peace,
harmony and development will be core principles.

Positioning India
The element of force as effective means for the
establishment of an ideal world union is ruled out in the
scheme of ideal human unity. History makes it evidently clear
that force may bring some kind of formal world unity but it
will not last long unless the mechanism of force gives way to
the means of harmony and order. Curry stipulated the
following conditions for the emergence of a genuine world
federation: independent control of foreign policy, common
armed force, common economic policy, common control of
communications, international control of currency, and
effective world public opinion. Streit emphasized on the
following points: union citizenship, union defence force, union
customs-free economy, union money, and union postal and
communications system. [27]

Though Sri Aurobindo analyzed the possibility of
administrative unity, common economic policy, common
military force, he did not give any specific guidelines
regarding the future structure of the world body. What he

emphasized most was the cultivation of the religion of humanity among the nations. The emergence of world unity for Sri Aurobindo is the manifestation of a higher consciousness in the world. The march from the state to the higher, world state can be explained as a movement of nature from infrarational to rational and then to suprarational forms of consciousness. Sri Aurobindo's ideal of human unity provides the rationale for the nation states to come out of the hegemonic ambitions and related foreign policy postures pursued by them as clearly reflected in turmoil of the past decade. Sidney Kartus observes: "The Western world knows far more of Marx's call to the working men to unite than it does of Sri Aurobindo's message to the humanity to unite. Yet it is a message such as that of Sri Aurobindo with which humanity must become familiar and which it must need in order attain human unity." [28]

An integral part of Sri Aurobindo's concept of nationalism was spiritualism. He advocated spiritual nationalism during the Indian freedom struggle. In his editorials in *Bande Mataram*, he demanded for complete independence from the British domination against the moderate demand for dominion status as, he argued, *swaraj* (self-rule) of India was not a factor sole to India herself but was an imperative for the larger cause of humanity. He, thus, demanded complete independence for India and for the achievement of that goal advocated spiritual nationalism, having four-fold dimensions: *swadeshi* (self-reliance), *swaraj*, boycott and national education. Such an approach, he argued, will arouse national consciousness for India's freedom so that India with her non-antagonistic posture can play an important role towards ideal human unity. In his message on the eve of first Independence Day on 15 August 1947, he outlined five dreams about India and humanity. While the third dream was about the formation of a world union, the fourth one emphasized India's spiritual role in promoting the ideal of human unity. India with its rich cultural heritage and pluralistic character could play a vital role towards bringing nations together for the larger objective of ideal human unity.

Once the principle of ideal human unity is embedded in the approaches of nations in their mutual conducts, though a difficult proposition in the current state of affairs keeping in view the post-cold war developments, then the world order free from aggressive tendencies will be stable and the question of force as a foreign policy tool will become largely obsolete. Whether it is 'peaceful rise of Chine' or 'rise of India' or 'rise of Asian powers' or 'decline of the West' these developments will not be viewed in the ambit of zero sum game in international politics as they will emerge as facts to contend with in evolving international politics. The power alignments meant to contain one power or the other will be viewed differently from the evolutionary perspective towards ideal human unity. India's relations vis-à-vis other powers particularly China with which India enjoys an asymmetric relationship can be analyzed in this context. India-China relations can be described by the biological aphorism as malnutrition of political relations and surfeit of economic relations.

China is India's second largest trade partner though they display disagreements on various issues including border, terrorism, principles governing bilateral and multilateral relationship. Lee Kuan Yew in an article analyzed how in March 2005 the US Secretary of State Condoleezza Rice in New Delhi lured Indian leadership to cooperate with the US to contain China and in return "America will help India become a world power," and posed the question with a sense of disagreement "Will India line up with the U.S. against its powerful neighbour, China, as Japan has? India has a deep sense of its separate destiny." [29] India's foreign policy in its core has the principle of accommodation and appreciation, clearly reflected in the statement by Indian Prime Minister Manmohan Singh, "The world is large enough to accommodate the growth and ambitions of both our countries

(India and China). I do not look upon our relations with the US as meant to rival China. I look forward to enhanced cooperation with China." [30]

In the coming decades the world's economic centre of gravity will move from the Atlantic to the Pacific and Indian oceans with the rise of India and China, but it does not predicate that the world will then be free from disorder, instability and violence unless a framework is evolved to contain the aggressive nationalist spirit that still looms large in the policies of nation-states. This further reinforces the ideal of human unity which is predicated on the premise that nation-states must come out of their aggressive mindset to make the unity feasible. India in the post-cold war situation has aspired to multi-task its foreign policy by simultaneously engaging diverse powers both perceived friends and enemies. India since independence has made rapid strides in development as much as that at least the 'grave doubts in the Western mind' [31] about India's capability to play an effective role in international politics has vanished in the post-cold war world.

The Nuclear Suppliers' Group's waiver on the recent Indo-US nuclear deal reflects India's acceptability as a responsible rising power. The philosophical as well historical background of India's foreign policy, with having roots as early as 6th Century BC, has in core promotion of peace and rejection of violence. This is well reflected in the teachings and philosophy of spiritual and political leaders including Mahatma Gandhi and Sri Aurobindo. This tradition was espoused and practised by the father of the Indian nation Mahatma Gandhi, whose influence on the making of India's foreign policy is indisputable as the first Prime Minister of India, Jawaharlal Nehru was his ardent follower. In fact the principles of non-alignment, peaceful coexistence have in their core India's non-antagonistic approach, which held in a very literal sense that human beings were the nation and that the behaviour of every individual ultimately moulded the fate of his country. [32]

The rapid strides in India's development and increasing

circle of its foreign policy have maintained synchrony with this traditional core of India's foreign policy. India has broken out of the 'claustrophobic confines of South Asia', [33] and looked forward to extend its neighbourhood across the Pacific and the Atlantic. The principle of accommodation and non-antagonistic postures embedded in foreign policy approach of India provide it a higher pitch to play a crucial role in crafting a framework in which nation-states can collaborate towards a world of harmony and order without a single centre of domination but with multiple centres of interaction and cooperation.

References
1. Sri Aurobindo, *The Human Cycle, The Ideal of Human Unity, and The War and Self-determination* (Pondicherry: Sri Aurobindo Ashram, 1962).
2. Ibid, p. 618.
3. Ibid, p. 797.
4. Ibid, p. 743.
5. Karan Singh, *Prophet of Indian Nationalism* (Bombay: Bharatiya Vidya Bhavan, 1991), p. 78.
6. Karan Singh, "Towards an Assessment of Sri Aurobindo as a Political Thinker", in Kishore Gandhi, ed., *Contemporary Relevance of Sri Aurobindo* (Pondicherry: Sri Aurobindo Ashram, 1972), p. 55.
7. Ibid.
8. E. J. Hobsbawm, *Nations and Nationalism Since 1870: Programme, Myth, Reality* (Cambridge: Cambridge University Press, 1993); and Benedict Anderson, *Imagined Communities: Reflections on the Origin and Spread of Nationalism* (London: Verso, 1991).
9. J.N. Mohanty, *Essays on Indian Philosophy, Traditional and Modern* (Delhi: Oxford University Press, 1993), p. 142.
10. W.B. Curry, *The Case for Federal Union* (Middlesex: Penguin Book Ltd., 1939), p. 65.
11. Sri Aurobindo, *The Human Cycle ...*, pp. 762-763.
12. Ibid, p. 617.
13. Ibid, p. 783.
14. Picco Giandomenico and et al, *Crossing the Divide: Dialogue*

Among Civilizations (New Jersey: Sheton Hall University, 2001).

15. Ibid, pp. 109-152.
16. Sri Aurobindo, *The Human Cycle* ..., p. 710.
17. Ibid, p. 782.
18. Ostrom J. Moller, *The End of Internationalism or World Governance?* (Westport: Praeger, 2000), p. 173.
19. Ibid, p. 146.
20. Alexandra Novosseloff gives some well-thought out suggestions for the reform of the United Nations. She holds the view that the UN has failed to anticipate emerging problems concerning globalization, ethnicism, poverty, migration, IT revolution, etc. She suggests for both structural and conceptual reforms of this world body. For details of her arguments see, Alexandra Novosseloff, "Revitalizing of the United Nations: Anticipation and Prevention as Primary Goals," *Strategic Analysis*, vol. 25, no. 8, November 2001, pp. 945-963.
21. Curry, *The Case for Federal Union*, p. 77.
22. Various non-governmental organizations such as World Constitution and Parliament Association, World Citizens' Assembly, World Association of World Federalists, International Registry of World Citizens and many others have launched movements to bring a just and harmonious union among the nations. For more information about these movements, see Samar Basu, *The UNO, the World Government and the Ideal of World Union* (Pondicherry: Sri Aurobindo Ashram, 1999).
23. Paul Martin, "A Global Answer to Global Problems: The Case for a New Leaders' Forum," *Foreign Affairs*, vol. 84, no. 3, May-June 2005, pp. 2-6.
24. Basu, *The UNO, the World Government* ..., p. 1.
25. Ibid, p. 4.
26. Giandomenico and et al, *Crossing the Divide* ..., p. 74.
27. For detail elaboration of Curry's and Streit's schemes of world federation see, Curry, *The Case for Federal Union* ..., pp. 107-114 and 147.
28. Sidney Kartus, "World Unity", in H. Chaudhuri and F. Speigelberg, ed., *The Integral Philosophy of Sri Aurobindo* (London: George Allen and Unwin Ltd., 1960), p. 314.
29. Lee Kuan Yew, "A Rising Asia," Forbes Magazine, 25 July

2005, http://www.forbes.com/forbes/2005/0725/039.html
30. Ibid.
31. To quote Vijay Lakshmi Pandit, India's Ambassador to the US from 1949 to 1952, "After eight years of independence India's foreign policy still gives rise to grave doubts in the Western mind" (p. 432). For detail elaboration of India's foreign policy in the initial years of its independence see, Vijay Lakshmi Pandit, "India's Foreign Policy," *Foreign Affairs*, vol. 34, no. 3, April 1956, pp. 432-440.
32. Ibid, p. 434.
33. Bhabani Sen Gupta, "India in the Twenty-first Century," *International Affairs*, vol. 73, no. 2, 1997, p. 309.

2

Towards Multipolarism: The Rise of BRIC

The last decade appeared eventful and brought before the players in international politics variegated dilemmas and challenges and also opportunities. Developments in the Balkans and the Trans-Caucasus such as the declaration of independence by Kosovo and later by the break way regions of Georgia may on surface appear disparate events but together they impacted the scales of balance in international relations. The re-emergence of Afghanistan post-9/11 shaped and continued to mould international politics. The terrorism menace remained unabated rather it became further protracted with new faces and new mechanisms. Apprehension of nuclear weapons falling into the hands of terrorists, and also rise of distinct aspirations in different parts of world emerged prominently. The regions of Central Eurasia and South Asia witnessed some of the intense play of forces in determining the geopolitical and economic contours of the global politics and, hence, analysis of the developments in these regions can help understanding of changing nature of international politics. The conflicts and conflicting interests in various parts of the world appeared more troublesome with the Iran episode, the issue of climate change and the issue of reformation of global bodies remaining intractable and in fact dividing the nations of the globe.

It appeared though the Berlin wall collapsed and the cold war ended, history did not end; rather new dimensions to the challenges confronting the world have emerged shaping the international politics in an unpredictable way. Amidst the new challenges, however, some incipient but robust developments also took place on the international theatre. The formal emergence of BRIC countries and the assertion of G-20 on global affairs raised the expectations on part of the nations that the prospects of accommodation and appreciation between diverse powers cannot be out rightly ruled out and the scenario is not as dismal as it appears to be.

The emergence of Barack Obama in the US and the emergence of Dmitry Medvedev in Russia dissipated much of the apprehensions about the prospects of new great game or new cold war. Obama's famous 'resetting button' reflected his accommodative gesture and was transformed into reality in declaring withdrawal of anti-missile shield plan from East Europe. The Afghan conundrum could evoke sense of cooperation between competing powers, and as the London Conference of January 2010 showed there is a possibility that the powers can devise a workable agenda to meet the Afghan crisis. On a broader scale, the world has appeared moving towards resolute evolution of multiple centres of power. Multipolarity seems to be knocking the door with Russia asserting itself and China with its fast growing economy becoming a strong contender to be a global power and India gearing up to play a global role. This chapter delves in detail into some of these developments that hold mirror to the evolving nature of international politics and the likely shape of the emerging world order.

Deciphering the World Order

In 2009 Germany commemorated the 20th year of the collapse of the Berlin wall that divided East Germany from West Germany for 28 years during the heydays of the cold war, thus sharpening the contours of rivalry between the cold war blocs driven by ideology. The implications of the collapse of the wall remained beyond its dismantling as it implied the beginning of end of the cold war. The collapse of the Berlin wall within a span of three decades had surprised plurality of people around the world. The incumbent German Chancellor, Angela Merkel who was working as a physicist in East Germany at the time of the collapse of the wall, observed she was hopeful about reunification of Germany 'but not necessarily during my lifetime.' [1] Probably that was the feeling in the air in one of the most uncertain phase of history when the East Europe was passing through turmoil in the final decades of the 20th Century. That the wall would not collapse at least in near future was emphasized by then East German President Erich Honecker, 'the Wall will still stand in 50 and also in 100 years.'

The wall symbolizing the famous iron curtain divided not only Germany, but also the whole Europe on the basis of ideology. The wall was built in 1961 to prevent the migration of East Germans into developed and prosperous West Germany. The wall not only created a physical barrier between the Germans but also created a sense of division in mindset and obstructed interactions among the people. As Jochen Alexander Freydank (from then East Germany) the Oscar Award winner for best short film stated, "I grew up in East Germany, behind the Wall...And the Oscar now...This is almost a surreal moment for me." The 20th year of the wall collapse was earmarked by huge celebrations in Germany in 2009. The 1.3 kilometre of the total 96 miles (155 kilometres) wall is still sanding erect and called East Side Gallery. Artists from different parts of the world painted their hearts and minds on the gallery. There are about 100 murals on the gallery. In 2009 under the Domino Project, Berlin planned to erect Styrofoam dominoes at the location where the wall stood, only to be collapsed to mark the occasion. The enthusiastic Berlin Mayor Klaus Wowereit said, 'we want to knock over the Wall once again' in order to forget 'aggressive divisions and separating walls.'

In a historical context, the collapse of the Berlin wall led to the gradual collapse of the regimes in the East Europe. The visit of then Soviet President Mikhail Gorbachev to attend the 40th year celebrations of the East Germany in 1989 appeared emphatic in this context as he cautioned the leaders of East Germany against tardy change as 'life punishes those who are too late.' [2] It is still a matter of debate how far the

Gorbachev's reforms of perestroika and glasnost led to the collapse of the communist bloc and subsequent collapse of the Soviet Union, but it remains a fact the reforms process affected the socialist regimes in East Europe. The protest march by about one million people at Alexander square of East Germany on 4 November 1989 pressurized its government to allow its citizens to travel to West Germany, thus fostering the collapse of the wall within a week. It may be a matter of rejoice that Germany got reunited in October 1990 aftermath of the collapse of the wall, but the more pertinent question that needs to be asked whether the world has emerged peaceful after the wall collapsed leading to end of the cold war or it is still passing through a phase of crisis as the recent developments in international politics unfold. Some of these factors in this context need special mention.

First, the East-West confrontation still appears raging. If during the cold war the issues were ideology driven, the post-cold war world is equally perturbed by the same old problems but with new forms. For instance concern about proliferation of nuclear weapons is still looming large. If during the cold war the intense space for competition was East Europe, in the post-cold war the space of intense competition is the emerging Central Eurasia, which has added to the concept of new great game waged between the players in the region. Second, the talks are not still dead about the cold war, rather it has added by a prefix 'new' as talks of a new cold war are gaining ground. As the anti-missile shield crisis, Luguvoi controversy, the Afghanistan turmoil, Kosovo and the Trans-Caucasian crisis indicate, the competitions and rivalries have reached a new height. Whether it is the Iraq war or Iran issue, or the North Korean issue or the UN reforms, there have been wider divergences in ideas and policies.

Though there are attempts to 'reset' relations, to embark on friendly relations with far off nations, to evolve a multilateral approach towards global issues of concern the international relations appear complex and unstable. Third, the rise of international terrorism has become dreadful. The complexity is further added when there are differing perceptions about the definition, nature and perpetrators of terrorism. In this case the Afghanistan turmoil has provided an ideal example of the sharp difference between various players in the region. Afghanistan which played an important pawn during the cold war has now become a hotbed of extremism and terrorism. Hence, the post-Berlin wall world is not free from complexities and ordeals. The global financial crisis and the issues like terrorism question the world order emerged after the collapse of the Berlin wall.

It may be difficult to categorize international developments into watertight compartments as international politics especially after the end of the cold war has witnessed variegated display of patterns least comprehended earlier. In this context, it may be an interesting as well as a meaningful exercise to analyze the generic terms unipolarism, bipolarism and multipolarism in contemporary discourse and see whether the current international scenario fits into any of these or any mixture of them. Unipolarism, simply defined, is the one pole of attraction around which international developments revolve. In international politics it can be translated as a kind of authoritarian system, in whatever guise, that dictates, rules and controls international developments with national, regional and global implications. The term basically has a negative connotation as it challenges the democratic premise on which inter-state relations are predicated. In the post-cold war scenario, the term has been widely identified with some of the policies of the US as the sole super power. The weak position of Russia in 1990s, lack of any alternative balancer to the US, the weakening of the UN lend credence to the proposition that the world is unipolar with the lone centre of power being the US. The Gulf crisis of early 1990s, the Kosovo crisis of the late 1990s and the Iraq war provided ground to the proponents of unipolarism to proclaim the world unipolar.

The term bipolarism gained much currency in post-second

world war scenario, in which both the superpowers the US and the erstwhile Soviet Union and the two blocs under their aegis perceived each other's goals as inherently antagonistic. Depending on the degree of the rivalries, the system could also be characterized as tight bi-polar or loose bi-polar. [3] Broadly, the system was based on fierce rivalry between the super powers without conceding required space to international organizations like the UN. The concepts like détente though popularized during this period, could function only as a fear-reduction technique, than as a genuine attempt towards reconciliation and peace. This is the phase which automatically led to unprecedented arms race, deep polarization of the world politics and fierce propagation of respective ideologies to increase their influence across the globe. Whether it was NATO or Warsaw Pact, these were groomed as frontal organizations to boost power, influence as well as dominance. This bipolar mechanism lacked any democratic structure, promoted power and group rivalry and consequent instability in the international relations.

In contrast to the concepts of unipolarism and bipolarism both of which have virtually been transcended in reality in the international horizon, the concept of multipolarism is in its nascent stage in contemporary international politics. This concept has gained currency in recent times and is predicted to bring substantial changes in the international sphere when translated into full practice.

In this system, international bodies like the UN are envisaged as the regulators of international stability and order. It implies not one or two poles of power but multiple centres of power. The rise of India, China and Russia is indicative of this emerging trend. Other developing countries like Brazil and South Africa are also emerging as crucial powers in the international scenario. The attempts towards Russia-India-China strategic triangle and BRIC quadrangle and the rise of regional organizations like EU, ASEAN, APEC and G-20 have provided credence to the concept of multipolarism.

Assertive Russia

The first half of 1990s witnessed Russia plunged deep into the morass of multiple crises, including economic and political. The so-called 'Atlanticism' faded its colour after a sudden glow as the promised Western assistance could not be materialized as expected. A weak domestic scenario and debilitating tendencies in the north Caucasus weakened and perhaps propelled Russia to follow an uncertain course in initial years after the Soviet collapse. It was in late 1990s that Russian policy makers could devise a clear cut policy making in both domestic and international arenas. Two factors- strong leadership provided by then President Vladimir Putin and growing economic muscle particularly in the sectors of oil and gas steered Russia to emerge as an assertive player in international politics. Particularly aftermath of the crisis in the trans-Caucasus in August 2008, the debates have gained momentum about a new equation emerging in the world. The 2008 US presidential debates got almost acrimonious while dealing with this subject. The Republican candidate, John McCain criticized Russia for its 'aggressive behaviour' in the trans-Caucasus and suggested driving it out from the G8 and advocated stringent measures to control its aggressive policies. Some sections of the Western media went vocal in criticizing 'brutishness' of the bear and labelled Russia 'a gangster state.' Some commentators compared the Russian actions to actions of Nazi Germany. These developments however did not lead to any kind of settlement of peace nor generated good will·but panoply of actions and reactions.

The Russian-Georgian face off could not be confined to local politics as it holds wider implications for international politics. It has also impacted the epistemological underpinnings of a new cold war discourse. Prime Minister Putin declared that the beleaguered Georgian president got a 'punch on the face' [4] as a response to his actions in South Ossetia. From a Russian perspective, Russia's action in trans-Caucasus is a decisive show of the Eurasian country as an assertive power which takes reciprocal actions against the developments in Kosovo guided by the West. Issues such as anti-missile shield in Europe and Luguvoi controversy further sharpened the polarizations. Russian President Medvedev's 26 September 2008 announcement of construction of 'guaranteed nuclear deterrent system' and a new 'aerospace defence system' by 2020 reflected Russia's aggressive response to the US policies in Europe. In another move, causing apprehension in the US and the EU, in Tehran on 21 October 2008 Russia, Iran and Qatar deliberated on issues in strengthening cooperation to set up a gas cartel in the style of Organization of Petroleum Exporting Countries (OPEC).

Russia has demonstrated its capacity to strike its perceived enemies and countering actions which are perceived against its interests in the region. Russia's Deputy Prime Minister, Sergei Ivanov, made it clear that Russia is not going to attack its neighbours as it respects their sovereignty, though it would not forgo its security concerns. Russia has also demonstrated that it can interrupt and challenge the energy security of the West, as the pipeline that passes through Georgia is not far from the Ossetian region. South Ossetia under its influence, Russia will be able to influence the West's energy policies in the region.

A lost power with a fragile economy and polity until a decade ago, Russia has emerged to play an important role in international politics. It appears to have adopted a calibrated policy by calling for the European integration without the American strings. That was what exactly in Putin's mind, when during his visit to Europe in September 2009 he envisaged European integration without support from the other side of the Atlantic. It is also well known that Russia has avowedly opposed the expansion of NATO towards its borders. However, it will be naïve to conclude that Russia will have a smooth sail in its policies towards the West. With the global slow down that considerably affected the world market and slashing of the oil prices, Russia's focus has become more inward.

Even on political front it continues to face insurmountable problems. In its support to South Ossetian and Abkhazian statehood so far no country has come forward except tiny Nauru, Nicaragua and Venezuela. The UN, the EU and the US aside, the SCO of which Russia is a member too adopted a couched language not to appear supportive of Russia's actions in Georgia. China's rising clout, its economic sinews, and its increasing influence in global affairs also contain in them the seed of probable confrontation between Russia and China. Russian Foreign Minister, Sergei Lavrov made it clear that Russia is going to shape the foreign policy discourse which is not going to revolve around a unipolar world order. His assertion that Russia is not going to turn a blind eye to the developments in its neighbourhood is an indication that a lot of churning will take place in Central Eurasian region in the coming years. Russia's actions in Georgia might have been generated by its perceived security interests, but its actions may lead to trade non-cooperation of some significant EU countries with Russia, which will likely affect Russia's economic development.

Rise of China

The rise of China has further dented the concept of unipolarism. The Chinese prowess as shown in the Beijing Olympics, its high booming economy along with its military power has pronounced it as a powerful player in Asian landscape. Though Chinese political system and its complicated cocktail of authoritarianism and socialism and capitalism have not won much appreciation from the democracies worldwide, its burgeoning economy and military prowess have nonetheless led it to play a decisive role in international politics. It may not be mere fortuitous combination of events that on 20 January 2009 China released its 2008 defence white paper while the new US President was taking oath of office. The timing of projection of China as an emerging power hence adds to multiple significance not only for China-US relations but also for the world.

The white paper aimed at developing a new paradigm of international relations in post-cold war era, in which the 'hegemonism and power politics' has eroded, leaving a calculated vacuum to adjust emerging aspirations. This paper, sixth after 1998 when China first promulgated such a paper, has been indicative of many new things. The 105-page document announced that China has come out of age with a new confidence that any threat to its territorial integrity and sovereignty will not be tolerated. The report emphasized the major threat to China comes not from out of its territory, but from within, an obvious reference to separatist trends what the white paper calls the 'splittist' tendencies in Taiwan, Tibet and Xinjiang. China in the paper proclaimed its relations across the Taiwan Strait have taken 'significantly positive turn' in recent years, at it has developed closer ties with the Kuomintang Party ruler, Ma Ying-jeou, who has adopted a non-confrontationist approach towards China.

However, China could not justify the positioning of hundreds of missiles towards Taiwan off east coast in view of what it calls the most favourable climate. The white paper also warned the Obama administration against any provocation towards Taiwan's independence as it will be thwarted with all might as it threatens territorial integrity and sovereignty of China. It may be noted the US-China standoff took a new turn in October 2008 with the proposed US arms deals worth US$ 6.5 billion with Taiwan.

Probably the most positive and appreciable aspect of the white paper was China's declaration of intent towards building a 'harmonious world of enduring peace and common prosperity.' [5] Without the support of international powers (in an obvious allusion to its relations with powers like the US, Russia and Japan), the paper argued, China cannot be peaceful and prosperous, but at the same time 'nor can the world enjoy prosperity and stability without China.' On an optimistic note this intent of complementarily may strike a chord of harmony in international relations thus moving the architecture of relations in a non-hegemonic friendly way and resolving contentious issues with US and Japan, as well as other powers like India. That China's leadership has clearly indicated the world is no longer unipolar and the emerging China will play an effective role towards international peace and prosperity may appear soothing for the time being for those who are apprehensive of a rising China and its ambitions.

What may cause consternation for China's neighbours and rivals is announcement of massive investment in defence. China's military expenditure in 2007 was US$ 46.8 billion, an official statistics disputed by many. China's defence ministry has expressed desire to develop an aircraft carrier to strike far off conflict areas. China is not only getting ready to keep Taiwan in mind, but also other regions in which it has conflicts such as with Japan over Senkaku islands having gas fields, and over Spratley islands in South China Sea. The paper's pronouncement that in the era of 'competitive bargaining and strategic fighting' China has to prepare its defence has raised heckles in Asia and Pacific. The traditional capital of hostility in the region may further witness a downturn with the Chinese manoeuvres in the Pacific region. Amidst debates as to China's revelation of statistics some analysts argue China's defence budget is in fact two to three times higher than the announcement. As the editorial of *Japan Times* of 28 January 2009 wrote, 'Despite this reassuring statement (that China's national policy is purely defensive), Chinese defence spending has risen sharply…China's real defence spending is two to three times the amount made public.' The Chinese experts counter the argument by saying the US military expenditure is three times higher than that of China even if the western estimate of China's military budget is taken into account.

The white paper expressed the Chinese ambition to make defence forces more 'informational.' Already the Chinese Beidou global navigation satellite system has accomplished the task partially, which is expected to achieve full global coverage by 2015. Announcing its 'leapfrog development' in military modernization, the white paper declared Chinese objective of 'winning local wars in conditions of informationization.' In the age of cyber warfare, the Chinese leadership well understands the significance of information technology in defence. In the age of economic diplomacy and globalization in which China aims to play an important role, its leadership understands both economic development and an integrated C4IS system (Command, Control, Communications, and Computers Information System) go together.

Undoubtedly, the white paper shows not only Chinese military assertion, but also its increasing international confidence. It recently demonstrated it prowess by sending its forces to the Gulf of Eden in Arabian Sea to contain Somali pirates. The Chinese President, Hu Jintao toured the Indian Ocean countries in 2009 to establish China's strategic leverage in the region. China's power projections in terms of extending its bases around the world and particularly in the seas, its emerging clout in Africa, its strong posture to separatist movements within its proclaimed territory, its inroads into Central Asian countries have undoubtedly made it clear that the rise of China is an inevitability which needs to be factored in international politics. The aftermath of the global financial crisis has put forth in the horizon the rise of China as a world power. China's economy has grown fast despite the financial crisis, and it has become the second largest economy in a short period. It is interesting to note that China played an important role in salvaging the US economy from the recession.

Besides China, India has shown impressive economic growth and has not hidden its ambitions to play a major role in global affairs. In fact there are occasions in 2009 such as deliberations at BRIC or BASIC at Copenhagen during climate change conference, in which India and China have coordinated their efforts to have a common bargaining agenda. But, the relations between the two countries cannot be termed cordial. There was a minor fracas between India and China in January

2009 when China accused India of tracking movements of its ships in Arabian Sea which India denied. China's relationship with Pakistan, its building of Karakoram highway to Gwader port in Pakistan, building of military base in Bay of Bengal, its 'string of pearls' strategy, and the border disputes are to be seen in the context of China's emerging clout in international politics. [6]

Despite the rise of China and its projection as a global power, it has still not been accepted by majority of nations as a transparent and responsible power. China is entering a new era but it seems 'ideologically and operationally ill prepared for it.' Short of protecting its narrow interests the communist regime still does not seem sure what it wants internationally, what are its broader foreign-policy goals and what kind of a world does it hope to shape. [7] The coming decade or two will be quite interesting in terms of emerging power equations in Asia and Pacific.

Rise of India

India in the last decade or so has emerged a crucial player, moving ahead of the earlier times when it had to use its gold reserves to repay loans. Its fast growing economy, robust human capital, democratic and pluralistic culture and non-antagonistic policy postures steeped in the tradition of peace and non-violence put India in good stead for a smooth rise in international politics without compromising core national interests. Lack of tag of being an irresponsible power helped it to rise to an acceptable position in international politics despite opposition from some of its neighbours. India has enjoyed working relations with almost all countries in the world. Its greater integration with the world economy was reflected by the trade openness indicator, the merchandise trade to GDP, which increased from 20 percent of GDP in 2001-2002, to 34.2 in 2006-07 and further to 40 percent of GDP in 2008-09. [8]

Despite the global financial crisis Indian economy was estimated to have grown by 6.7 percent in 2008-09 following a growth of 9.2 percent in 2007-08. The current rates in savings and investments will likely propel India to cross over to double digit growth rates in the next four to five years and surpass China as the world's fastest growing economy. [9] India's success story might not have expectedly impacted its rigid societal structure and political culture towards a vibrant polity and society, the fact remains that the rising political consciousness on the part of Indian people particularly the rising middle class, the vigilant media, the dynamism of the youth to adopt and inculcate innovative ideas bereft of old social practices and rigidities, its culture of debate and criticism place India on a higher platform towards the ideal human unity. The rise of media friendly spiritual leaders, not communal leaders, and their propagation of values of peace, tranquillity and development with an Indian traditional spin has impacted the modern India of the 21st century and its policies. India's rising clout in international politics has been dealt in detail in later pages.

Emergence of BRIC

The meeting of foreign ministers of Brazil, Russia, India and China, for the first time officially, in the Russian city of Yekaterinburg on 16 May 2008 was a defining moment in the annals of international politics. Russia which is part Europe and part Asia has emerged as a strong power despite hurdles. Similarly, India and China are emerging to be the major economic power houses. The South American Brazil's joining the group adds not only an international and polycentric dimension to the initiative, but also opens up the possibilities of the group emerging as a global balancer and economic power house. [10] The Russian foreign ministry spokesman observed at the sidelines of the meeting, "BRIC unites the major economic growth centres with more than half the world's population, the role of which in international affairs will grow." [11] Besides economics, international politics too remains a core concern for BRIC countries. In its very first meeting the members called for a fresh opening of talks between Belgrade and Pristina to moderate the violent situation in the Balkans. Similarly, on the Iran issue these countries called for international mediation and to find a middle ground, instead of using any kind of coercion.

The advantage of the four countries coming together is enormous. It is in retrospect one can say what Goldman Sachs predicted in 2003 [12] is now a reality. Goldman Sachs predicted that by the year 2035, the combined economy of BRIC countries will surpass the economy of the most prosperous group of G-7 (G-8 minus Russia). These countries possess enormous human resources along with a huge and fast growing consumer market. In the two years of 2006 and 2007 stocks in these countries have risen 70 percent and markets have grown at the rate of 42 percent. Hence, when the US says that the Indian and Chinese middle class are growing fast and consuming fast, this in a way indicates the American recognition of the fast rising economies of India and China.

All these four countries can work together to meet each other's requirements. Russia has the largest reserves of natural gas and second largest reserves of oil. On the other hand, India and China are energy hungry countries. It is but feasible when India and China can fill the consumer market voids in Russia and Brazil, Russia and Brazil can meet energy and raw material needs of the two countries. India's high IT skills and manpower and Chinese massive production of goods can complement Russian and Brazilian economies. While Russia and China are permanent members of the United Nations Security Council, India has strong clout among the developing countries. It is indubitable that the collective political will of these four powers can checkmate any unilateral actions in contravention of the UN Charter. These countries can work together to tackle international menaces such as drug trafficking and terrorism, and formulate common stand on issues such as climate change, non-proliferation issue and food and energy security. All of these countries have suffered from the menace of terrorism. Whether it is Kashmir in India, Chechnya in Russia, or Xinjiang in China, these countries have faced terrorist violence.

Brazilian President Lula da Silva in his article published in an Indian daily on 16 June 2009 [13] observed that BRIC is seeking fresh answers to old problems. In his words, the first BRIC summit in Yekaterinburg in June 2009 "marks a major turning point in how our countries engage in a world undergoing profound change...amid broken paradigms and failing multilateral institutions." Russian President Dmitry Medvedev echoed the similar view point at the press conference at the end of the summit when he stated, "All the decisions important for the international community—economic, security and political—should be taken on fairer basis...this fairness is the key word for our interaction. BRIC should create conditions for a fairer world order." [14] The first summit meeting of BRIC held lot of promises for a better and fairer world. Undoubtedly, through equitable partnership BRIC can play a dynamic role and assert itself in international politics. The 16-point statement issued at the end of the summit dealt with divergent issues of international concern ranging from food crisis to UN reforms.

The BRIC countries constituting 40 percent of world population with 40 percent of world GDP no doubt can play an effective role in remoulding international order by opening multipolar centres of dialogue and reconciliation. In these multipolar centres the developed countries must come forth to adjust to the changing circumstances by taking into account divergent view points and accommodating the emerging powers in international framework. It is in this context the grouping emphasized on accommodating emerging powers in a reformed United Nations. The joint statement clearly stated the importance the grouping attaches 'to the status of India and Brazil in international affairs, and understand and support their aspirations to play a greater role in the UN.'

Another important issue that the BRIC confronted during

the summit is the prospects of a new currency and the reform of Bretton Woods structures such as World Bank and IMF. The joint statement argued for a strong need for a stable, predictable and more diversified international monetary system. It reiterated the grouping's demand that the emerging and developing economies must have greater voice and representation in international bodies. It made explicit its demand that the leadership of these bodies 'should be appointed through an open, transparent and merit-based selection process.' Regarding food crisis the joint statement argued that it is not only the issue of developing countries consuming more, but it is a matter far complicated and multifaceted. The grouping urged the Western countries to give up protectionism and emphasized on the need for a comprehensive and balanced outcome of the WTO Doha Development Round. However, on the issue of alternate currency, no concrete decision could be taken. Perhaps on the issue of a supranational currency or a world reserve currency the grouping will have to deliberate further to reach at a concrete and unanimous decision.

Indian Prime Minister, Manmohan Singh before departing to Yekaterinburg in June 2009 to attend the SCO meeting and the BRIC summit told the press in New Delhi his visit testifies to the "high regard we have for Russia's Presidency of the SCO and our desire to intensify our engagement with countries of our extended neighbourhood in Central Asia." [15] While expressing optimism that 'the volume of trade among BRIC countries has grown rapidly in recent years, Intra-BRIC investments have also grown,' Singh advocated for the creation of a BRIC Joint Business Forum that can cooperate in diverse areas such as agriculture, aviation, energy, pharmaceuticals and services. The Indian prime minister's argument that the group members need to further coordinate their effort at official level towards evolving a multilateral financial system has also been taken well by the grouping. This can be a successful idea provided the parties adopt a consensual approach on the issue.

The most pertinent question that needs to be asked is how far this nascent body (though the idea came earlier, and the foreign ministers of these countries met at the sidelines of the UN meetings in 2006 and 2007) will evolve in making the collective dream a practical reality. Its sustainability and robustness will depend on how far the four countries manage their interests with a broader objective of economic cooperation in a non-zero sum format. The member countries will have to rise above bilateral rivalries in order to play a more responsible and responsive role in international arena. Whether it is India's border issue with China, or China's likely encirclement of India through Karakoram and Pakistan's Gwader port, or through the Indian ocean; or the Chinese-Russian rivalry and the issue of Chinese mass migration to southern Siberia and other issues of contention need to be looked from a broader perspective. There are apprehensions that high corruption rates in these countries and strident regulations against foreign investment may hamper the prospects of fast growth of these economies.

If BRIC intends to rise as a global balancer and as a repository of economic power, the member countries have to work together in a more constructive and collaborative framework. The members need to develop a common agenda with effective will to push that agenda. Any divergence of goals might defeat its purpose to achieve a fairer multipolar world order. In the changing world order which is more economically bargaining oriented, the counties need to redesign their goals to suit the common objectives without sacrificing their national interests. The BRIC countries which represent a significant percent of the total world population with high growth rates and resources indeed have the potential to lead global economic growth and shape new world order. Whatever the stature and effectiveness of the BRIC at present may be, it has no doubt emerged with prospects of an alternative voice in the international politics.

It has provided a platform to voice diverse aspirations and to exchange ideas for a 'more democratic and just multipolar world order'. It is another point of debate how far the resolve of this grouping to dawn an equitable world order will be translated into reality, as it will depend on the kind of coordination and commonality of interests among the members of the grouping. Only a coordinated approach can foster BRIC's agenda for a fairer world.

References

1. Mike Swanson, "Fall of Berlin Wall came as a Surprise to Germans," http://www.monstersandcritics.com/news/europe/features/article_1466425.php/Fall_of_Berlin_Wall_came_as_a_surprise_to_Germans_Feature.

2. Igor Bukker, "Berlin Wall was levelled 15 years ago to unite East and West," http://english.pravda.ru/main/2001/09/07/14565.html.

3. Morton A. Kaplan applied systems analysis to the study of international politics. For details see, Morton Kaplan, *System and Process in International Politics* (New York: John Wiley and Sons Inc., 1957).

4. Bridget Kendall, "Putin Defends Georgia Offensive," http://news.bbc.co.uk/2/hi/europe/7611482.stm.

5. The White Paper is available at http://news.xinhuanet.com/english/2009-01/20/content_10688124.htm.

6. Debidatta Aurobinda Mahapatra, "The Pearls and String of the Theory," Strategic Culture Foundation online magazine, 5 June 2009. http://en.fondsk.ru/article.php?id=2203.

7. Fareed Zakaria, "The Beijing Blues," *Newsweek*, vol. 155, no. 24, 14 June 2010.

8. M. Veerappa Moily, "Painting by Numbers," *Indian Express*, 21 June 2010.

9. Ibid.

10. Debidatta Aurobinda Mahapatra, "BRIC Building," Strategic Culture Foundation online magazine, 19 May 2008. http://en.fondsk.ru/article.php?id=1395.

11. Quoted in Carl Mortished, "Russia Shows its Political Clout by

Hosting BRIC Summit," *The Times*, 16 May 2008. http://business.timesonline.co.uk/tol/business/markets/russia/arti cle3941462.ece.
12. Goldman Sachs Report 2003 is available at http://www2.goldmansachs.com/ideas/brics/book/99-dreaming.pdf.
13. *Indian Express*, 16 June 2009.
14. Quoted in Siddharth Varadarajan, "BRIC should Create Conditions for Fairer World Order," *The Hindu*, 17 June 2009.
15. *The Hindu*, 16 June 2009.

3

New Great Game

For years to come, Central Eurasia will remain one of the most happening areas in international politics. Though the situation there is in flux and the principle of certitude fails in analyzing the developments, it will be naïve to ignore the importance of the region due to its geo-strategic location and vast resources. Interestingly, Central Eurasia as a concept has eluded the scope of a proper definition. Geographically, on a wider scale, it includes 'lands from the Iranian Plateau, the Black Sea, and the Volga Basin through Afghanistan, Southern Siberia, and the Himalayas to Muslim and Manchu regions of China and the Mongol lands.' The advocates of 'critical geopolitics' [1] challenge the realist and neorealist theories of international politics and emphasize on role of non-state actors, such as international financial institutions, in both conceptual and material construction of the region. From a wider perspective the concept can be seen more an interactive than an integrative one. It is a landscape traversed by not only diverse empires but also by diverse cultures. [2]

The impact of the former Soviet Union, and earlier of the Tsarist rule, on the formation of the socio-political and economic personality of the region can not be ignored. The rule of the Russian empire and the subsequent Soviet Union had brought a kind of uniformity in most parts of the region. After the Soviet collapse, the region underwent a radical transformation. A host of forces including clan politics, religion, fundamentalism and feudal system of governance came up or refashioned. Myriad diversities aside, the collapse of the Soviet Union brought these states to the brink of uncertainty. The old communist apparatchik took over the reigns of power. Some of the regimes in this region, especially in Central Asia, are seeking to build legitimacy through adoption of cultural ideologies. There was no requisite formation of civil society structures to promote democratic norms and practices. The weak political institutions appeared increasingly unable to channel the growing energies of the masses in constructive directions.

Another crisis that struck these emerging nations was economic backwardness. Besides the demerits of segregated economic developments inherited from the Soviet Union, these societies did not get adequate international aid or investments to boost their economy. Worse still, the resources remain unexplored and the fear of rising Islamic extremism discourages potential investors. Though many territorial disputes in the region are resolved, the remaining conflicts as in the case of Nagorno-Karabakh, Abkhazia or South Ossetia have played havoc in the region.

In the post-Cold War scenario, Central Eurasia assumed importance as a bridge between East and West with strategic importance transcending the concerns of immediate neighbours. When energy resources are added to this strategic equation, the region faces a challenging future. Parts of the region such as Caspian Sea basin are rich in energy resources and there are prospects of opening trans-Central Eurasian routes. It is estimated that the Caspian Sea basin contains about 250 billion barrels of proven petroleum reserves. [3] In the emerging scenario the following four major influences in the region can be identified: Russia, the West, led by the United States and EU, China, and the 'new Islamic pole', involving theocratic and fundamentalist regimes.

Among the four, while the first three have more or less political and economic ambitions in the region, the fourth seems to have subtle underpinnings, endeavouring to drive the region towards radicalism. Interestingly, though there is diversity of religious practices in Central Eurasian states, of late the influence of radical Islam has come to forefront. The Wahabi variety of Islam, stemmed from the soil of Saudi Arabia, has made enough dent in the region. It is widely perceived that entrenchment of Al Qaeda in Afghanistan and Pakistan, the rise of the Taliban and the international drug racket owe their existence partly to fragile politics in the region.

Whether it is Chechnya or Kashmir or Xinjiang, the international network of Islamic terrorism has significantly drawn its sustenance from the difficult mountain terrains in the region. While the United States has endeavoured to fill the power vacuum in the Central Eurasian region to suit its interests, Russia and China perceive it as encroachment into their sphere of influence. In 2001 for the first time deployment of the American combat troops took place near the Kyrgyz capital Bishkek as part of the anti-terror campaign in Afghanistan. China is worried that the US presence in the region might encourage internal unrest in its disgruntled regions such as Xinjiang. In October 2003 Russia's Defence Minister, Sergei Ivanov, demanded publicly that the Americans pull out from the region within two years. Then Russian President Vladimir Putin signed new security pacts with the Central Asian rulers, allowing Russian troops to set up a new military base in Kyrgyzstan, which lies only 35 miles away from the US airbase. The east ward expansion of NATO and inclusion of former Soviet countries in the European Union have made the region an intense playground of power politics.

Turkey and Iran are the major local influences in the region. The Iranian and Turkic influence stem from geographical contiguity of the region and also due to historical ties. Interestingly, the great power involvement in the regional dynamics has further complicated the regional politics. The alignments of Iran with Russia and Turkey with the US have led to further alignments of local nature. For instance, in the regional conflicts like Nagorno-Karabakh the standpoint of the countries of the region are marked by their equations with these alignments. While the Iranian influence is distinct in Central Asian countries, the influence of Turkey is more prominent in Caucasian states like Azerbaijan. Central Eurasian languages are also based either on Turkic or on Persian roots, with later Russian influence. But, this impact has also led to sullen memories of rivalries, conquest and empire-building. It is difficult to predict whether various regional organizations such as Commonwealth of Independent States, Eurasian Economic Community, Black Sea Economic Cooperation and Shanghai Cooperation Organization can provide the needed sinew to keep the states together on a single platform to raise and address common issues.

Though these organizations can provide opportunity to work together for enhancing security and coping with the future challenges but mutual differences between the countries seem to make difficult the prospects of cooperation. While the states like Georgia and Ukraine have significant differences with Russia, other states of Central Asia and the Caucasus are embroiled in internal problems. Any instability in Central Eurasia is a matter of common concern for several reasons. First, instability in the region provides fertile ground for the growth of radical movements that often have a global reach. Second, the surge of illicit narcotics trade in the region provides a major source of funding for these groupings. Third, the Caspian Sea basin is an emerging oil producing region which can play an important role in future energy security. Any rivalry of interests in this energy rich region may jeopardize prospects of stability. Finally, regional conflicts in this volatile area have the potential of developing into major power confrontations. Central Eurasia has for a number of years been in the process of becoming a region of major strategic importance. Given the increased competition in the region its importance is set to grow. The attempts by the West to fill the power vacuum left by the fall of the Soviet Union, and the attempts by Russia to regain the lost ground, have accentuated the power politics.

Challenges and Prospects of Co-operation

The politics of hardcore realism creates obstacles in the

materialization of the ideal of a peaceful world despite the US President Barack Obama being awarded the Nobel Prize for his peace overtures. His call for friendship with Muslim world in Cairo in June 2009 notwithstanding, [4] the tensions across the divide have intensified or at least sustained. One of the most important developments in 2009 was Obama's announcement of 'resetting' relationship with Russia. The newly elected US President Barack Obama did send feelers that he is interested to develop close ties with the Russia to steer amicable resolution of contentious issues. This was well received by Russian President, Dmitry Medvedev. The visit of Obama to Russia in July, and the later announcement of the US administration to withdraw anti-missile shield plan from Eastern Europe did achieve significantly in terms of cooling down the animosity and tension in the Central Eurasian region for a while.

Analysts who feared the prospects of new cold war brewing between the two powers especially after the US move to expand NATO in Central Eurasia, with the players in the region collaborating to reduce Russian influence by developing alternate pipelines and promoting anti-Russian regimes, now at least for the time being could avoid predicting doom for dialogue in international politics. The withdrawal of the US anti-missile system from the Eastern Europe has led to debates about the prospects of a cooperative security system in Central Eurasia. The anti-missile system announced by the George Bush administration in 2007 had led to much blood boil in the region almost akin to the cold war rivalry. As Obama's focus on resetting relations with Russia pans out, the prospect of Russia-US cooperation appears bright in the Central Eurasian region with Russia already allowing its territory for supplies to Afghanistan and refashioning its stand towards Iran regarding nuclear disarmament.

The anti-missile shield unveiled in January 2007 aimed at deploying a radar system in Czech Republic and 10 interceptors in Poland by 2012. The main purpose of anti-missile shield, from the perspective of the US, was to intercept potential missile attacks from 'rogue' states such as North Korea and Iran. To the objections that the countries like Iran do not have range missiles which can target the US or Europe, the advocates of the shield argued it may possess these weapons in near future. Both Poland and Czech Republic expressed willingness to host parts of the US missile-defence system on their territories. Russia considered the move as a threat to its security to undermine its sphere of influence. The US rejection of Russia's proposal for joint use of Gabala radar station in Azerbaijan gave rise to the Russian suspicion of the use of anti-missile system against Russia and its allies. The Russian opposition found strong resonance in the Munich conference in February 2007, where then Russian President Vladimir Putin termed the US plans a disturbing factor and warned the inevitability of an arms race. [5]

Putin also challenged the argument of prospective missile strike by 'rogue' states such as North Korea through Western Europe as it 'obviously contradicts law of ballistics', as it can target the US through the Pacific. The situation got a new twist after Obama came to power in January 2009 as he endeavoured to change the policies of his predecessor. The prevailing scenario too necessitated a course correction. As per reports, the missile programmes were getting difficult to sustain on the face of its apparent non-success. Since the late 1980s, the US has spent about US$150billion to develop such systems. The revelation in *Wall Street Journal* of 17 September 2009 that, "Iran's plan to get hold of long-range missiles has not made as rapid of progress as what had previously been expected" might have encouraged the US administration to withdraw the plan. The other factors such as eliciting Russia's support to counter terrorism and extremism in Afghanistan, to bring Iran to the orbit of nuclear non-proliferation, and differences with the European powers like Germany and France, might have motivated the Obama administration to withdraw the anti-missile plan despite opposition from some of the European allies particularly Poland and Czech republic on the territories of which the system was to be based.

Whether the withdrawal will herald a new era of cooperation between the US and Russia or not the coming days will reveal but the fact remains the withdrawal has infused confidence and trust in both the players to devise common approach on a variety of issues among which the two are very important. First, both the countries have come closer to develop a common approach on the Iran issue. At the G-20 summit in Pittsburgh in September 2009, Russian President Medvedev described the construction of the second uranium enrichment plant at Qom in Iran as a matter of 'serious concern.' [6]

Russia has already delayed plan to deliver S-300 defence system to Iran. It has refused to sell Iran more advanced S-400 defence system. It has urged Iran to comply with international rules and regulations regarding nuclear non-proliferation. In this context, the meeting of the six parties with Iran on 1 October 2009 in Geneva was a positive step. In the meeting Iran agreed to open its uranium enrichment plant at Qom for inspection and to send most of its enriched uranium to Russia and France for turning it into fuel for production of medical isotopes. The IAEA Director, Mohamed El Baradei rightly mentioned in an interview that in the case of Iran 'the language of force is not helpful. It leads to confrontation' [7] Russia's attempts towards transparently guarding nuclear programme in Iran may be a positive indication towards the emerging cooperative security in the region.

Second, Russia has expressed its support to the coalition forces to fight against Taliban forces in the region. Of late the US has realized the Afghan conundrum cannot be resolved by acting solo and it must take into confidence other players in the region. The US realization of mutual cooperation and Russia's forwardness to seize the opportunity has led to an atmosphere of mutual cooperation to fight the Taliban menace.

It is realized with an international framework, and with the cooperation of regional powers, it will be feasible to contain the Taliban menace in Afghanistan. The Geneva meeting of six-party on the Iran issue is a step in right direction as it enhanced the prospects of cooperative security in the region after a prolonged and intense rivalry. The European Union report pointing finger at Georgia for initiating the August 2008 war too has emerged as a balancer in moderating tensions in trans-Caucasus. It may not be farfetched to argue that the Obama-Medvedev duo is capable to shed much of the past animosities and move forward towards building cooperative architecture.

Hub of the New Great Game

The developments in and around Afghanistan since 2001 indicate a new architecture of relations emerging in Central Eurasia, further reinforcing the theory of great game in which the major stakeholders vie with each other to have control over the geo-strategic space of the region. The debates regarding supply routes to the war torn Afghanistan have provided enough clue that the NATO led International Security Assistance Force in the trouble-torn region will not be able to follow the old policy of solely relying on Pakistan for supply of enforcements, especially after repeated obstructions by the radical elements in the route from Karachi port to Afghanistan, particularly in the Khyber pass. The complexity of the situation came to picture after the announcement by the new Obama administration in Washington that it will seek help from Russia and the countries of Central Asia to supply goods to the war torn country.

The tenure of George W. Bush administration witnessed tense US-Russia relations, particularly after the intense efforts of the US to woo the Central Asian countries, attempts to draw the countries like Ukraine and Georgia into NATO fold, announcement of anti-missile shield in Czech and Poland and the irritants like Luguvoi controversy. These developments had dramatically affected the relations. The bonhomie in relations expected to grow aftermath of the 9/11 had withered away gradually with the uncompromising and antagonistic policies in the strategic and energy rich Central Eurasia. The Kosovo crisis and the later Georgian crisis too marked the differing contours of the US-Russia policies in the Central Eurasian region. The Afghan issue was not exception to this overall ambit of the US-Russia relations.

The Afghan problem, particularly the issue of supply routes, can be a scope and at the same time a lost opportunity in the context of US-Russia relations. The NATO forcers lost 90 supply lorries in December 2008 on a bridge in Khyber Pass from Pakistan due to the Taliban attacks. Needless to mention, the Taliban has viewed the NATO forces a thorn on the flesh of its ascendancy not only in Afghanistan but also in the border areas of Pakistan. Russia too is concerned by the rise of radicalism in Afghanistan and surrounding regions as it apprehends these forces might challenge its federal and pluralistic structure.

Regarding how the Russian cooperation can help the US led NATO better its prospects in Afghanistan, following factors must be kept in mind. First, this region is well connected by the Soviet era rail road system. The route from Russia, and then through Kazakhstan, Turkmenistan and Uzbekistan to Afghanistan can help the NATO to achieve its targets with Russian cooperation. Moscow has given the green signal to NATO by allowing 'non-lethal' supplies to use Russian territory as transit to Afghanistan. In November 2008, it allowed the forces of Spain and Germany to use its territory to transport their goods to Afghanistan. Such a partnership between the US led NATO and Russia would defuse much of the tensions in the region, besides help tackling the radical elements and menaces like drug trafficking. The Soviet experience in late 1970s and 1980s in tackling the Afghan guerrillas can also be used to control Taliban elements in the region. Moscow's participation in this venture will provide

Russia a share in contributing to peace efforts in the region, and at the same time it may lead to success in many diverse areas such as arms control.

Any US policy to bypass countries of influence in the region including Russia may lead to tense atmosphere with wide-ranging consequences. The US option to avoid the easiest Iran route can be attributed to the nuclear issue. Similarly, the US may not be much enthused about another route that starts from Shanghai port straight across China to Tajikistan and to Afghanistan. The proposed plan to build a new route from Black Sea to the port of Poti in Georgia to Azerbaijan, and then onward to Kazakhstan and Turkmenistan to Afghanistan will likely lead to further rivalry in the region.

Some analysts argue such a route will provide occasion for further NATO expansion in the region, and help the US to completely bypass Russia and China. As some reports suggest this route may later be developed as an oil route thus having bearing on oil politics in the region. This may also affect the prospects of anti-terror operations as the politics of the region will be further contested intensely. In this context Russia's proposed plans to sell Iran S300 missile defence system and SA-20 missile systems need to be juxtaposed. It will also be a difficult task for the US to bring the countries of Central Asia on the supply route without Russia's cooperation. Situations like the Kyrgyz government's decision on 4 February 2009 to ask its Parliament to approve closure of the US military base will likely hamper the NATO efforts to go solo in Afghanistan. The challenges in Afghanistan will define the emerging contours of power politics in Central Eurasian region and set new rules for new great game in Central Eurasia.

The AfPak Strategy

The US President Barack Obama in March 2009 unveiled the AfPak strategy, which called powers like India, Russia and China to collaborate with the US in combating terrorism in Afghanistan and Pakistan. He called terrorism 'an international security challenge of the highest order,' and appealed these nations to be part of a contact group to tackle the menace in the region that has 'descended into chaos.' Perhaps for the first time since the 9/11 in 2001, the US leadership called for collaborative effort in forming a Contact Group comprising powers with diverse policy orientations to fight terrorism. On the occasion, Obama's emphasis on the role of the United Nations in the task is reflective of his difference of policy approach from the previous administration. [8]

The main idea underlying AfPak strategy is the consolidation of the whole Afghanistan-Pakistan region as a single point of agenda in countering terrorism and religious fundamentalism. The Obama initiative would have multiple implications not only for the future of AfPak, or the immediate neighbours, but also for other powers of the region and for the world. One of the first premises on which Obama developed the strategy is his realization of the difficult enterprise of going solo in AfPak in fighting terrorism and religious fundamentalism. Since 2001 when the US sent forces to defeat Taliban in Afghanistan, the situation has been protracted and after about nine years it has been further precarious. The US has lost 700 personnel till early 2009 while civilian casualties number thousands. Afghanistan has become a hotbed of terrorism and religious fundamentalism, further widening the tentacles to borders areas of Pakistan particularly the Federally Administered Tribal Areas and the North West Frontier Province. Many believe that the rugged mountain terrains of these areas have sheltered Al Qaeda leader, Osama bin Laden.

As the terror attack in Pakistan's police academy in Lahore on 30 March 2009 demonstrated, just within four days of announcement of the US strategy, the Taliban has further encroached into Pakistan's eastern areas. The Pakistani Taliban claimed responsibility for the attack which killed about ten people and injured many. President Asif Ali Zardari admitted the increasing influence of Taliban in Pakistan's border areas. Hence, when the US resolves to 'disrupt, dismantle and defeat Al Qaeda in Pakistan and Afghanistan, and to prevent their return to either country in the future', it realizes the necessity of a collaborative approach for the task. Obama under the new strategy deployed 21,000 troops (14,000 already ordered, further 7000 to train Afghan forces) in Afghanistan. The strategy targeted to build an Afghan army of 134,000 and a police force of 82,000 by 2011. Without mincing any words, Obama made it clear Pakistan must be accountable for every dollar the US pays it to counter terrorism. He committed US$ 1.5billion annually for a period of five years to support Pakistan. The US intelligence agencies confirmed the complicity of Pakistan's intelligence agency with terrorist organizations and the Taliban; hence it would be interesting to see how the new strategy rejigs to break the collusion.

Another aspect of Obama's strategy was to include Iran in the contact group. Obama probably intended to draw Iran to the US orbit by invoking its important role in Afghan crisis. Iran too seems to be worried about terrorism and drug trafficking in its neighbourhood. Its distaste of the Saudi, Sunni influence on Taliban in Afghanistan might motivate Iran to join the collaborative effort. It will be also interesting to see how Obama will co-opt Iran in its new strategy while the US has differences with it on many issues particularly the nuclear issue. Equally important aspect of the strategy is to invite India to be a member of the contact group on AfPak. India has traditionally enjoyed good relations with Afghanistan, though Pakistan has viewed it with suspicion. In July 2008 the bomb blast at Indian embassy in Kabul killed 40 people with senior Indian diplomats. India accused Pakistani intelligence behind the attack, which was further corroborated by the US intelligence. The special envoy of Obama for AfPak, Richard Holbrooke visited India on 7 April 2009 to deliberate with India's foreign secretary and national security advisor for constructive diplomacy between India and Pakistan to resolve bilateral issues. India expressed interest in AfPak strategy but with regard to Obama's advocacy of constructive diplomacy between the two nuclear rivals it adopted a wait and watch approach.

On the sidelines of G-20 meeting in London on 2-3 April 2009, Obama met with Russian President, Dmitry Medvedev, India's Prime Minister, Manmohan Singh and Chinese President, Hu Jintao and appeared to have reiterated the same collaborative approach before these leaders. However, the success of the new strategy will depend much on how it is implemented. Regarding the new strategy, Russia will be looking at the issue from a fresh perspective as Obama has advocated for friendly relations with it. Besides terrorism other factors such as geopolitical dynamics of the region and power rivalries will come to picture when the new strategy will be put into operational mode. The point that needs to be factored in foreign policy discourse of all the powers including India, Russia and China that the AfPak region has witnessed the proliferation of Al Qaeda, Taliban and their ilk, which need to be tackled. The world powers perhaps have the right opportunity to show their unity in approach to tackle one of the deadliest scourges of the 21st century.

Revamping the Strategy

Obama in December 2009 announced a 'surge' of troops in Afghanistan as a measure to further bolster AfPak strategy unveiled in March. An analysis of Obama's new strategy and the reactions to it brought forth the complexities the new plan will likely confront in the trouble torn region. Obama planned to increase the number of US troops by 30,000 (thus further adding to already stationed 71,000 US troops in the region) to help tackle the Taliban menace by providing training and strengthening the Afghan security and police forces. It will also help, the Obama administration argued, building stability and development in the trouble-torn region. The new plan envisaged luring the Taliban to join the political process by applying carrot and stick policy. It envisaged employing the moderate Taliban as foot soldiers in an effort to wean away them from extremism.

The plan indicated that the US led NATO does not want to station forces for a long overhaul. It also indicated for a gradual withdrawal after 2011 from the territory that is supposed to be peaceful without the menace of terrorism, religious fundamentalism and drug trafficking by that time. International response to this new policy was guarded. The Russian government took the new Obama initiative in a 'positive' way, but argued that the initiative must be undertaken in collaboration with international bodies like the UN. The responses of the US' NATO allies and other major powers appeared supportive. The UK announced to increase its troops to the tune of 500 (thus totalling its contribution to 10,000) to the NATO troops in Afghanistan. The Prime Minister of UK appealed the international powers to contribute and support the Obama initiative. Poland also became enthusiastic and announced increase of its troop by 638, in all probability to prove to the US that it is a strong ally despite the US negligence of it. In fact the Obama decision to withdraw anti-missile defence plan from the Eastern Europe caused much embarrassment to Poland.

With the troop 'surge' the total number of NATO troops in Afghanistan will be about 140,000 to fight about 25,000 strong Taliban extremists. But the issue appears to be far more complex. How far AfPak strategy part II will be successful is yet to be seen. Pakistan, undoubtedly, is the front state which can aid the process to curb the terror menace in the region. In fact the Afghan Taliban and Pakistan Taliban have in their common agenda to promote radical Islam and to target everything that oppose their global agenda. After their retreat from Afghanistan in post 9/11 period the extremist forces have deeply entrenched into the north west of Pakistan. The Pak policy of using these elements in some places and deterring them at other places has already proven dangerous. Pakistan must guard its policies in terms of cutting off all kinds of supports to Taliban and their ilk.

In this context, Obama's two-pager letter in November 2009 to the Pak president, Asif Ali Zardari, which urged the Pak leadership to stop the use of the terrorist elements to pursue policy goals needs special mention. [9] In return, the US promised Pakistan partnership, arms and aid. The question remains how far the US, which is viewed with suspicion by many people in Pakistan including sections in its establishment, can achieve the objectives unless the Pakistan army and civilian establishment come forward together to support the strategy.

Some analysts have compared Obama's plan to increase troops in Afghanistan to Bush's policy to increase troops in Iraq. The comparison can not sustain long as the geography, political situation, ethnic set up and regional factors in both the cases are different. At the same time, the mountain terrains in the border areas of Pakistan and Afghanistan that shelter many terrorists make it difficult to fight these elements that are well equipped and trained to continue and sustain guerrilla type warfare for long. Further, the malaise of corruption and mismanagement that afflict the Karzai government feed to the popular suspicion whether the new policy will be able to effectively impact the situation. There is also another shred of argument that the Taliban will now adopt a cool and calibrated policy of hiding and gather strength till the NATO withdraw troops, and then return with the bounden force to control Afghanistan, and spread its tentacles to other regions. For the success of any strategy to contain Taliban the region needs an international strategy with the involvement of the international as well as regional players.

Besides, the Afghanistan people and various tribal leaders must be taken into confidence for any policy measure to be successful. The complex Afghan situation cannot be resolved by mere increasing troops unless the confidence of the local people is won. There need to be attempts to create a political platform which can help bring diverse parties in the conflict towards a common goal. The majority of Afghans do not like Taliban, but also they do not have many options to choose from. Hence, it is the responsibility of international and regional players to see that there is a transparent, effective governance system which can cater to the needs of the common people of the region.

London Conference on Afghanistan

In a venture to assess the situation in the AfPak and devise strategies, UK organized an international conference on 28 January 2010, in which all 43 NATO members took part. The leaders of seventy countries including the NATO members met in London to deliberate on the future strategy to be adopted for 'secure, prosperous and democratic Afghanistan.' Afghanistan, which throughout major parts of its history remained vexed, ruled by authoritarian regimes and emerged as a playing field for control of its strategic depth, has probably not been as turbulent as aftermath of the 2001. The London conference while taking into account the complicated nature of the transition process in the war ravaged Afghanistan unveiled a complicated strategy. Important among them were to reintegrate moderate Taliban into the mainstream, to streamline administration by weeding out corruption and handing over the system of administration to the Afghans by phasing out foreign forces, and most importantly bringing to the realization the adoption of a regional strategy to resolve the regional issue. [10]

As a precursor to the London conference, the Istanbul regional conference on Friendship and Cooperation on 26 January 2010 too emphasized on a regional approach for the resolution of the complicated issue. Afghanistan, particularly aftermath of the terror surge in 2001, has become a peculiar hotbed of contesting powers who vie to have strategic lever over the region in the 'heart of Asia.' Pakistan particularly has evinced major interest as it views the region as its strategic backyard, and its past record of supporting the radical forces against the erstwhile Soviet Union has endeared it to the US and NATO. Turkey's interest has been in salience with the NATO, its patron organization, and as the Istanbul conference portrayed Turkey has not hidden its aspirations to play a major role in the region. India, especially recently, has played an important role in the reconstruction of the war ravaged Afghanistan. Conspicuously, the absence of Iran in the London conference clearly indicates that not all is well in the international endeavour aiming to develop a multilateral approach in working out a regional solution suitable to the geopolitical and economic matrix of Afghanistan. Importantly, perhaps for the first time the London conference communiqué mentioned the regional organizations like SCO, SAARC and ECO which can play important role in bringing peace and stability in Afghanistan.

Whatever might be the shortcomings, the London conference was a significant step towards finding a feasible solution to Afghan issue. Outlining some of the prominent features of the conference communiqué [11] makes it clear. The conference participants nearly agreed to include the moderate Taliban into the mainstream Afghan society. President Hamid Karzai of Afghanistan emphasized that unless the moderate Taliban, who comprise a major chunk of the Afghan population mainly Pushtun, are included in the peace process it will be difficult to smooth sail the peace process.

It is thus crucial to note that the conference endeavoured to draw a line of distinction between the hard line and moderate Taliban as to the degree of their ideology and violent practices, and wedge a tussle between the two by providing support both monetary and political to the later while alienating the former. The UN representative had a discussion with representatives of Taliban in Dubai on 8 January 2010. Organizations like OIC and countries like Saudi Arabia have expressed keen interest to mediate between the Taliban and the Afghan government. The London conference has also set up a Peace and Reintegration Trust Fund to steer the peace and integration process further.

The kind of coordination between varied elements and the mediators, success or failure of efforts to alienate the hard line elements, and the extent of support the Afghan government and the donors receive from players will determine the success of the peace efforts.

Another important dimension of the conference was to let the Afghans manage affairs on their own. This agenda is predicated on the principle of gradual phasing out of International Security Assistance Force, and gradual shifting of power to Afghan National Security Forces and other Afghan government agencies. As per the communiqué the provinces which are less turbulent can be handed over to the ANSF by late 2010 or early 2011, and in other turbulent provinces the international force will gradually withdraw by playing a supportive role, while simultaneously training and enlarging the Afghan forces. It will be a Herculean task, and the outcome will depend on how things actually work on the ground, and how the immediate neighbours reshape their strategy towards Afghanistan. It is no hidden fact that Afghan Taliban and Pakistan Taliban are sister organizations. The Pakistan Taliban circulated pamphlets to the effect that there will be rapid surge of attack on Pakistani installations as well as other civilian centres if Pakistan mounts another series of attacks on the Taliban.

The killing of Pakistan Taliban leader, Hakimullah Mehsud [12] on 14 January 2010 may come as a respite, but it may be farfetched to argue that the killing will sound death knell to the dreaded organization, as there are many such Mehsuds preparing to lead the organization. Equally importantly, the conference communiqué urged Karzai to rein in forces of corruption, nepotism and favouritism with which his government is much associated. Much of the aid money is siphoned off by the government officials thus leaving paltry amount for the common Afghans. The conference urged the Afghan government to establish an oversight committee to work against corruption. Issues of providing employment to the common Afghans, establishing a civil service organization to create an administrative cadre in Afghanistan and to speed up infrastructure and other development projects also prominently figured in the conference. Conference participants supported the idea of Karzai government to set up Afghanistan Reconstruction Trust Fund and the Law and Order Trust Fund to speed up these activities.

Tehran Declaration: Potential Game Changer?
The Tehran summit on 24 May 2009 involving three Muslim nations is significant in terms of demonstrating the growing clout of Iran among the neighbouring countries-Pakistan and Afghanistan- with which the US has developed special relationship. Iran's strong criticism against the foreign troops (an indirect reference to the presence of the NATO troops in Afghanistan) might not match well with the policies of the West particularly the US which has invested heavily in the region. The Tehran declaration signed at the end of the summit called for a trilateral approach amongst the three countries to fight the menace of religious extremism, terrorism and drug trafficking, thus giving rise the possibility of exclusion of other powers in solving regional issues. The holding of the Tehran summit was perhaps due since the beginning of 2009. It was on expected lines after the meeting of the leaders of three countries at the sidelines of 10th ECO Summit in March 2009 in Tehran and the meeting of their foreign ministers in April in Kabul.

At the Tehran summit, Mahmoud Ahmedinejad, Asif Ali Zardari and Hamid Karzai, leaders of Iran, Pakistan and Afghanistan respectively, while emphasizing their deep historical, religious, cultural bonds, common heritage and geographical commonalties expressed concern about insecurity, terrorism, extremism and drug production and trafficking in the region. The 24-item declaration [13] in its first point aimed at establishing a mechanism for holding regular and periodical trilateral consultations on special issues by senior officials, foreign ministers and the heads of state/government of the three countries. The declaration also emphasized on trilateral institution building to establish economic and industrial planning commissions and Chambers of Commerce. Item 2 stressed on the joint commitment to make every effort to tackle the regional issues and address their root causes.

There are fundamental issues which need to be analyzed with regard to feasibility of the trilateral approach as envisaged in the declaration. Whether Pakistan and Afghanistan will follow the line of Iran, which perceives the US role in the region as antithetical to their interests, is a matter that needs to be taken into account while analysing the regional dynamics. On the eve of the summit Ahmedinejad was highly critical of the presence of foreign troops in the region. He stated, "Although the presence of foreign forces in our region was under the pretext of establishing security...it has not been much of a help to the establishment of permanent security and political and economic growth." [14]

On the next day of the summit he challenged the US President for face-to-face debate at the United Nations. The US congress, under the Biden-Lugar Bill, has tripled civilian aid to Pakistan and also enhanced the assistance to fight terrorism and fundamentalism. It is a temptation hard to be resisted by Pakistan. The same is the case with Afghanistan. There are tens of thousands of US and NATO troops stationed in Afghanistan. In this context it will be interesting to see how far the trilateral platform, if at all it comes to life, succeeds to fight the menace of religious fundamentalism and terrorism without external support. Similar is the case in the context of fighting drug trafficking and smuggling. Afghanistan alone is the home to about 90 percent of poppy cultivation in the world.

Just one day before the summit, one of the largest-ever drugs seizure in Afghanistan was undertaken in a Taliban stronghold and opium-production centre in the south of the country that led to the killing of 60 Taliban fighters. The point that needs emphasis is whether Afghanistan or Pakistan or the combined force have the wherewithal to fight the menace of terrorism, fundamentalism and drug trafficking that are so much embedded in their systems? Also, from a broader point of view, it may be factored whether the US and the NATO presence in this region will suffice to counter the growing menace of these forces? Or there needs to be the urgency to tackle these issues by evolving an international approach which will have the acceptability by the countries of the region as well as other regional and international powers?

The nuclear angle also might make the balance of relations among the three countries a difficult enterprise. In April 2009 Russia, the US, and other powers such as China, France, UK and Germany invited Iran for deliberation and dialogue to find a diplomatic solution to the nuclear tangle. Their joint statement on 8 April 2009 read, "we strongly urge Iran to take advantage of this opportunity to engage seriously with all of us in a spirit of mutual respect." [15] While the West has expressed concern at Iran's nuclear programme which might be channelled to build nuclear weapons, Iran has rejected all these charges and argued its nuclear programme is meant for civilian purposes. However, after North Korea's test of nuclear device on 25 May 2009, the international pressure on Iran to stop its nuclear programme has increased. The new US administration may use its leverage over Pakistan and Afghanistan in persuading Iran to stop its nuclear programme. In this likely mounting pressure Iran may find it in a fix to balance its relations with these two neighbours. Iran the fifth largest exporter of oil in the world is no doubt a regional power in Central Eurasia. Its huge resources, its cultural capital, and policy projections have become a matter of concern as well as attraction for other powers.

That Iran and Pakistan have not been always in good terms owing to their sectarian differences (Pakistan is Sunni dominated while Iran is Shia dominated), as well as their approaches to international issues may make the success of the trilateral framework a difficult proposition though not impossible. The implications of the Tehran declaration for international politics, particularly for the politics of Central Eurasia cannot be overlooked. That Iran has asserted itself as a regional power and that it could attract immediate neighbours despite differences is no way a mean achievement. It has shown its increasing clout in the region as well as its increasing acceptability by the neighbours. It is no surprise, hence, the summit took place just after a few weeks Zardari and Karzai attended the Washington summit hosted by Obama. Iran's rich natural resources, its nuclear programme, its approach to domestic and international issues and its regional clout need to be factored in the geo-strategic calculus of the region. The declaration will no doubt affect the policy orientations in the region and add a new dimension to the new great game in Central Eurasia with global implications.

References

1. Mehdi Parvizi Amineh, "Towards Rethinking Geopolitics," *Central Eurasian Studies Review*, vol. 3, no. 1, 2004, pp. 7-8.
2. Debidatta Aurobinda Mahapatra, "Central Eurasia: The Concept and Dynamics," *Journal of Eurasian Studies*, vol. 1, no. 3, July-September 2009, pp. 156-167. Also see, Debidatta Aurobinda Mahapatra, *Central Eurasia: Geopolitics, Compulsions and Connections, Factoring India* (New Delhi: Lancer's Publishers, 2008).
3. For details of the resources in the Caspian Sea basin see, Renaud Francois, "Caspian Sea: The Headache of Sharing it Out," *European Strategic Intelligence and Security Centre (ESISC) Analysis*, 22 October 2009. http://www.esisc.org/documents/pdf/en/caspian-sea-the-headache-of-sharing-it-out-449.pdf.
4. For the text of Obama's Cairo Speech see, *The New York Times*, 4 June 2009.
5. For the text of Putin's February 2007 Speech at the 43rd Munich Conference on Security Policy in Munich see, http://www.wakeupfromyourslumber.com/node/646.
6. Anatoly Medetsky, "Medvedev Bristles at Iran's New Plant,"

The Moscow Times, 28 September 2009.

7. Peter Symonds, "New York Times Recycles Fabrications about Iran's Nuclear Programs,"
   http://www.wsws.org/articles/2009/oct2009/iran-o06.shtml.

8. Debidatta Aurobinda Mahapatra, "The AfPak Strategy and its Implementation," *Journal of Alternative Perspectives in the Social Sciences*, vol. 1, no. 3, September-December 2009, pp. 1003-1009.

9. Karen DeYoung, "U.S. Offers New Role for Pakistan," http://www.washingtonpost.com/wp-dyn/content/article/2009/11/29/AR2009112902934.html.

10. Debidatta Aurobinda Mahapatra, "London Afghanistan Conference," Strategic Culture Foundation online magazine, 3 February 2010. http://en.fondsk.ru/article.php?id=2748.

11. For the conference communiqué see, http://www.isaf.nato.int/images/stories/File/factsheets/Documents_Communique percent20of percent20London. percent20Conference percent20on percent20Afghanistan.pdf.

12. Debidatta Aurobinda Mahapatra, "What Death of Baitullah Mehsud Means for Terrorism," Strategic Culture Foundation online magazine, 12 August 2009. http://en.fondsk.ru/article.php?id=2389.

13. For the text of the declaration see, http://www.tehrantimes.com/index_View.asp?code=195443.

14. "Iran Says Foreign Troops no Help to Region's Security," http://www.reuters.com/article/idUSTRE54N0HM20090524.

15. Damien McElroy, "Iran is Offered New Nuclear Talks," http://www.telegraph.co.uk/news/worldnews/middleeast/iran/5128000/Iran-is-offered-new-nuclear-talks.html.

4

International Challenges and Debates

Will Kosovo independence affect other conflicts across the globe? What will be the future international order as other disgruntled regions in different parts of the world aspire for independent status, thus posing challenge to the existing state system? The scenario aftermath of the Kosovo independence in February 2008 raised such pertinent issues. Kosovo came to light since the Balkan crisis gained momentum in the 1990s. The Milosevic regime's ruthless suppression might have exaggerated the crisis but it is power politics between regional and global powers that further aided the crisis. Russia's desire to maintain the unity of Serbia is not only characterized by its Slavic attachment to the region but also due to fear of ripple effect of independence on its regions and neighbourhood.

Putin's statement "Kosovo is a terrible precedent, and it breaks up the entire system of international relations that existed for decades and even centuries" can be seen from a Russian perspective as Russia faces similar challenges in its south. From this perspective, the Kosovo independence might affect the structure of international relations if not properly balanced. Independent Kosovo has been recognized by countries like US, UK, France, Germany and Turkey while countries like Russia, China, Spain, Georgia, and Greece have differing viewpoints on the issue. Among the former Soviet republics, the Baltic States have expressed their support where as countries like Belarus, Moldova, Georgia, Armenia and Azerbaijan have declared their opposition to recognize Serbia's breakaway region.

The impact of Kosovo independence on the Caucasian region has already been felt as Abkhazia the breakaway region of Georgia demanded recognition of its self-proclaimed independence. Georgia had earlier expressed apprehension that any recognition of Kosovo independence may fuel similar sentiments in Abkhazia and South Ossetia. Similarly the Armenian Foreign Minister Vartan Oskanian complained of international double standards, arguing "Granting independence to Kosovo, the international community violated the legal norms but forgot Karabakh." [1]

Both Armenia and Azerbaijan have conflicting interests in Nagorno-Karabakh and the developments in Kosovo will be interpreted differently by both these countries. Azerbaijan declared the independence of Kosovo 'illegal'. The Central Asian states like Kazakhstan, Kyrgyzstan, and Tajikistan expressed opposition against the declaration of independence. India too expressed reservation over this issue as any recognition of independent Kosovo might encourage separatists in its north and north-east to raise their demands more violently. This region in the past has witnessed much bloodshed and now it may prove difficult for India to risk supporting Kosovo's independence. Similarly, Russia's problem in its southern part such as Chechnya and Dagestan is well known. The debilitating potentials of Kosovo developments in fomenting religious fundamentalism and terrorism in the guise of self-determination cannot be ruled out. The Chechen radical leader Doku Umarov has already revealed his vision of a Caucasian caliphate and he may well use the Kosovo incident to further his activities in the region.

The question that needs to be elicited is not that of Kosovo or Abkhazia or South Ossetia, but it is the larger question of the effectiveness of the existing state system. There are around the world numerous disgruntled regions which, if granted independence, will radically alter the existing state system. The Kosovo episode not only polarized the perceptions of powers but also posed a challenge to the existing state system in theory and practice. This episode is crucial in the evolving order of international relations as it posed challenge to multiethnic and pluralistic societies. It has generated a huge churning process in international political order. It is true that right to self determination is a noble principle, but its misinterpretation may bring devastating consequences in an era in which religion and ethnicity based violence has become widespread.

With the rise in aspirations of regions to get independence and with their recognitions amidst contestations, the state system vogue almost for three and half centuries further received a jolt with the episodes of South Ossetia and Abkhazia and earlier that of Kosovo in 2008. The modern state system derives its existence from the treaty of Westphalia, 1648, which recognized the sovereignty of nation states. The treaty which encompasses the two peace treaties of Osnabruck and Munster, signed on 15 May and 24 October of 1648 respectively, ended both the Thirty Years' War in Germany and the Eighty Years' War between Spain and the Netherlands. It initiated a new order in Europe based on the concept of national sovereignty. Earlier, it was not the state per se in the sense of its modern usage, there were empires and kingdoms, whether Greek, Roman, Mongol, Ottoman, Persian or Russian that were reigning over huge chunks of territory. The medieval era was particularly called dark phase as it witnessed tussle between temporal and papal authorities at its height. The Westphalia treaty among then major powers led to the emergence of the current state system. [2]

The two world wars were fought on the pretext of fighting imperialism and making the world safe for democracy. President Woodrow Wilson propounded fourteen points in 1918 as postulates of peace and order. [3] The Second World War that led to the defeat of Nazi totalitarianism was also declared to make the world free from retrograde forces, and to provide rights to emerging nations to live in peace. The UN Charter of 1945 was an improved version of the League of Nations, which ostensibly failed to address the complicated international issues due to non-compliance of its terms by the members. The United Nations is facing unprecedented challenges including that of contested state sovereignty. The question of balancing national sovereignty and right to self determination has become a difficult enterprise. The concept of nationalism too has been highly contested and the same is the case with the concept of right to self determination. The cold war, much driven by ideological considerations, witnessed colossal losses over trivial issues.

The world was polarized into two camps, with some of the developing countries adhering to a policy of non-alignment. The military blocs such as NATO and Warsaw Pact and erection of the Berlin wall on ideological basis- affected the state system. The end of the cold war did not witness any significant changes in international system, though it witnessed change in the patterns of the global politics. It appeared that the old rivalry has not died down, rather it has refashioned itself. Though scholars like Fukuyama has argued that after the end of the cold war liberal ideas would emerge victorious, the international politics appeared complicated with tussles revolving around geo-strategy and geo-economics. The ethnic diversities of various nation-states have challenged the structure of state. Whether it is Nagorno-Karabakh, South Ossetia, Abkhazia, Kashmir or Balochistan in Pakistan the ethnic groups resurfaced to assert their identities, at times by adopting violent methods and getting labelled as terrorist groups.

Two issues need to be focused in the above context. First, whether federalism is still a plausible and workable framework for distinct units in a multi-ethnic, pluralistic society to work together? Or every distinct unit in a federation must enjoy the right to have self-determination at will? This is a matter of common concern for all pluralistic countries, as the domino-effect of secession in societies can well be imagined. Second, how can the differences between the Centre and the unit be resolved amicably in a federation without pulling the relations in opposite direction beyond adjustable limits? Arend Lijphart's 'consociational model' can be considered a device to bring different units with divergent aspirations on a platform to work under certain commonly agreed principles. [4]

However, there can not be any fixed formula as every situation has its own dynamics. As the theory of cultural relativism holds, it is not only precarious but also disastrous to apply a particular set of principles to resolve all the crisis situations. The dynamics of the new world order do not portend the disintegration of state system, but rather accommodation of diverse demands in a framework of resilient federal structure. In the modern world, no particular state is absolutely homogenous in its structure. Diverse aspirations exist, but it is the resilience and flexibility of the federal state to accommodate assorted aspirations or its rigid and totalitarian control over regions- that will determine the shape of the state system. The crucial question is: if harmonious coexistence of the diverse identities within a broader framework of national sovereignty is not adhered to, will the theory and practice of the state system remain unchanged? The issue gets complicated when the power politics dominate the recognition or non-recognition of the newly found states; leading to the polarization of the world community.

In the case of South Ossetia and Abkhazia, the question can be formulated whether these regions could have stayed within the Georgian framework or the break away was inevitable? While the two were not recognized by the US and other European countries Russia was quick to recognize them. It argued that the Kosovo episode set the precedence for the independence of South Ossetia and Abkhazia. It also argued, if Kosovo with a distinct identity within the larger Serbian state system could not be accommodated, then how could the two republics within Georgia? Any irreconcilable tussle between the two principles- national sovereignty and territorial integrity and right to self determination has seeds of major clashes with drastic global ramifications. In this rapidly developing fragile scenario, the responsibility of international powers will be put to test to protect the state and affiliated vibrancy instead of accelerating its demise.

Crisis in Tibet

An interesting case in the context of state sovereignty vs. right to self determination is that of Tibet, the history of which is not free from contestations and varied interpretations as any other history. Tibet the land locked Himalayan region was an independent kingdom till it was conquered and assimilated by the Yuan dynasty of China in 13th century, which was reinforced throughout the next two dynasties, the Ming and the Qing. In 1904, a British force under Francis Younghusband invaded Tibet and occupied its capital Lhasa. The invasion led to a peace treaty between Britain and Tibet, a document that some Tibetan historians see as recognition of their independence but resented by China. During the first decade of the 20th century the matter came to a turn as the 13th Dalai Lama took the advantage of the civil war in China by declaring independence of the Himalayan kingdom in 1912.

After the communist revolution in China in 1949 and establishment of the People's Republic, Chairman Mao Tse Tung ordered the 'liberation' of Tibet by the People's Liberation Army. The Tibetan independence did not last long as the Communist regime under Mao attacked Tibet in 1950 and brought it into the Chinese fold. The Tibetans called this occupation by the Chinese, though the Chinese called it 'People's Liberation' from serfdom. Under the 1951 agreement China agreed to keep Tibet's traditional government and religion in place but later the Chinese policies kept the situation uneasy. The Dalai Lama demanded greater autonomy for the Tibet only to be rejected by Mao. In 1959 the 14th Dalai Lama led an uprising which brought the disenchantment of the Tibetans to a new high. The Chinese government started a massive crackdown of the movement, thus leading to the exile of the Dalai Lama. On 10 March 2010 the Tibetan crisis marked its 51st anniversary. The same year the Tibetan spiritual leader the 14th Dalai Lama observed fifty one years of his exile in India and establishment of his Government in Exile in north Indian town of Dharmashala.

"For nearly six decades, Tibetans in the whole of Tibet known as Cholkha-Sum (U-Tsang, Kham and Amdo) have had to live in a state of constant fear, intimidation and suspicion under Chinese repression. Nevertheless, in addition to maintaining their religious faith, a sense of nationalism and their unique culture, the Tibetan people have been able to keep alive their basic aspiration for freedom." [5] This was a part of the statement of the Tibetan spiritual leader, Dalai Lama on the forty-ninth anniversary of the 'Tibetan National Uprising Day' on 10 March 2008. It was also the day when violent protests erupted in the Tibetan capital Lhasa and later spread like rapid fire throughout the whole region. On the same day about five-hundred monks from the Drepung monastery defied Chinese authorities and marched into Lhasa. Monks from Sera and Gamden monasteries in Lhasa joined the protest.

On 12 March thousands of Chinese security personnel fired tear gas to disperse more than 600 monks from the Sera monastery taking part in street protests. Violent protesters damaged public property by setting fire to shops and vehicles. Chinese authorities sealed off Drepung, Sera and Gamden monasteries. On 15 March Chinese authorities declared that the violent protestors would be shown 'leniency' if they stop protests by midnight of 17 March. On 16 March armed police patrolled streets of Lhasa and China suspended foreign travel permits to Tibet. Protests spread to ethnic Tibetan areas in Sichuan and Gansu provinces. In Gansu's Machu town, a crowd of about 400 people carried pictures of the Dalai Lama while protesting Chinese policies. In the whole episode hundreds of innocent civilian lives were lost.

While the Tibetan government in exile claimed it was the Chinese authorities that provoked the Tibetans to rise in protest, as the promised autonomy was diluted with gradual passage of time with massive Chinese migration to Tibet and building of military garrison in the region, the Chinese authorities argued it was a well calibrated move by international powers in collusion with the Dalai Lama to instigate the Tibetans to show Chinese in a poor image just before few months of the Olympics in Beijing. Both the sides traded vituperative charges, while radicals in the Chinese communist party called Dalai Lama 'wolf in a monk's garb,' the Chinese premier Wen Jiabao accused him for 'inciting sabotage',

Dalai Lama categorized Chinese action 'cultural genocide', and challenged the Chinese Premier to prove his alleged involvement in instigating the protests. While some Tibetans favour continuation of the peaceful protests by giving up the path of violence, the other group is of the view that violence is the only language that China understands. This view was reflected in a TV interaction programme on the Indian *Times Now* channel on 21 March 2008. Ran Yan, the Chinese correspondent of *People's Daily* in New Delhi, called the international community to criticize the Tibetans violent protest as 'anti-religion, anti-human kind, anti-Buddhist and anti-society.' In the same programme the Tibetan representative Sherab Woeser criticized the Chinese authorities for not granting the Tibetans their rights and argued that it is sheer frustration that moved the Tibetans to take part in violent protests.

There were protests world wide against Chinese authorities in the cities across the globe including New York, Sydney, Singapore and Berlin. Protesters in Sydney attempted to replace the Chinese flag at the Chinese consulate by the Tibetan flag. The Tibetan protest took a new turn as about 15-20 young Tibetans jumped over the high security wall of the Chinese embassy in New Delhi and tried to set fire to the Chinese flag on 21 March 2008. They were arrested by the Indian police and taken into custody. The protests prompted many world leaders to issue statements in favour of peaceful resolution of the protracted Tibetan crisis. India expressed serious concern over the violence and the counter violence that engulfed the region. India's concern of the Tibetan crisis is characterized primarily by three factors.

First, the region neighbours Indian north, in which both India and China are engulfed in a border dispute. Second, the violent protests, as the Tibetan government in exile operates from Indian town of Dharmasala, may affect India-China relations. Third, the growing burden of refugees from Tibet is an important area of concern for India. Australia urged China to guarantee basic rights and freedoms of the Tibetan people. Then US Secretary of State, Condoleezza Rice appealed Chinese authorities and Tibetan protestors to exercise restraint and to work for a negotiated settlement. The Speaker of the US House of Representatives, Nancy Pelosi, met the Tibetan leader, Dalai Lama in Dharmasala on 21 March 2008 and demanded for an independent probe for the protests. On the same day, the Chinese Ambassador to India asserted that Tibet is an internal affair of China, and issued stern warning against any interference by any country, organization or person. Whatever may have prompted the violent protests it cannot be overlooked that the Tibetans have raised voice against the Chinese rule from time to time.

Despite the troubled history of Tibet, the present situation seems much gloomy than before. In the present context, especially when China has established virtually absolute control, it is unlikely that Tibetan issue can be addressed earnestly in the near future. Dalai Lama himself has virtually given up the demand for complete independence. In January 2007, in an interview he said "What we demand from the Chinese authority is more autonomy for Tibetans to protect their culture." Dalai Lama has abandoned any claim for absolute independence of Tibet; since 1979 he has advocated for a middle path in the Buddhist tradition, in which a way can be discovered by accommodating Tibetan demands for greater autonomy and independence of their cultural and religious traditions within China. The Chinese government rejects Dalai Lama's 'middle path' approach. Since 2002 six rounds of talks have failed between the Tibetan leaders and the Chinese government. The failure of talks between Dalai Lama's representatives and Chinese government has led to hardening of their respective stances. Chinese government's policy of media blackout after the uprising of 2008 has made happenings in Tibet least known to the outside world.

The China's defence white paper, as elaborated in the second chapter, has emphasized on the Chinese policy of intolerance of any 'splitist' tendencies in the country. This has an obvious reference to the Tibetan movement led by Dalai Lama, besides the Taiwan issue. The defence doctrine made it clear any such movement will be dealt with an iron hand. From the Chinese perspective that may be understood as a matter of national sovereignty, but the Tibetan sentiment especially in terms of protecting identity as reflected in distinct culture and traditions is endangered. China's attempt to change the Tibetan cultural heritage and distinctness has made matter complicated and worrisome. Under newly launched 'patriotic re-education' programme, Chinese government has attempted to change the Tibetan cultural discourse by underplaying the role of Dalai Lama, and other distinct cultural marks of Tibet. Photos of the Dalai Lama were banned in China in 1994 and the decision was fully implemented in Tibetan capital Lhasa in 1996.

The demographic policy of China in the region has added to the concern of the Tibetans. The Tibetans argue that the massive migration of Han Chinese into Tibet has led to worsening of situation as they fear becoming minority in their own land in near future. In the emerging scenario, it will be an interesting pointer how China, one of the fast emerging powers, will address the Tibetan concerns. Application of crude force to suppress the Tibetan movement may have its boomerang effect in the long run. Aspiring to be a global power, China's unravelling of policies towards Tibet will also determine its future projections towards the region in particular and towards the world in general.

Tackling Piracy
Can there be an effective international approach which can

actually tackle the menace of piracy? The matter has assumed special significance particularly after the overwhelming incidents of piracy in the Gulf of Aden and off the Somali coast. About 20,000 ships pass through the Gulf of Aden every year. Though piracy is an age old phenomenon, it has never been as horrendous as the repeated hijacking of ships by the Somali pirates indicate. In 2008 there were 293 incidents of piracy against ships worldwide, which witnessed a rise of 11 percent in comparison to previous year. However, piracy off the Somali coast and in the Gulf of Aden has almost trebled within one year. About 80 percent of trade takes place through sea routes. The major choke points like the Gulf of Aden have major sea routes passing through them.

While some of the earlier sea routes passing through Straits of Malacca could be controlled and managed from the attacks of the pirates, it is the Gulf of Aden that has become the centre stage of debate and action. Some of the analysts have argued that the piracy is not an isolated issue in international politics rather it is a complicated issue with wider implications. The poverty of Somalia, the curtailment of fishermen's rights by big foreign trawlers, dumping of toxic waste, or more nascent development of nexus between pirates and Islamic fundamentalists in Somalia such as Al Shabaab have further spurred piracy as a business. As per a report only in the year 2008 the pirates earned 100 million US dollars as ransom. The big money without much risk might have provided the incentive behind the increasing incidents of piracy. In 2008, 42 vessels were hijacked in the Gulf of Aden and off the coast Somalia. In 2009 till June out of 143 attempted attacks 31 became successful. International Maritime Bureau estimated that in the first quarter of 2009 piracy incidents surpassed that of 2008. [6]

The US, Russia, India, China and Japan have sent their patrolling vessels to guard the sea route against the possible attacks by the Somali pirates. However, it has become difficult to tackle the problem, as the pirates have no well knit organizations; they work in small groups and their expertise at sea in hijacking ships is remarkable. Equally importantly the lack of international coordination has virtually given a free hand to pirates to increase their business. The situation may become further murkier with the rise of Islamic fundamentalist group in Somalia. Some of these pirates have developed close links with Islamic radicals of the group Al Shabaab which is engaged in a fierce battle with Somalia government and African Union forces. The African nation since 1991 has entered into a phase of turmoil. Its government collapsed in the same year leaving 3,330 kilometres of coastline unguarded and subject to all kinds of violations.

Various international organizations have expressed concern and argued for developing an international mechanism to tackle the menace. It needs mention that the activities of pirates are no more confined to hijacking, hostage taking and looting but have been extended to other disruptive activities. For instance, Seacom, the fibre optic cable network, has expressed concern that the pirates have disrupted the optic fibre cables laid under the sea. The cable pipes were supposed to connect Africa particularly the countries of South Africa, Mozambique, Madagascar, Tanzania, Kenya and Ethiopia to India and Europe through internet. [7]

The disruptive activities will likely continue unabated as any stringent action or step in a collaborative format against them is not appearing in the horizon. This brings the urgency for international cooperation to tackle the menace. There are two options in this context. First, the UN can initiate a mechanism to address the issue with a focus on alienating the pirates from the Islamic radicals. The issue of fishing rights of the local fishermen and dumping of toxic materials off the coast need to be looked at from a humanitarian point of view. Second, this policy can be taken up collectively by powers who share common interests in the Gulf and Africa. What is more important these countries can come forward and make a common agreement while taking into confidence the Somali government and patrol collectively the sea lanes. In the world where the financial crisis has ravaged the most, it is the time that the international trade and business must go smooth without disruption for which the sea routes need to be protected. There has been no such urgency as of now to evolve a commonly agreed international framework to tackle the piracy problem.

Climate Change and the Polarization

The climate change conference at Copenhagen in December 2009, which witnessed participation of delegates from 193 countries and by 110 heads of states, virtually yielded no substantial result primarily owing to widely held differences and perceptions and also due to the divide between the developing and the developed countries. Though the agreement on 18 December after hectic parleys was called to be 'meaningful' and historic it was neither in true sense of the term as nothing was legally binding on the members regarding their commitment to reduce emission of green house gases, nor did it set a framework for the countries' commitments to be strictly monitored. The Brazilian president expressed frustration during his speech in the conference that probably an angel could come and bestow required intelligence in the negotiating parties to realize the gravity of the problem and achieve a meaningful agreement. The fact remains that the Copenhagen conference achieved trifle and it will be the future course of developments that will determine the fate of climate change discourse and also the fate of the struggling planet.

On 13 December the African countries boycotted the talks with the argument that their plea before the developed countries to bear the cost of climate change measures by providing finance and technologies was not appreciated by the developed countries. Similarly the chairman of G-77, Sudan expressed unhappiness at the conclusion of summit after hectic parleys but without substantial result. Many drafts were made, many cancelled and many individual drafts such as that of

Denmark were criticized, but finally there was none of the consensual agreement about how to go for a safer and secure planet for future generations. The main argument of the developing countries is that the developed countries which are responsible for about 75 percent of the green house gas emission must fix the target for themselves to reduce carbon emissions and help developing countries in terms of green technology and finance to tackle the problem. They further argue that the guiding principle behind any agreement on climate change must recognize the equitable sharing of responsibility and global commons and differentiated capabilities to contribute towards a better planet by targeting reduction of green house gases.

Two major disagreements emerged during the conference. First, the developed group mainly represented by Japan and EU argued for going beyond Kyoto protocol of 1997 mandated till 2012, which bound both developed and developing countries to reduce the green house gases. They insisted that a new agreement should be established replacing the present Kyoto Protocol. They further argued that the developing countries must fix the targets so that the global warming must not increase by two degree Celsius by 2050. China has declared 40 to 45 percent reduction by 2020 compared to the 2005 level, India 20 to 25 percent by the same period and Brazil 38 to 42 percent.

However, the arguments made by Japan and EU appeared to put the sole onus on the developing countries to reduce carbon emissions. At the conference Brazil, South Africa, India and China made a strong case for the developing countries and argued that unless there is equitable sharing of burden there can not be any progress towards working climate change architecture. Rather they emphasized on Bali Action Plan of 2007 which focused on the principles of equity and equitable burden sharing. The 13th Conference of Parties at Bali emphasized on an Action Plan to enhance the implementation of the UN Framework Convention on Climate

Change. The plan aimed at full, effective and sustained implementation of the climate convention through long term cooperative action of the Parties up to and beyond 2012.

Second, the developing countries argued that the developed countries must provide technology and capital to the developing countries to share and mitigate the hazards of climate change by reducing the green house gases. Indian Prime Minister, Manmohan Singh, articulating the voices of the developing countries, argued "climate change cannot be addressed by perpetuating the poverty of the developing countries. Every citizen of the globe has equal entitlement of the global atmospheric space." [8] Hence, in order to fight global warming the developing countries need assistance from developed countries. Japan has pledged US$ 15 billion, the EU US$ 11 billion, and the US has pledged to raise US$ 100 billion by 2020 to assist developing countries to face the challenges of climate change. The point of concern is unless the green houses gases are not curtailed the vagaries of climate will hurt the planet and by 2050 the temperature may rise up to 6 percent, causing catastrophe to the world particularly to the nations at sea and ocean coasts. There will be more cyclones, floods and droughts due to melting of ice caps, scanty rains, etc. thus posing serious challenges to the survival of humanity.

The agreement reached on 18 December was neither satisfactory nor result oriented though it contained a ray of hope. Obama's argument that the developing countries' commitments to reduction of carbon emission must be monitored by an international agency was opposed by BASIC countries. The developing countries fear such a move will only strengthen the hand of developed countries by providing them an upper hand in the international decision making body. Rather they emphasized on the principles as stipulated by the Kyoto Protocol and Bali Action Plan.

However, a face saving formula was adopted at the end of the summit. A non-binding agreement was drafted by members after the US-BASIC and US-EU deliberations. The non-controversial principles that the increase in the global warming to be confined to 2 percent by 2050 and the developing countries should share information about their green house gas reduction measures were commonly agreed upon. The Copenhagen Conference of Parties that took place for about two weeks after two years of announcement of Bali Plan will be remembered for hectic parleys but without any significant achievement. Its success, if there is any, lies in the fact that it did not close the future scope for dialogue and deliberation for better climate change architecture. However, the achievements of two-week deliberations appear trifle in view of the magnitude of the threat the climate change poses before the humanity.

Cyber Politics in Inter-State Relations

The famous scientist Albert Einstein, while deeply perturbed by the use of nuclear weapons during the second world war, had lamented that though he could not predict the kind of weapons to be used in any probable third world war, he was sure the fourth world war, if the humanity survives after the third one, will be fought with archaic weapons like stones. This Einsteinian prediction about complexities involved in future wars and their horrendous consequences could be well comprehended in recent times with the increasing use of different kinds of 'weapons' by the nations, among which the application of information technology is a prominent one. The US-Chinese brawl over the allegation of the largest search engine Google against the hacking of its source codes has in fact widened the complex web of international politics with likely wide ranging socio-political and economic implications. While China out rightly denied any role in the hacking episode and accused US of imposing diktats on other countries, US sought further explanation from China and some of the US based organizations threatened to drag China to WTO over the issue.

The issue came to the forefront on 12 January 2010 when

the California based web search engine Google accused the Chinese government of accessing email accounts of its email holders in a 'highly sophisticated' attack. It threatened to withdraw its operations from China on this account. On 19 January 2010 Google postponed the launch of Android phones in China. China has the largest number of population at about 350 million who use internet with a huge search engine market. In 2009 this market stood at about US$ 1billion. In this emerging market Google holds about one third of the share, only second to the Chinese Baidu which holds more than 60 percent of the market. Google's rise to prominence within a span of four years, as it opened its office in Beijing in 2006, is not a small feat. Its success story in the different setting of China was followed by other companies.

Hence, Google's threat of withdrawal from China not only raised alarm about its business prospects in China, but also about bilateral trade between the US and China with implications for the world. The US President Barack Obama declared that he is 'troubled' by the developments and the Secretary of State, Hilary Clinton asked China to provide further information about its activities in the matter. Chinese official daily *Xinhua* quoting a spokesperson of the Chinese Ministry of Information and Technology denied any charges of violation of cyber laws and stated that accusation of their participation in cyber attack was 'groundless' and aimed to denigrate China. China accused US of 'double standards' and claimed that it was the victim of cyber attacks. Official data of China showed more than one million IP addresses were under control by overseas sources and more than 42,000 Chinese websites had been hacked in the year 2009 alone. Besides, China criticized the US of imposing its values on other countries. The official *China Daily* newspaper observed that the strategy of the US was "to exploit its advantages in internet funds, technology and marketing and export its politics, commerce and culture to other nations for political, commercial and cultural interests of the world's only superpower." [9]

China also argued since the Chinese law is not followed by many foreign companies including the IT ones; hence they invite attention from the authorities. The main US contention is that the Chinese authorities committed cyber attacks by hacking the codes of Google engine, while the Chinese argument as stated above is it has not done any such attacks and whatever it has done it is within the purview of the Chinese law. The problem is that these kinds of standoff between the two major powers may not only affect their political relations, but also trade relations thus affecting the global financial situation and in the log term global political situation.

There is an increasing trend of allegations by nations about their web servers having classified information being hacked by other nations. India has revealed that sensitive information from the ministries of foreign affairs and defence have been hacked from distant sources. With the increasing allegations as well as threats of cyber warfare, it is undoubtedly an increasing factor of concern in international politics that the national rivalries will be reflected in the cyber domain. With the increasing use of information technology the millions of lines of programming instructions, known as source codes, have become vulnerable to hackers. These hackers can be used by rivals, including rival nations, in stealing key instructions and copying them, thus making advantage of the opponent in information technology defunct. The attackers can make undetected changes to that code, and hence give themselves secret access to the activities of the company or the nation. The complexity of software system created by thousands of professionals also makes it difficult to be absolutely confident about security of any program.

The rogue elements like terrorists have started using this complex nature of information technology in their activities and have increasingly shown their keenness to use it to further widen their inhuman operations. The nations will likely no more engage in direct warfare but wars at other planes such as at subtle cyber plane. The use of cyber technology by nations to fight their rivals is certainly a novel development in international politics. This technology has become a new tool in the hands of nations to settle scores with each other with a potential of destruction not only of nations but also of the humanity unless there is a genuine attempt on part of the nations to coordinate their cyber laws and develop coordinated mechanism to prevent misuse of the technology.

Is NAM Relevant?

Can Non-aligned Movement, a movement that emerged in the heydays of the cold war, play a role in a changed post-cold war scenario? The 15th summit at the Egyptian Red Sea resort Sharm el Sheikh in July 2009 engaged policy makers as well as scholars to seek a plausible answer as to the relevance of the organization in the 21st century. The indications are positive as the utterances, except few grumblings such as that by Libyan ruler Muammar Gaddafi, were free from verbose and rhetoric, and marked by practical sense of recognition of the changed world and the required reorientation in the approaches.

The evolution of NAM can be traced back to the Afro-Asian conference at Bandung in Indonesia in 1955. The prominent leaders- Indian Prime Minister Jawaharlal Nehru, Yugoslavian leader Josip Broz Tito, Egyptian leader Gamal Abdel Nasser, Sukarno of Indonesia and Kwame Nkrumah of Ghana played crucial role to give the movement an organizational form. NAM emerged as the voice of the developing countries amidst the tense cold war environment. Further back in 1947, the Inter-Asian Relations Conference in New Delhi called for Asian solidarity to fight against the nemesis of colonialism, imperialism and other menaces like racism. These objectives with their moral implications were covered by the NAM agenda, which also emphasized on a de-weaponized, non-hostile, and non-discriminatory world. NAM did play a significant role during the cold war. India's role in

Korean crisis and Nehru's world vision of peaceful world order and coexistence did promote its objectives.

The organization's massive presence in the UN enhanced its role. The first summit at Belgrade in 1961, further promoted its agenda of a non-discriminatory world. Throughout its summit declarations the NAM echoed its voice as a moral harbinger of peace in the tumultuous world in which the horrors of star wars and nuclear weaponization programmes had struck mankind. Besides its political role, the NAM indeed played an important role in raising the concerns at the economic monopolization by the developed nations. Through its summit declarations NAM called for south-south cooperation for a new international economic order by forging alliance of the developing nations of the world.

The end of the cold war raised questions about the validity of this mechanism evolved during the cold war, which was then labelled 'immoral' by some quarters. There are now no blocs in a rigid sense, no super power rivalry, no nuclear weaponization by big powers and no colonialism in an apparent sense. Hence, what is its relevance, the antagonists of this organization continue to ask. Some even predicted the demise of NAM with the end of the cold war. Even during the cold war, the antagonists argue, NAM failed as a conflict resolution mechanism. For instance, they point out the Colombo plan mooted by the NAM members to ease tensions between India and China failed to broker peace. Similarly, despite its proclaimed non-aligned character plurality of the members had their links with either of the ideological blocs.

Whatever may be the shortcomings, undoubtedly, it is a matter of common agreement that NAM played a significant role, at least a balancing one among the power blocs with its moral edge. In a broader sense it gave voice to the voiceless on a broader platform of peace, friendship and non-violence. There may be the end of the cold war but the motives that spurred the cold war have not died down and as the politics of the post-cold war world shows the power politics has assumed new dimensions. Second, though there has been no massive build up of nuclear weapons by the developed countries, there has been illegal arms trade and nuclear weapons build up by other powers, which have not only acquired nuclear weapons but the unsafe location of these weapons has given rise to the fears of their falling into the hands of devious elements. Third, the menace of terrorism and its increasing sophisticated nature in this post-cold war world has shown the world that the problems have not ended, rather they have multiplied. Fourth, as the recent global financial crisis has shown, what Indian Prime Minister, Manmohan Singh in his speech at Sharm el Sheikh in 2009 referred, the worst economic crisis 'in living memory' further hunts down the global politics and has necessitated a collective, multilateral approach to tackle the crisis.

Relatedly, as the Indian prime minister pointed out in his speech, the developing countries have been hit by the policies of the developed countries such as protectionism. "If the aftermath of the (financial) crisis is not carefully managed, and if the abundance of liquidity leads to a revival of speculative activities, we may well see a period of prolonged stagflation," [10] he cautioned.

NAM, a group of 115 nations, representing two-thirds of the UN with more than half of world's population, bears a resemblance to its old self as its moral standing still appears vivid, but, needless to add, it has to reorient its approach to suit changing world order. Probably, the 15th summit has made the right utterances in this direction. The outgoing Chairman of the grouping, Cuban President Raul Castro, rightly called for a new economic order to face the global financial crisis. Castro also called NAM to be more active in the areas of health, human rights and non-proliferation.

The summit in its deliberations also rightly emphasized that the terrorist menace must be tackled, and 'there should be no safe haven for terrorists in the world.' It also talked about expeditious reform of the UNSC and finalization of draft on comprehensive convention on terrorism. The joint declaration issued at the end of the summit on 16 July 2009 incorporated all the above issues. Regarding climate change the declaration emphasized on 'mitigation, adaptation, finance and technology transfer, capacity building' to tackle the problem according to the principle of 'differentiated responsibilities.'

NAM has to play a renewed role in a changed global context. It still plays a moral guide but it has to develop pragmatic approaches to confront reigning problems afflicting the world. It will be irrational as well as unethical to grade NAM as an anti-cold war mechanism as it means more than that. The cold war of the past might have gone away but the politics of power and the Hobbesian rules of game persist in the post-cold war world. The changed world with its old and new set of problems not only justifies NAM and necessitates its existence but also heralds for it the imperative to create a comprehensive, balanced and equitable world order.

Can G-20 Replace G-8?
After the widely publicized and effective G-20 summit of the world leaders in Pittsburgh, there are speculations making round whether G-20 will replace G-8 in near future as a better alternative to deliberate on common issues of the globe. The G-20 summit in September 2009 primarily to discuss the global economic issues has emerged as a premier international forum to bring the economic power houses of the world, including the emerging ones like India, China and Brazil to deliberate on the issues of global economic slow down and the measures to come out of the crisis. G-8 (earlier G-7), a conglomeration of the rich and industrially developed countries mostly from the Western hemisphere emerged in 1975 to deliberate on the issues of global concern such as health, economic and social development, energy, environment, and terrorism. Dominated by the West, this grouping controlled levers of the world economy with major saying in the affairs of global financial institutions like WB

and IMF. It is the richest club of the world. In order to further broad base its scope and nature, the grouping in 2005 formed G8+ 5, in which countries like India and China were included though these outreach countries do not have any say in the decision making process of the grouping.

The emerging realities in the post cold war world need to be taken into account while emphasizing the role of G-20. The first reality particularly from an economic perspective is the rise of BRIC countries. As per an estimate the combined economy of BRIC countries would surpass the economy of the most prosperous group of G-7 by 2035. These countries particularly India and China have huge population with a large and fast growing consumer market; making them crucial players in this emerging matrix. Despite the global economic slow down Indian economy has grown in the period of 2008-2009 at more than 6 percent and expected to grow at a similar rate in 2009-2010. China's role in aiding the US in fighting slump in its economy is noteworthy. Since its inception in 1999 G-20, which also includes all the BRIC countries, has played an important role 'to strengthen the international financial architecture and to foster sustainable economic growth and development.' As its official website states, "the G-20 now has a crucial role in driving forward work between advanced and emerging economies to tackle the international financial and economic crisis, restore worldwide financial stability, lead the international economic recovery and secure a sustainable future for all countries." [11]

The rise of Asia has been well pronounced at the summit of the G-20 in Pittsburgh. Affirming the role of Asia, Indian Prime Minister Manmohan Singh emphasized the rise of Asia with both political and economic clouts, which must be recognized and factored in the politics of the nations. To quote him, "With the rise of Asia, with growth of India, China and Brazil, the economic decision-making has to take into account the views of these countries if it is to have an optimum impact." [12] The G-20, formed by both the developed and the developing, in contrast to the G-8 dominated by the rich industrial nations, can provide a base for equitable international playing field for the countries of the world. As Singh observed, "Interdependence in a globalized world means that no country, however powerful it may be, can take on the entire burden of economic adjustment and economic decision-making."

It may be too early to predict the replacement of the G-8 by G-20. There are many challenges which the larger group must confront. Though the G-20 communiqué stated, "We designated the G-20 to be the premier forum for our international economic co-operation" the question arises whether the grouping with differences within the members, with diverse political and economic set ups and aspirations can rise as a single player in international politics. G-20 is quite divergent when the issues of global climate change, non-proliferation and financial regulation reform come to picture. However, it will be difficult to ignore the clout of rising economies of the world. It is also equally important to remember the G-20 represents 90 percent of the GDP of the world. The Asian drivers outpace the European counterparts in terms of growth. While the global financial crisis hit hardest the US and Europe, the Asian powers particularly India and China managed well the crisis.

It may not be far fetched to project G-20 as an alternative to the G-8. While the G-8 deliberates on both political and economic issues, the overwhelming economic nature of G-20 keeps it out of political ramblings and keeps it in good stead as the major forum to sort out, and to deliberate on the global economic issues. The recent global financial crisis, probably the severest since the recession of the inter war period of 1930s, has goaded the world leaders to think broadly in terms of common goals and achievements. The emerging power equations and configurations in the post-cold war era will definitely impact the shaping of international order. In this emerging scenario, the emerging clout of the G-20 and the clout of its leading members can not be ignored.

References

1. http://www.panarmenian.net/eng/politics/news/24958.
2. Treaty of Westphalia (Peace Treaty between the Holy Roman Emperor and the King of France and their respective Allies), http://avalon.law.yale.edu/17th_century/westphal.asp.
3. Woodrow Wilson's Fourteen Points Speech, http://usinfo.org/docs/democracy/51.htm.
4. For Lijphart's Theory on Consociational Democracy see, Arend Lijphart, *The Politics of Accommodation: Pluralism and Democracy in the Netherlands* (Berkeley: University of California Press, 1968); and *Democracy in Plural Societies: A Comparative Exploration* (New Haven: Yale University Press, 1977).
5. Statement of His Holiness the Dalai Lama on the 49th Anniversary of the Tibetan National Uprising Day, 10 March 2008, http://www.tibet.org/march10-hhdl.html.
6. http://www.bairdmaritime.com/index.php?option=com_content &view=article&id=3887:imb-issues-latest-quarterly-piracy-report-&catid=113:ports-and-shipping&Itemid=208.
7. Debidatta Aurobinda Mahapatra, "Need for International Cooperation to Tackle Piracy," Strategic Culture Foundation online magazine, 1 July 2009. http://en.fondsk.ru/article.php?id=2280.
8. For the Prime Minister's statement before proceeding to Copenhagen summit for climate change see, http://www.ndtv.com/news/india/pms_statement_as_he_heads_t o_copenhagen.php.
9. Wen Guang, "Google Incident and US Internet Strategy," http://www.chinadaily.com.cn/cndy/2010-01/23/content_9365524.htm.
10. Statement by the Prime Minister at the 15th Summit of the Non Aligned Movement, http://www.indianembassy.de/template.php?mnid=103&inclpag e=170720092.htm.
11. www.g20.org/.
12. *The Economic Times*, 27 September 2009.

5

Facets of Terrorism

Terrorism in South Asia, with having wider implications, can be termed a hydra headed monster with deep roots. In fact the interesting phenomenon is that there is no commonly agreed format in tackling the menace, and when its potentials as a weapon of national interest is explored then the issue becomes further murkier and challenging. The events after the terror attack in Mumbai show that the conflicting interests of neighbours, and the conflicting perspectives on the issues pertaining to borders, have added complexity to the issue and the challenges it puts forth. Pakistan's predicament is that it suffers violence from radical elements that it itself has nourished. The matter of concern with the unfolding of the so called Karachi project is wider with graver implications. The project intends to draw Indian Muslims into the orbit of extremism and terrorism, thus challenging the very Indian fabric of pluralism, secularism and multi-ethnicism.

That the Mumbai Muslims did not allow the culprits of November 2008 attacks, also Muslims, to be buried in Mumbai soil is no mean portrayal of Indian pluralistic national identity, which the Karachi project intends to target. India-Pakistan cooperation, expected to take a shape with the launch of the 'irreversible' peace process, weathered away after the Mumbai attack as the issues were raised to endless trivialities without genuine concerns and actions to bring to justice the culprits. India in the past decade became a victim of terrorism perhaps unmatched by any country. But, the terror menace is not confined to India or Indian subcontinent rather it is much wider in its reach. Terrorism laced with religious fundamentalism not only challenges Indian state but also challenges any state which has multiethnic and pluralistic character. At the same time, the nature of terrorism and motivation the radical elements draw will depend on the state policies as to how far they accommodate diverse aspirations.

Fatwa against Terrorism

A major event made many protagonists of global war against terrorism perplexed when a fatwa (edict) against terrorism was issued by the oldest and second largest Islamic university, Darul Uloom situated at Deoband in India on 31 May 2008 at a conference in Ram Lila ground of New Delhi. The conference was attended by more than one hundred thousand people from different Islamic sects as well as religions including Hinduism, Jainism and Sikhism. Besides India, host of Islamic scholars from Uzbekistan, Afghanistan, Pakistan, Sri Lanka, Maldives, Jordan, Lebanon and Indonesia participated in the conference. The fatwa was endorsed by all Muslim sects in India. Various respected Islamic bodies such as Nadwatul Ulama at Lucknow, Jamaat-e-Islami Hind and All India Muslim Personal Law Board ratified the fatwa against terrorism. The fatwa stated: "Islam is a religion of peace and security. In its eyes, on any part over the surface of the earth, spreading mischief, rioting, breach of peace, bloodshed, killing of innocent persons and plundering are the most inhuman crimes." [1]

The fatwa differentiated between jihad and terrorism: "There is a world of difference between terrorism and jihad. Jihad is constructive and terrorism is destructive. Jihad is for the establishment of peace... terrorism is the gravest of crimes, as held by the Koran and Islam." One of the most important aspects of the conference was the attempt at defining the much controversial concept of terrorism. The fatwa defined the concept as "Any action that targets innocents, whether by an individual or by any government or by a private organization anywhere in the world constitutes, according to Islam, an act of terrorism." [2]

For the first time in the history a fatwa was issued by an Islamic school in unequivocal terms. Though the Deobond

School issued another fatwa in its 'All India Anti-terrorism conference' in Deobond on 25 February 2008, in which it took into account diverse politics accompanying terrorism and called for a united Muslim front to fight the rust in Islam; it was the New Delhi conference, named 'Anti-terrorism and Global Peace conference' (the words global and peace added in the second conference) which set the tone for a more clear cut and straight forward criticism of terrorist violence. The subtle underpinnings of the fatwa are varied. It is common knowledge that radical organizations and movements such as the Taliban in Afghanistan and Jaish-e-Mohammad in Pakistan avowedly draw their ideological sustenance from the Deobond School. Hence, the school's distancing from the violent propaganda may disrupt or at least discourage the ideological connection between the two. The Taliban imposed a medieval kind of orthodox rule in Afghanistan in the late 1990s and the Pak-based Jaish-e-Mohammad played havoc in India, including attacking its parliament in 2001. Hence, the distancing of Deobond from these groups might turn the radical organizations as mere terrorists, renegade, pervert elements, which have no religion.

The international ramifications of the fatwa are far reaching. One of the common elements in international political discourse revolving around Islam includes the prospects of building an Islamic state, purely governed by Islamic rules. According to this view, this can be possible only when Islam rules, and which can be achieved by means of force. Hence, when the terrorist organizations give the call for establishment of Islamic Caliphate, they draw heavily on perverse interpretations of Islam. Interestingly, the anti-terrorism conference in February had called all Muslims to continue their loyalty towards the motherland and love and respect towards humanity. The Deobond fatwa, both first and second, were warnings for the terrorist organizations that they are not Islamic in spirit and they just play havoc on the path of international peace and order. A participant from Pakistan,

Muhammad Hashim Babar, openly admitted in the conference that the Pakistan border along with Afghanistan has madrasas which produce hordes of terrorists every year. [3]

The fatwa by the Deobond School, considered the most important Islamic institutions after the Al-Azhar University in Cairo, was expected to impact these madrasas for better. The timing and place of the edict was also crucial. It is true that terrorism in many instances all over the world have been linked with Islam either by design or by a fortuitous combination of terror act and religion of the culprit. The fatwa, hence, in a sense made an attempt to absolve the Muslim community from this connection and show that Islam, like any other religion, loves peace and tranquillity. The message of the conference was clear that some Muslims may be terrorists, but all Muslims cannot be victimized for acts of perverts in the religion. The Deobond fatwa might have seemed an indication that from the acts of some perverted Muslims, the whole community or a particular country can not be castigated.

Needless to emphasize the fatwa was much needed in the current global turmoil. Its place of issue in India bears special significance in the sense that India is a multiethnic, pluralistic and secular country, and which too has witnessed horrendous scenes of terrorist violence. Muslims make up about 13 percent of India's population, making it the third largest Islamic population after Indonesia and Pakistan. The Deobond School took the lead in a true sprit of Islam to fight rotten elements within its frame.

This effort of the Deobond needs to be supported not only by India but also by the countries around the globe. In order to make the world terror-free, all the religions must come out openly to denounce violence, and emphasize on peaceful resolution of conflicts. The Deobond School must be congratulated in taking such a bold step. However, the most important thing that still needs to be done is the genuine implementation of the fatwa. That will be its real test. The Mumbai terror attack after few months of the fatwa and before that terror attacks at many places in India and other countries, as discussed later, serve the indication that the Islamic extremists have not fathomed the true teachings of Islam.

Terrorism Unabated

Bomb blasts in China, India, Russia, and many other places in 2008 vindicated the tactical astuteness and technological strength of the terrorists to strike targets including hospitals, schools, busy markets and public festivals. In the month of June and July 2008 India witnessed three major terror strikes in three of its major cities: Jaipur in June, Bangalore and Ahmedabad in July. Terror strike in another Indian city, Surat also known as the diamond hub of India, could be avoided in last minute due to prior information and timely defuse of live bombs planted in public parks, garbage, and hanging from tree branches. The 21 serial bomb blasts in Ahmedabad killed 56 people and seven blasts in Bangalore killed 6 people, besides injuring hundreds. For the first time in India, the terrorists targeted a hospital, killing not only doctors and nurses, but also pregnant women and children.

The gory act displayed barbarity of the terrorists and their ghastly designs to generate fear among common people. The National Security Advisor of India claimed that till the middle of 2008 about 800 sleeping terror cells were discovered in Indian territory. [4] The fragile situation in Pakistan will ensconce the terrorist morale to foment violent activities. The terror strike at the Indian embassy in July 2008 in Kabul, killing about 40 people, showed the Taliban resolve, along with the support of Pakistan (as Afghanistan and the US corroborated it), to obstruct Indian humanitarian activities in Afghanistan.

In August 2008, China in news for grand Olympic celebrations, witnessed three terror strikes in its Xinjiang province, a region majority of inhabitants of which are Uyghur Muslims. The bomb blasts on 4 August 2008 in different parts of Xinjiang including in the Silk Route town of Kashgar killed

31 people including 14 policemen and injured hundred others. The motive behind the attack was to spoil the spirit of Olympics and use the occasion to bring a new and fresh colour to the already insipid terror movement. The spectre of terrorism in Afghanistan, not far from China's Xinjiang, in these months witnessed intense revival. The leader of Pakistan-Taliban, Baitullah Mahsud (later killed by the US drone attacks) said that his fighters will aid their Taliban brothers. In an interview aired on Al-Jazeera TV on 26 May 2008 he declared that his men "are proud that we are the enemies of Jews and Christians, and we are also proud that we are fighting them with all our strength." [5] Terror strikes in Chechnya and Ingushetia and other parts of globe indicated the resurgence of terrorist activities throughout the world with renewed vigour.

To contain terror, one of the first steps must be to check its proliferation by discovering and nullifying its epicentres. But when the governments appear to patronize terrorist activities, it becomes difficult to contain the menace. From this point of view, the South Asian region has become a matter of special focus. For instance the HUJI of Bangladesh, which has a large network especially in Chittagong hill tracts of the country, and Hizbul Mujahideen, Lashkar-e-Toiba and United Jihad Council active in Pakistan and in Kashmir under Pak control with well functioning training centres have become matters of concern. Though Pakistan claimed to have killed the dreaded Al Qaeda number 3 leader, Abu Saeed al Masri in second week of August 2008, it appeared like offering sop to the US to garner favour and get assistance. The situation is neither better in north towards Afghanistan. Known for its poppy cultivation Afghanistan is an international hub for drug trafficking and smuggling through its porous borders with Central Asian countries.

These networks use the traditional Silk Route for drug peddling to countries west and north, and to Europe. The situation has got further murkier due to the region's embroilment in power politics due to its geo-strategic location. In this context, states need to adopt a well calibrated policy to tackle the menace especially by applying soft methods. The July 2008 international conference on Sufism (the tolerant and peaceful variant of Islam) in Gudermes in Chechnya to counter the values of the radical Salafism, much prevalent in North Caucasus, can be seen as a step in this direction. [6] But, how far the menace of international terrorism will be tackled globally is a moot question that needs to be addressed. Great hopes in this direction were pinned after the 9/11, when the leaders of the world called to align global forces to fight the menace. But the spirit frittered away as the later developments witnessed. It appears that the solemn hopes were crushed under the labyrinth of the so called new great game in which geo-strategic ambitions, competition to control energy resources, expansion of zone of influence became more prominent, than to counter the global menace of terrorism.

Mumbai Terror Attack

The terror attack in Mumbai in November 2008 is critical in many ways. It was the first attack on India which assumed multinational character as the terrorists held hostage of British, US, Russian and Israeli nationals and their email message espoused the cause of international conflicts for perpetrating the barbarous act. Second, the attack targeted India's commercial centre, Mumbai. Not the common places in city as in July 2006 but its luxury hotels and restaurants usually visited by businesspersons, affluent and foreign tourists were targeted. Though the mastermind behind this inhuman act was traced to Pakistan, the implications of the act became worldwide and the world leaders while pronouncing their support for India displayed unity in criticizing the act in most unequivocal terms.

It all started in the dusk hours of the 26 November. The terrorists in a well orchestrated manner, after duping the Indian marine police, coast guard and Mumbai police reached

Mumbai through a hijacked trawler named Kuber and split after reaching Mumbai. One group attacked the Chhatrapati Shivaji Terminal railway station and targeted the people in the terminal, then turned to Cama hospital and fired indiscriminately. Other groups targeted the posh hotels Taj Mahal Palace (a hundred year old heritage hotel, with about 800 rooms with its new wing combined) and Oberoi-Trident, and the Nariman House (mostly housed by Jews). About 200 people got killed in the heinous terrorist attack. The terrorists not only killed civilians, foreign tourists and senior police officials but took the whole city to ransom, bringing the buzzing city of Mumbai to a standstill. India's National Security Guard, Army and Mumbai Police continued the operation till the morning of 29 November to eliminate the terrorists from the Taj, and the other two places. The old and regal structure of the Taj provided the terrorists enough space for manipulation to avoid the gaze of the Indian forces.

No clear estimation of terrorist strength, their accomplices and sources could be made for quite some time, though the findings of Indian intelligence agencies revealed role of Pakistan based organizations and estimated the number of terrorist to be ten. The magnitude of this terror act indicated the long term plan of the terrorists with links with terrorist organizations based in Pakistan. Al Qaeda and organizations like LeT, JeM and a host others consider India as inimical to their interests and designs. They see India as a collaborator with the West which they highly despise and on many occasions they have poured venom on India due to its cooperation with the West. They too see Kashmir as a part of their agenda. The targeting of Jews in Nariman House appeared to have an explicit objective to highlight the issue of Palestine.

The holding of hostage of other foreign nationals was not only aimed at magnifying and protracting the issue at a global scale, but also to show the world their might, technology and strategy in perpetrating such barbarous acts. The strategy to target India's commercial hub can be seen as intended to break India's economic backbone and discourage foreign investors. The role of Pakistan based LeT in complicity with Pakistan's intelligence agencies was quite perceptible in perpetrating the terrorist act. In its meeting in Pakistan town Muridke on 23 November 2008, its Chief Hafeez Saeed had criticized India for its role in Afghanistan and its involvement in reconstruction works. He exhorted the members of the Lashkar to punish India. The attack could be seen in a wider framework of global terrorism, epicentre of which could be traced to Afghanistan and Pakistan's border areas with it which are infested by Al Qaeda and Taliban elements.

The US, Russia, UK, France, almost all countries of the world strongly condemned the terror attack. Russian President, Dmitry Medvedev condemned the attack in most unequivocal terms, "the monstrous crimes of terrorists in Mumbai arouse our wrath, indignation and unconditional condemnation," and "the inhuman terrorist attacks on hospitals, hotels and other public places aimed at killing civilians, taking and murdering hostages are crimes directed against the foundation of civilized society." [7] For the first time the Indian political elites came above the sectarian vote bank politics, took a united stand irrespective of ideologies. Though some analysts might call the tragedy the 9/11 of India, the priority was to successfully manage its economic loss and concurrent loss of confidence of foreign investors and build an effective mechanism to counter the menace. The heightened situation also required enough introspection in bringing the neighbourhood into orbit of genuine cooperation so that the crushing and maiming of humanity is not repeated though on this front the complexities are enormous.

The perplexing nature of the Mumbai terror attack that took place in November 2008 continues unabated. The magnitude of the attack in terms of death and destruction and the results so far in countering its fallouts are equally horrendous. It may not be exaggeration to say the covert nature of the terror design still remains invisible under the overt ambiguities floated by the terrorist organizations and their patrons. Instead of bringing the perpetrators to justice, it appears the players are still in a mood to add grist to their mills out of the one of the most barbarous crimes against humanity. As a result unsurprisingly the flurry of activities in countering the attack has produced little and the process seems unending. Indian government's dossier of evidence presented to Pakistan on 5 January 2009 was categorized as a set of information which could not be counted as evidence. India in its dossier, divided into three sections, demanded three things. The first section of the dossier outlined details of the dates and locations of the attacks, the number of casualties and the names of the people who lost their lives, the second section included details of the route to Mumbai and the planned route of return after the attack and used GPRS pictures to corroborate the findings, and the third section mentioned the complicity of Pak mechanism in perpetrating the attacks and made threefold demands.

First, Pakistan should hand over the culprits engaged in the attack to face trial in India. Second, Pakistan should dismantle the terror networks operating in its soil and prevent attacks on India. Third, it must abide by bilateral, multilateral and international agreements against terrorism. The result on the ground corroborates the posture of non-cooperation of Islamabad in dismantling terrorist organizations based on its soil. The banned Jamaat-ul-Dawa (it was banned by the UNSC aftermath of the Mumbai attack), the frontal organization of the LeT, and its leaders openly participated in a rally in Lahore on 12 January 2009. The banned Jamaat donned a new garb named, Tehrik-e-Tehfuz. Pakistan initially attempted to dismantle the proof of Kasab's Pak citizenship by saying that his name is not found in the national citizenship register. It is not plausible how in a country in which about 20 percent of names are registered, Kasab's name would be definitely found in the list? However, under the international pressure Pakistan later admitted Kasab's Pak citizenship.

The contrast between the civilian government in Pakistan and the army is a crucial factor that needs to be kept in mind. The civilian government's intention however feeble in cooperating with India has been thwarted by the army. When Pakistan President, Asif Ali Zardari ordered the ISI Director-General Ahmed Shuja Pasha to visit India aftermath of the attack to get apprised of the evidence, the decision was cancelled after the interference by the Army Chief Ashfaq Pervez Kayani. When the civilian government purportedly wanted to look at the incident from a broader viewpoint of terrorism, the army wanted to confine the incident into India-Pakistan orbit as a scoreboard, and detach the event from global war against terrorism. The Pakistan National Security Advisor, Mahmud Ali Durrani was suspended after his information to a local TV channel confirming Kasab's Pak citizenship. Zardari's wish to keep his suspension on hold went unheeded. The dialogue process between India and Pakistan has restarted but action on the terror elements is missing. The inaction on part of Pakistan perhaps also reflects the weakness of the Indian diplomacy to garner sufficient support in pressuring Pakistan to act.

It also reflects the fragility of international order to take concerted action against the menace of terrorism. It is difficult to explain that despite acceptance by international players like the US and the UK of Pak complicity in fomenting terrorism, terrorist organizations still thrive on the soil of Pakistan while it remains a crucial ally of the West in fight against terrorism. The US establishment seemed to have underplayed the importance of the Mumbai incident, and that partly explained why the Indian establishment's policy of international cooperation led to frustration and helplessness. The US' probable intention to dissuade Pakistan from Taliban and its current engagement in Afghanistan and equations with the Muslim world might have led it to adopt an ambiguous policy in South Asia. India with its multicultural and pluralistic society might be resilient enough to absorb shocks of violence as in the past, but the costs of incoherence in tackling terrorism at international level will be too heavy if not appropriate actions are not taken in time. The international community needs to adopt a broader perspective in fighting the menace in an international framework. Any narrow perspective will lead to such heinous activities recur again in any part of the world.

The British Foreign Secretary, David Miliband's observations linking terrorism with Kashmir conflict received a sharp reaction from the Indian establishment. On 21 January 2009, Indian Prime Minister, Manmohan Singh wrote a letter to his British counterpart objecting the link. India reiterated its commitment to resolve the Kashmir issue bilaterally and peacefully. By a strange coincidence on the same day Manmohan wrote to Brown, the Taliban demolished 170 schools in Swat valley in the North West Frontier Province of Pakistan, and issued a diktat which barred girls above nine school education and ordered all males to grow beard. It is important to bear in mind while countering terrorism in Mumbai or elsewhere, whether this Taliban act is linked more to the issue of Kashmir or to other issues which need urgent attention.

From Mumbai to Chicago to Brescia
The arrest of David Headley and Tahawwur Hussain Rana in Chicago airport in October 2009 and Mohammad Yaqub Janijua and his son Aamer Yaqub Janijua in the northern Italian town of Brescia next month brought to the picture the deep entrenchment and spread of terror networks. David Headley, a US citizen, was born to a retired Pak army official. In 2006 he changed his name from Dawood Gilani to David Coleman Headley to give his name a veneer of un-Islamic identity in order to make the terrorist linkages and operation covert. It will, he might have calculated, also help escape the eyes of security agencies. He along with Tahawwur Rana, another person of Pakistani origin, but currently a Canadian

national, was arrested for plotting the attack on the Danish cartoonist and the newspaper named *Jyllands-Posten*. The newspaper had portrayed cartoon of Prophet Mohammed in 2005.

On interrogation, the involvement of Headley and Rana in terrorist activities was found deep rooted, including in Mumbai attack. Both Headley and Rana had visited India several times in 2007 and 2008. They travelled across India including the city of Mumbai. Headley visited in addition to Mumbai other Indian cities including Cochi, Lucknow and Pune to establish links. During these visits they also gave concrete shape to the designs for the terror attack in Mumbai in 2008. Headley had stayed in the hotel Taj in Mumbai before few days of the terror attack for a reconnaissance purpose to make the attack a success. It has been conclusively established that Headley with close links with Pak based banned LeT played an important role in the Mumbai terror attack. As further investigations revealed, Headley and Rana had in their agenda to facilitate terrors attacks on India's national defence college and other government establishments.

With the Italian connection to the terror designs the plot has become much thicker. On 21 November the Italian police arrested the Janijua father son duo for their involvement in the attack. Mohammad Janijua, the owner of the business centre, Madina trading corporation, was found culprit mainly owing to two reasons. First, on 25 November 2008 the centre transferred money electronically to US for voice over internet protocol telephone service, which was in fact used by the terrorists and their handlers while the terror attack was going on in Mumbai. The internet voice service facilitated the smooth conduct of the attack. Second, Janijua transferred money to the US in the name of a Pakistan national who in fact never visited Italy. Hence, it was illegal.

The Italian police arrested two more Pakistani nationals in Brescia in this connection while another wanted Pakistani national went missing. The alleged involvement of a retired

Pakistani army official Ilyas Kashmiri with the plans of Headley and Rana has led to finger of suspicion towards Pakistan army and intelligence agency of involvement in this whole process. Kashmiri was arrested by Pakistan investigation agencies and detained for questioning in a move to show its cooperation in the anti-terror operations. There are some other personnel in its army with likely involvement that Islamabad is not willing to further explore or wants the matter to be investigated in a low profile manner within its official investigation process.

More than one and half year lapsed since the Mumbai terror attack without any concrete action against the culprits of the attack. The LeT, banned since 2001, played a major role in orchestrating the Mumbai terror attack. Its leader, Hafeez Saeed is a free man in Pakistan. The India-Pakistan logjam for a long time further complicated the matter and provided the terrorists the alibi to further disturb peace and stability in the South Asian region. With further effective probe and investigations by Pakistan there will be likely more skeletons getting revealed in the cupboards. Needless to say the revelation of the whole plot, its masterminds and their trial is crucial not only for India but for the whole international community as the terror plans are not only India-centric – they are interconnected, driven by same ideology and similar devious designs.

The terror network from Mumbai to Chicago to Brescia may be just a small spot in the terror map. But it is an indication that the terrorist network, manpower, intelligence, money power all are so richly cultivated in the terror designs, it is simply impossible on part of one country to tackle the terror menace. Here comes to picture the necessity of international collaboration to tackle the menace by dismantling terrorist training camps, targeting their leaders, and by preaching the values of coexistence and harmony. Probably that was the message on the first anniversary of the Mumbai terror attack when hundreds of people from all religions gathered at different places of the city, including the Gateway of India, to pay homage to the victims of the attacks.

Drug Trafficking and Terrorism

The discourse on Mumbai attack received a twist after the Russian news agency *Rossiskaya Gazeta* in an interview published on 10 December 2008 traced the financer of the Mumbai terror attack to the international drug mafia don, Dawood Ibrahim. [8] The news agency quoting Victor Ivanov, Director of Russia's anti-narcotics service, made it amply clear that the super profits generated from drug trafficking in Afghanistan run by the Dawood gang, were utilized to fund the terrorist attack on the Indian commercial hub. Dawood, originally a citizen of India, has eluded the grasp of Indian authorities since 1993.

Though Pakistan officially denied the residence of Dawood in the port city of Karachi, the non-official reports as well as many international agencies confirmed his presence in Pakistan. Dawood was at Murree, 35 km from Islamabad when the terror attack in Mumbai took place. There were reports that Dawood later shifted his base to FATA, a Taliban stronghold in Pakistan. The terrorists sailed from Karachi to Sasool dock in India from where they were taken first to Cuff Parade and later to Gateway of India in boats arranged by a frontman of Dawood, who ran several custom clearing houses in Mumbai. For India, it was the second largest attack supported by Dawood. After the 1993 Mumbai bomb blasts India has been demanding from Pakistan to extradite Dawood who is also in Interpol's list for organized crime and counterfeiting and considered by Forbes the fourth most dreaded person in the world.

Undoubtedly the revelations almost stirred a hornet's nest in the context of global discourse on international terrorism and its links with drug trafficking and religious fundamentalism emanating from Afghanistan, which comes handy while discussing the context, contour and reach of international terrorism. The Operation Enduring Freedom in 2001 might have temporarily defeated Taliban forces, but their resurgence in Afghanistan and the north west areas of Pakistan has added to the fear of emergence of Taliban like activities engulfing the whole region with its spill over effects in the surrounding areas. Afghanistan's role as a bridge between Central and South Asia is illustrated most clearly in its ethnic divisions. Roughly half its population consists of Pashtuns; nevertheless, more Pashtuns reside in Pakistan than in Afghanistan.

Likewise, Baluchs live on the territory of Pakistan, Iran and Afghanistan. On the other hand, over a quarter of Afghanistan's population is composed of Tajiks, Uzbeks and Turkmens, residing in the north of the country, on its border with Central Asia. These ethnic links have a considerable impact on the security of the concerned states. Especially in an age of increased global ethnic awareness, ethnicity has become a major challenge to the security of multi-ethnic states. Afghanistan shares border with three countries of Central Asia- Tajikistan, Uzbekistan and Turkmenistan, and with Pakistan and Iran. Hence, the developments in Afghanistan have their impacts in these countries as well as the whole of Central Eurasia. One of the serious issues that the Central Asian states have to confront is the issue of drug trafficking. The erstwhile Soviet Union and its control over borders with Afghanistan had precluded the possibility of spread of drug trafficking into its regions, including Soviet Central Asia.

After the Soviet collapse, especially after the Russian withdrawal from Tajik border with Afghanistan in 2005 drug trafficking and religious fundamentalism have become a major concern for the region. The simultaneous tightening of border by Iran and Turkey has provided the trafficker the only option to use the porous border with Central Asia through the famous Silk Route to Russia and Europe. According to 2007 World Drug Report released by the Vienna-based United Nations Office on Drugs and Crime, in 2006 the opium cultivation in

Afghanistan increased 49 percent over the earlier year placing the country as the world's leader in opium production with an estimated share of 92 percent of the global production. [9]

Any violent propagation of religion enmeshed with terrorism is not only horrifying for India, but also for other countries, as it impinges on peace and security of multiethnic and pluralistic societies. With international linkages of extremism, terrorism and drug trafficking becoming more and more evident there is no denial that international peace and security is under major threat.

New Project of Jihad

The reach of international terrorism has become wider than the conceivable imagination a decade or two earlier. Starting from the North Caucasus region of Russia to Central Asia to China's Xinjiang to Kashmir region, its reach is phenomenal. Chechen terrorists like Shamil Basayev had travelled as far as Pakistan, Central Asia and to China's Xinjiang region to propagate radical Islam and terrorism. That Al Qaeda still invokes attention of the globe in its pronouncements of jihad is corroborated with its call for a new front of jihad against China. Abu Yahya al-Libi, a Libyan national and a top ranking leader of the radical organization, in Arabic broadcast on 8 October 2009 called for jihad against China's 'oppression and injustice.' [10]

The Al Qaeda leader accused China of suppressing the right of minority Uyghurs in its Xinjiang province. Expectedly, the Chinese reaction was sharp and confident that with the international cooperation it is capable enough to tackle the terror menace in its far western province. The Al Qaeda pronouncement reflected the organization's machination for escalation of violence by invoking religious sentiments. It also reflected resolve of the organization to challenge the might of rising China. At the same time the Chinese resolve to fight the menace, and to take steps to address the minority issue reflect the Chinese apprehension that the pronouncement may cause further trouble in its far west. A court at Shaoguan in southern China on 10 October 2009 delivered death sentence to a Han Chinese for the brawl which had fostered the July 2009 unrest in Urumuqi, the capital of Xinjiang. In this brawl in July two Uyghur workers were beaten to death. The verdict is seen widely as a corrective action to address the concerns of the Uyghur Muslims.

The July 2009 violence in Urumuqi had led to death of about 200 people with more than a thousand injured. The Al Qaeda as a matter of 'co-religionist' concern took up the issue into its hands and called for 'reprisals' against the Chinese. In the same month, the north African arm of Al Qaeda called Al Qaeda in the Islamic Maghreb gave a call to target Chinese installations in Africa particularly in Algeria, in which about fifty thousand Chinese workers are engaged in commercial activities. As a result the Chinese government had to issue an alert to its citizens in that country. It is important to mention that China which is a rapidly rising power, with huge investments in oil and gas in African countries, has to confront the issue with serious concern. The Chinese foreign ministry spokesperson, Ma Zhaoxu, while rejecting Al Qaeda's theory of suppression, argued "Xinjiang has fully implemented the policies of equality of all ethnic minorities and religious freedom." [11]

While the Uyghur leaders allege suppression of their rights and deprivation from opportunities, the Chinese government has argued in the contrary by saying there is equality among citizens throughout its territory. In fact, the Chinese government has become increasingly apprehensive of the separatist movements in its territory, particularly after the Tibetan violence in 2008 and July 2009 violence in Xinjiang. As already discussed in earlier pages, China's defence white paper of 2008 has strongly taken exception to these separatist tendencies and vowed to target elements that support or are involved in separatist activities.

The location of Xinjiang in the Central Eurasian matrix

adds to its fragile nature. Having common borders with Central Asian states of Uzbekistan, Tajikistan and Kyrgyzstan, the region sits on a violent political and religious volcano. The turmoil in Afghanistan too contributes to the volatile scenario. With the NATO onslaught in Afghanistan the terrorists have proliferated to other regions of Central Asia. The Islamic Movement of Uzbekistan is a case in point. The extremist organization with links with Al Qaeda has aimed at Islamization of the whole region. In fact the terror networks in Central Eurasia spread from the North Caucasus region to further south to Central Asia to Xinjiang and further downwards towards Kashmir. The call of Libi to Muslims 'to stand by the side of their wounded and wronged brothers in East Turkestan (referring to Xinjiang)' was an addition to this radical agenda of Al Qaeda to challenge multiethnic and pluralistic societies.

On an exuberant note, the Al Qaeda leader exhorted the radicals to overthrow the 'atheist regime.' All these add to the grand Al Qaeda design and further raise the prospects of conversion of Xinjiang to a hotbed of radical Islam. The Chinese call for international cooperation to fight the terror menace needs to be taken earnestly by global and regional players. The terror menace transcends national boundaries and national interest perimeter; hence, it needs international collaboration to tackle the menace. Though the SCO has in its agenda fighting terrorism, it is time to widen the network of anti-terror operation. The Chinese state might be a rising power in international politics to reckon with, but the terrorist network is global in nature with complex layers. From north in Russia to south to Central Asia and China, to further south to South Asia, there need to be a collective and commonly agreed network to fight terrorism and religious fundamentalism.

A New Route to Terror
Terrorist organizations are acquiring new weapons and adopting new methods including exploring new routes from

various countries to the centres in the AfPak region. The Uzbek Islamic radicals using Islamabad and other airports in Pakistan en route their camps in Waziristan came to light in 2009. The terrorists from Uzbekistan used these airports in the garb of traders to travel to their bases at Mirali and Wana in North and South Waziristan tribal agencies. The radicals take flights from Dushanbe, Baku, Istanbul, Dubai and Sharjah to Islamabad and other air ports in Pakistan and then travel to Waziristan by hiring taxi or other vehicles. Referring to the briefing of FATA Additional Chief Secretary Habibullah Khan to Senate Standing Committee on States and Frontier Regions *Daily Times* of Pakistan on 13 September 2009 reported the Uzbek terrorists were known to travel to Waziristan through various routes. [12]

This strategy of using air routes may be new, but the link of Uzbek terrorists with their brethren in Pakistan is decade old. After the Uzbek extremists under the banner of IMU founded in 1998 were hounded by the US led forces aftermath of the 9/11 they had to shift their bases to Tajikistan and tribal areas of Pakistan. The shift has also provided new avenue to the terrorists to conglomerate and devise their agenda. This new revelation has also reflected the lax security measures by Pakistan. The Federal Investigation Agency of Pakistan revealed that Islamabad airport was thoroughly checked by the immigration officials with high priority given to visitors from India and Central Asia. It is yet to be revealed how despite high security measures the extremists could penetrate the security mechanism and dupe the officials. Habibullah Khan in his report to the Senate committee, mentioned earlier, revealed that the strength of Uzbek terrorists in North and South Waziristan tribal agencies is not less than 5,000. This rising number of terrorists has caused serious concern in the security establishment of Pakistan. This new route will further raise the terror spirit, and will likely cause further terror problems in Pakistan with implications transcending its borders.

Since the establishment of IMU its leader Qari Tahir

Yuldashev used links with Al Qaeda and Taliban to boost the radical Islamic agenda in the former Soviet republics, which are professedly secular. It is partly due to the impact of Soviet atheistic state policy, all these republics inherited secularism as a cardinal virtue in state governance. However, with the rise of Taliban and its alliance with Al Qaeda, the states of Central Asia having common border with Afghanistan have become prone to radical Islam. These states, having majority Muslim population, are victims of an intensive radical propaganda, controlled and guided by terrorist organizations with international network. Hence, one can find in Waziristan, now an international base of terrorism, the Chechens, Libyans, Uyghurs, Uzbeks, Tajiks and Afghans with an aim to fight the governments of the region and impose radical Islam. The new route to terror through the very capital of Pakistan brings into picture that the terror element has almost become all pervasive in Pakistan state though its concentration has been confined to its north west.

With the further intensification of Taliban activities and with the Taliban march towards Islamabad Pakistan government swung into action with the support of the US. A drone attack killed the Uzbek leader of the Islamic Jihad Union, Najmiddin Kamolitdinovich Jalolov in September 2009. Notwithstanding the achievements, the terror threat looms large all over the AfPak region and beyond. As the Pak forces fight a long drawn battle with the Taliban in difficult regions the task will be really gruelling. Pakistan has been in a fix while fighting the terrorist forces in its territory. There appears to be a perplexity in the Pak policy while the issue of containing terrorism rises. The Taliban once pampered by Pakistan and recognized as the legitimate ruler of Afghanistan, has now become its archrival. But, there appear to be elements within the Pak establishment who are sympathetic to Taliban, and explore to draw a line between good and bad Taliban.

This distinction, probably in a genuine sense is motivated to bring the Taliban to moderation, has witnessed setbacks with the rising force of Taliban and the lack of Pak control over it. The increasing number of terrorists in the region and their proliferation to parts of Pakistan may further worsen the situation. The noted terrorist organization JeM known for its anti-India activities has opened its new base in Bahawalpur area of southern Punjab, ostensibly under the nose of Pak establishment. The new camp is poised to be centre for training in radical Islam and for training in arms operations. Despite the Pak army's manoeuvre with the US led NATO forces to tackle these forces; it will remain an uphill task unless Pakistan changes its fundamental approach towards terrorism. It needs emphasis that terrorism per se can not be divided into shades; it must be fought without any value or strategy attached to it. The methods of terrorism go against the democratic methods of dialogue and deliberation. The Pak determination to fight the terror menace may be lauded, but at the same time it needs to fill the gap between covert intentions and overt actions while tackling the menace.

A Terror Deal

The world exclaimed in surprise when the NWFP government in Pakistan with support from Islamabad signed a 'Peace' deal on 16 February 2009 with the pro-Taliban organization Tehrik-e-Nifaaz Shariat Muhammadi known for its extremist ideology in establishing Nizam-e-Adal (Islamic system of justice) in the Malakand region of the province which included the Swat valley once called Switzerland of Pakistan. The deal fostered by the terrorist violence added to the worries of the world regarding the future of Pakistan and also the future of war against terrorism in general and in Afghanistan in particular. The terror violence has led to the killing of thousands of people and displacement of about one third of the population in the region.

Tehrik-e-Nifaaz Shariat Muhammadi was founded by Maulana Sufi Mohammad in 1980s for the promulgation of Sharia law in Swat. The Maulana led an armed uprising in

1994 that pressurized then Benazir Bhutto government in Islamabad to concede his demands and impose Sharia law in Swat. The Maulana got support from the Taliban which came to power in Kabul in 1996. But the situation became precarious after the 9/11 terror attack, when the US led NATO forces attacked Afghanistan and defeated the Taliban with the support from Pakistan. The Maulana led thousands of his supporters to fight alongside Taliban against the NATO. He was sent to jail due to the Pak cooperation with the US against the global menace of terrorism.

The Maulana remained behind bars for six years and was released in April 2008 under an agreement that he will promote peace in the region. In the meantime, the Maulana's son-in-law, Mohammad Fazlullah became a leader of the Tehrik-e-Taliban, the Pakistan segment of the Taliban in Swat in 2007 and launched terrorist offensive in the region. The Taliban used illegal FM Radio station in Swat to sharpen their propaganda machine. The 3000 strong Taliban forces in Swat made summary executions in public, established own Islamic courts and bombarded about 180 schools to ground. The presence of 10,000 strong Pakistani forces in the valley could not deter such barbarous acts. Since 2007 when Fazlullah stepped up terrorist activities in Swat about 1,200 civilians lost their lives and about 500,000 people fled the region. The valley once a tourist attraction was turned into a hub of terrorism with the Taliban having its base at Matta village just 18km away from Mingora, the main town in the Swat valley.

What was more perplexing was the nature of collusion between extremism and terrorism in Swat. The demand for Sharia law might be explained as a kind of indigenous movement that the Maulana led, but the recent collusion of religious extremism with terrorism added to the devious strategy of the Taliban which intended to promulgate Sharia in the whole of Pakistan. This collusion is the most worrisome aspect of terrorism in Pakistan with wider implications for the world. The Taliban, especially after the November 2008 terror attack in Mumbai has been emboldened to carry out its terrorist activities and it is no surprise that the whole of South Asia is concerned about its ambitions. India has expressed concern at the Taliban adventure. The Taliban in Pakistan has warned India of further terror attacks in its territory. [13]

The likely success of the Taliban in the Swat will encourage such acts of barbarism to be replicated in other parts of Pakistan, Afghanistan and other regions. The Pakistan Taliban has not concealed its ambition to capture Islamabad, just 250km south east of Swat. The terrorist base will be further increased with the terrorists getting a safe haven in the Swat. The Taliban's declaration of ceasefire on 15 February, just a day before the deal, can be construed a clever strategy to chart out its strategies in the region. Though President Asif Ali Zardari stated Pakistan is not going to approve the deal unless peace returns to the valley, the deal that stipulates the forces of Pakistan to withdraw from the valley can provide enough time and space to Taliban to widen its network. The NATO led forces will find it difficult to adjust to the rise of Taliban in Pakistan. It will be really a difficult manoeuvre how the NATO forces will face the rising Taliban in Afghanistan and its border regions in Pakistan. The Afghanistan situation with the further strengthening of Taliban will give a new headache not only to the US but also to Pakistan itself.

In view of the emerging developments it will really be interesting to see whether the peace deal will really promote peace or ensconce the terrorist spirit in the region. On 18 February 2009 Sufi Mohammad led the cavalcade having about 300 vehicles with thousands of supporters to Mingora wearing black turbans (symbol of Taliban) and holding white flags, symbols of peace, to persuade the Taliban to adopt peaceful approach. It is really a strange paradox to see Taliban and peace go together. Such deals in the past have failed and as a consequence terrorism constituency has been further strengthened. It is not explicable how this deal will promote peace in the region, develop democratic spirit, open educational institutions, promote gender equality, and after all help defeat terrorism in the region when a party to the deal openly adheres to the principle of violence. It is really a difficult balance to see Pakistan with the US fighting against terrorism while approving the deals with what the US Special Representative to Afghanistan and Pakistan, Richard Holbrooke calls 'murderous thugs and militants,' and with which Pakistan President Asif Ali Zardari agrees. [14]

Swat has proved to be a test case for the international community to gauge the situation in its appropriate weight and breadth, and help Pakistan to fight the terror menace. If this situation goes out of hand the border of terror will not be confined to Pakistan but spread to other vulnerable spots in the world. In this sense, the rise and consolidation of terrorism is not only a challenge to Pakistan but also to the humanity as a whole.

Baitullah Mehsud and Terrorism

The death of Baitullah Mehsud, the leader of Tehrik-e-Taliban Pakistan in August 2009 in the southern Waziristan brought to light significant achievements of anti-terror operations in Pakistan. The incident checkmated the rise of the Taliban though it will be premature to say the death has ended Taliban in the region. Complete decimation of the Taliban ranks in Pakistan is far from sight particularly when they have, besides deep roots in the region, a strong nexus with other terror groups including Al Qaeda. Al Qaeda had shown keen interest to decide the succession issue probably with an Arab successor to lead the Taliban forces in Pakistan.

For Pakistan the killing of Mehsud was reflection of its increasing assertion against the Taliban. Under an implicit understanding, though Pakistan government never acknowledged it officially, the US drones from time to time target the radical elements in Pak territory. On 5 August, Mehsud had gone to his father-in-law's house in Zangara village in South Waziristan to see his wife. Mehsud and his wife along with 40 militants got killed when missile fired from a drone hit the house. Mehsud had emerged a formidable force in the Taliban ranks in the late 2000s. With a US$ 5 million tag on his head he played a significant role to bring cohesion to the disparate militant groups in Waziristan. In December 2007 he formed and led the TTP by bringing together about five militant groups, inspired by the Taliban ideology.

Mehsud in his 30s emerged supreme leader of TTP within a short span of time. He led a group of about 5000 radical fighters, a force to be reckoned with in the region. He wanted close links with the Pak army and tried to strike a deal with it by sending his envoys like Shah Abdul Aziz, a former member of Pakistan parliament. Though he might have some connections with the army and intelligence agency of Pakistan, the civil society of Pakistan were against the Taliban forces hence they had to bear the brunt. It was Mehsud who formed the suicide squad to target leaders and activists who opposed Taliban activities. Benazir Bhutto was killed by TTP in December 2007 while she was in the midst of an electoral campaign. Similarly, the attack on the Marriott hotel in Islamabad in January 2009 was allegedly carried out by TTP cadres.

Mehsud rose to prominence with his terrorist activities and patronage. He appointed deputies in various regions to spread Taliban ideology and carry out operations. His deputy in Swat, Maulana Fazlullah, also called Radio Mullah played a major role in the Tabilanization of the region by enforcing orthodox rules and regulations. The Pakistan government had conceded under the Swat Deal the promulgation of Sharia in Swat. The Buner district about 67 miles from Islamabad was captured by the Taliban in April 2009. Millions of people fled Swat, Buner and other surrounding regions to become internally displaced. With the raging apprehensions that Islamabad would ultimately fall under the control of TTP, the Pak army was finally forced to act. The Pak army could successfully repel the Taliban from Swat in July 2009 after about a 10-week offensive that killed more than 1,700 Taliban fighters. The TTP too played a dominant role to checkmate the NATO forces and their transports through Pakistan to Afghanistan. Mehsud supported the Taliban fighters in south-western Afghanistan to fight the NATO forces. The radicals attacked the transport vehicles from Pakistan to Afghanistan on hilly and mountainous routes including the Khyber Pass.

The significance of the killing of Mehsud transcends beyond the territory of Pakistan. For India, Pak based Taliban has been a source of threat since its emergence. The Taliban pushed from Buner and Swat and other regions have shifted their base to Kashmir under the control of Pakistan, besides to other areas. Mehsud had promised support to Pak army in the eventuality of a war with India aftermath of the Mumbai terror attack. The Taliban also supported the terrorist groups active in Kashmir and other parts of India. In many cases the Taliban forces aided infiltration of radicals into Kashmir from across the line of control to play havoc in the country. The killing of Mehsud will likely discourage these forces at least for some time.

The killing of Mehsud definitely gave a fatal blow to the Taliban forces and broadly to terrorism emanating from the Pak soil. The incident might bring temporary respite but the long drawn war on terrorism is far from over. The disparate Taliban groups will take some time to again rally behind a single leader. This intervening period can be used by Pakistan to pursue a calibrated policy to further weaken the Taliban. What is more important is to address the fundamentals of Talibanism in Pakistan. There needs to be the strengthening of democratic forces and mechanisms in Pakistan. The democratic mechanisms such as separations of powers and rule of law and the strengthening of the civil society groups will definitely help counter terrorism. Otherwise the killing of Mehsud will only bring temporary respite, which afterwards will subside with the rise of the ilk of Mehsud on the northwest horizon of Pakistan.

The Karachi Project

The Karachi project aims to further up Pakistan's strategic lever against India by using Indian Muslims as pawns. So far, till about mid 2000s, the terror attacks in India were perpetrated by the foreign nationals including Pakistani nationals. The Karachi project aims at changing this foreign dimension to the terrorist violence in India and attempts to give it colour of a home-grown movement led by Indian citizens. Its operational aim was to recruit disenchanted or otherwise Indian youths particularly Muslims in Pakistani camps in Karachi, and train them with deadly activities such as making and planting bombs, tackling the police encounter, etc. and send them back to India for action.

The tracing of David Headley's emails by the agencies clearly reveal that the Karachi project is not a very old idea. The office of the ISI in Karachi promotes these activities. In a distinction between good and bad jihadi (good are those who do not target Pakistan, but free in fact prompted to target India or other countries; the opposite is bad). Since 2008 Pakistan's intelligence agency has thrown its full weight behind this Karachi project, mainly mooted by LeT. The emails of Headley to his Pakistan handlers clearly reflect his reference to the Karachi project. During his visits to India in 2008 and 2009 Headley had visited Pune and in fact stayed in a hotel named Surya Villa Hotel near the site of the attack in 2009 and made a survey of the area.

The terror attacks in 2008 in Indian cities of Bangalore, Ahmedabad and Hyderabad, besides Mumbai, clearly brought into picture the existence of what is called Indian Mujahideen, with direct allegiance to their recruiters in Karachi. The Indian Mujahideen, involved in the Pune attack, mainly the Bhatkal brothers, Riyaz and Iqbal, played an important role in strengthening Indian Mujahideen. They have been given shelter in Karachi. The Indian Mujahideen had a strong presence in Pune as some of its prominent members like software engineer and head of the media wing of the group

Mohammed Mansoor Asgar Peerbhoy, Mohammad Atiq Mohammad Iqbal, Anik Shafiq Sayyad, and Anwar Abdulganj Bagwan were arrested and imprisoned in Pune.

India which is a multiethnic and pluralistic society with all the political and legal features of a secular country did not promote violence as a means for conflict resolution. In fact Muslims in India have abhorred violence as a means of their grievance redressal. This aspect of Indian polity came to light when the Muslims of Mumbai refused to allow the bodies of slain terrorists, also Muslims, to be buried in Mumbai. But, with the gradual strengthening of Indian Mujahideen, with the active support from across the border, Indian policy makers have expressed concern about the future prospects of stability, order and communal harmony in India. Probably, the terrorists with the religious fanatic zeal aim at exploiting the religious balance in Indian society and by targeting the innocent civilians in the name of jihad they want to perpetrate their devious designs.

Pakistan's complicity or at least apathy in curbing terrorism comes to picture on the eve of Pune terror attack. The attack killed ten people including three foreign nationals- an Italian woman, an Iranian student and a Nepali waiter. Abdur Rehman Makki, the Deputy Chief of Jamaat-ul-Dawa, a branch of LeT, in his public speech in Islamabad on 5 February 2010 called Indian Prime Minister 'evil,' and ordered his fellow jihadis to target Indian cities like 'Delhi, Pune and Kanpur.' He called Jihadis to 'teach India a lesson.' [15] Pakistani authorities did not take any action against him. Indian government is looking at this statement as a probable precursor or instigator to Pune terror attack, which has nothing in store but potential to further spoil already sullen bilateral relations. Another terrorist organization called Lashkar-e-Toiba Al Alami (a breakaway group from LeT) on 16 February 2010 claimed responsibility for orchestrating the attack in Pune. Some analysts argue that these kinds of attacks were only aimed to instigate India to lose patience and attack

Pakistan, thus resulting in another war in the subcontinent and letting the prospects of peace and development in the region go to oblivion.

State within a State

With the Taliban writ running large in FATA of Pakistan a retrograde medieval practice has come to life with utmost impunity with the imposition of religious tax (Jizya) on the minorities in the region. The Sikh families living in Qasim Khel and Samma Feroz Khel areas of Orakzai agency in FATA fled the area as the TTP devastated their houses and shops because they could not pay the tax fixed to the tune of 50 million Pakistani rupees, about one million US dollar (there are varying reports on the exact amount), before the stipulated date of 29 April 2009. These Sikhs were living in their ancestral land for centuries. The partition trauma of the Indian subcontinent, the creation of Pakistan on the basis of religion had not deterred these minority people to leave their ancestral land. However, with the recent Taliban onslaught their fate seems to have changed almost irretrievably.

The TTP argued that the Jizya imposition is justifiable under the Sharia Law, promulgated in the Swat region under an agreement between the NWFP of Pakistan and the TTP in February 2009. Under the agreement, the constitution and other rules will not be enforced in the region but the Sharia laws. Under Sharia the Taliban opened its own courts and delivered its own justice. Under its dispensation the whole world was horrified to see the public flogging of a teenage girl. About one hundred thousand people fled the region due to the reign of terror. As per a conservative estimate over 150 Sikh and Hindu families arrived at Gurdwara Panja Sahib in Hasan Abdal and Rawalpindi from places like Buner, Swat and Orkazai in May. [16] The Pakistan government has made arrangements for accommodation, food and security for the displaced. The loot and plunder filled the Taliban coffers and further ensconced their radical spirit. Under the Sharia law, the

Taliban argued the minority religions have to pay Jizya, which they interpret as 'protection tax' (but protection against whom, the Taliban did not elaborate).

The deal between the TTP and NWFP, referred to as the Swat Deal, signed in February 2009, came upon the minorities as their refugee decree, forcing them to leave their native place. The Taliban kidnapped Sikh leaders Kalyan Singh and Sewa Singh in April 2009 to force them to pay the ransom. The community was given two options: either to pay the amount before 29 April 2009 or leave their native place. Only after paying Rs 3.5 million the Sikhs could rescue the kidnapped leaders but not their homes and hearths. On 30 April 2009, under the orders of Haikmullah Mehsud the local TTP leader, the Taliban hoodlums torched 11 houses, ransacked 10 shops and auctioned goods at 0.8 million Pakistani rupees. The Sikhs fearing for their lives shifted to comparatively safer Minni Khel area in the agency. The fraternity the Sikhs enjoyed with the local Muslim people of the Minni Khel tribe, who too earlier protected the Sikhs, got ruptured with the Taliban terror. This region, particularly the FATA, bordering Pakistan-Afghanistan has become a dangerous belt of extremism and terrorism.

The victimization of the minority community has seen not only misuse of Islam by the Taliban in the region, but has also threatened any vestige of pluralism in Pakistan. The larger issue is: the Taliban rule based on extremism and retrograde system of laws has challenged the Pakistan state. It has emerged as another centre of power within Pakistan thus threatening its very core as a sovereign state. The civil society of Pakistan has been outraged at this instance of barbarity. *The News International*, one of the prominent news papers in Pakistan in its edition on 1 May 2009 deplored these elements. Labelling the Taliban a 'State within a State' [17] it severely criticized this act in the following words, "This of course is extortion. There is no other name for it. Over the past weeks it has become obvious the Taliban are engaged in a game of plunder. This too is how they inspire desperate young men to join them. The motive is base greed and not religious zeal." The report further stated how the Taliban ranks have almost overnight accumulated enormous wealth. Luxury items taken away from the homes of families forced to flee adorn the homes of the Taliban members. The newspaper criticized the legislators for their inefficiency or inactivity to stand up for the rights of the minorities who live in Taliban-controlled areas.

Another prominent newspaper, *Dawn* on its edition of 30 April 2009 displayed the pictures of devastated houses and narrated how Taliban had asked the Sikh community living in the tribal area for centuries to pay annual Jizya because 'Sharia had been enforced in the area and every non-Muslim had to pay protection money.' [18] As per a report the Taliban's devastating activities have increased hundred percent within a year. Perhaps that itself brings forth the necessity for international cooperation to tackle the menace. India, the home to the largest number of Sikhs, has officially protested against the victimization of the Sikhs. The Sikh religious place, Amritsar in India has witnessed huge protest rallies and burning of effigies representing Taliban. Pakistan has promised to protect its citizens including the minorities, but its actions so far lack the needed momentum.

Revival of a medieval retrograde practice must bewilder any conscientious citizen of the world, irrespective of their religious identities. This also shows the ominous future of minorities in Pakistan as well as the future of Pakistan state as well. The issue of Taliban barbarism is not only a matter of concern of the peace loving citizens of Pakistan, but also of the humanity at large. The Taliban is a scourge which must be contained at any cost. They are not only hindrance to religious freedom, but also hindrance to free thinking, democracy and associated values. It is time that the international powers must take coordinated actions to counter the Taliban menace. In the mean time the life and death question of the minorities in Pakistan must be the issue to be dealt with expeditiously.

Terrorists with Nuclear Weapons

The developments in Pakistan point at the feasibility of a scenario in which terrorists wield nuclear weapons with grave consequences for the world. These developments are going to add a new dimension to international terror discourse. Pakistan's Dera Ghazi Khan nuclear site and its adjacent compound have become the target of terrorists on many occasions. It has faced at least one ground attack by more than a dozen gunmen. The area, also known for sectarian violence, witnessed a suicide attack triggered by the Taliban on 5 February 2009 that killed more than 30 people. The turmoil in Pakistan, in which the army is engaged with the Taliban in border areas, has given rise to apprehension that the terrorists might take advantage of the volatile scenario and get hold of the nuclear weapons and target the perceived enemies.

The chief architect of Pakistan's nuclear programme A.Q. Khan has been interrogated on many occasions for his complicity in transferring nuclear technology illegally. The reported complicity of some of other Pak nuclear scientists with terrorist and extremist organizations and some countries has raised alarm not only about the safety of these weapons but about the impending tragedy that might befall on the nations of the world.

Under the Biden-Lugar bill the US has tripled the civilian aid to Pakistan. However, a significant section of policy makers in the US have expressed fear that the aid given for humanitarian and counter terrorism purposes has been used by Pakistan to develop and expand its nuclear programmes. Admiral Mike Mullen, Chairman of the US Joint Chiefs of Staff, at a congressional panel earlier in February 2009 confirmed that Pakistan is expanding its nuclear weapons systems and warheads. The satellite pictures taken by the US have shown clearly how Pakistan has developed new nuclear weapons facilities at Dera Ghazi Khan and Rawalpindi. The satellite images show a major expansion of a chemical plant complex near Dera Ghazi Khan, and development of a plutonium separation plant adjacent to the old one near Rawalpindi. Pakistan, particularly in installing additional capacity to produce nuclear materials for weapons, has the fastest weaponization programme in the world.

Pakistan's diversion of funds to nuclear weapon programme may be another subject of debate. Some analysts may argue Pakistan is expanding the programme for civilian use such as production of energy, but the credibility of such an argument might be put to test because first, these programmes have dual use, i.e. the same technology can be used for building nuclear weapons; and second, the issue of safety of the nuclear weapons. Besides, Pakistan's nuclear facilities expansion programme at a time when the army is engaged in a battle with the Taliban has also raised suspicions behind the motive to expand the facilities.   Speaking at the Pacific Council on International Policy, the US' CIA Director Leon Panetta observed on 18 May 2009 that the US does not know the location of the weapons nor the US has the intelligence to know where they all are located. However he added that "The last thing we want is to have the Taliban have access to nuclear weapons in Pakistan." [19]

Similarly, the meeting of security chiefs of SCO members in Moscow on 20 May 2009 expressed concern at the proliferation of nuclear technology from Pakistan. Russian Security Council head Vladimir Nazarov observed, "The SCO states have legitimate worries that nuclear weapons in Pakistan may fall into the hands of terrorists." [20] Pakistan has about 60 to 100 nuclear weapons deliverable by attack aircraft and ballistic missiles. The opaque character of nuclear programme in Pakistan, and its dominant control by the army, has further strengthened apprehensions of opening of nuclear material traffic to the terrorists groups like Al Qaeda and Taliban.

The international community and organizations like the UN and its agencies can play an effective role in ensuring the safety of nuclear weapons and technology in Pakistan. The US, which has been directly involved in the country by investing heavily in fighting the terror menace, needs to play an effective role in this direction. It needs to take steps so that the aid given to Pakistan is utilized for the intended purposes. It must make the policy makers accountable so that the aid is used effectively without diversion of funds for nuclear programmes or without corruption. A mechanism can be developed in Pakistan with the support of the international organizations particularly the IAEA, which can assist the Pak establishment in ensuring the safety of the nuclear weapons and prevent any leakage of these weapons and technology.

Unless swift actions are taken against the expansion and likely proliferation, the world may suffer consequences much wider and much graver than that of the 9/11. It will pose a mortal danger against the very survival of Pakistan and its fledgling democracy, besides impacting the regional politics with international ramifications. As the terrorists do not have any religion nor do they recognize the human values of compassion and dignity, the costs of a possible nuclear terror strike will definitely transcend boundaries of religions as well as nations. The likely capture of these weapons and technology by the terrorists either by means of theft or by forceful capture or by the complicity of corrupt officials will put the human life and its creations in jeopardy.

References

1. "Islamic Body Issues Fatwa against Terrorism," *Daily News and Analysis*, 31 May 2008.
2. Zia Haq, "Darul's Global Fatwa on Terror," *Hindustan Times*, 1 June 2008.
3. For details of the fatwa and the conference see, Debidatta Aurobinda Mahapatra, "Fatwa against Terrorism," Strategic Culture Foundation online magazine, 24 June 2008. http://en.fondsk.ru/article.php?id=1448.
4. "800 Terror Cells Active in Country," *Times of India*, 12 August 2008.
5. http://forum.pakistanidefence.com/index.php?showtopic=76058 &mode=linearplus.
6. For details of the conference and its implications see, Andrei

Smirnov, "Salafists and Sufis Square off over Chechnya," *North Caucasus Analysis*, vol. 9, no. 27, 11 July 2008. http://www.jamestown.org/programs/ncw/single/?tx_ttnews percent5Btt_news percent5D=5051&tx_ttnews percent5BbackPid percent5D=169&no_cache=1.

7. http://news.xinhuanet.com/english/2008-11/28/content_10425381.htm.

8. "Dawood's Network Financed Mumbai Attacks: Russia," *Indian Express*, 18 December 2008.

9. Details of the report are available at "U.N.: Opium Production Soaring in Afghanistan," http://www.msnbc.msn.com/id/19431056/.

10. Ishaan Tharoor, "Al Qaeda Leader: China, Enemy to Muslim World," 9 October 2009, http://www.time.com/time/world/article/0,8599,1929388,00.htm

11. "China Reacts to Al-Qaida Threat," http://www.peopleforum.cn/viewthread.php?tid=2099&extra=page percent3D222.

12. *Daily Times*, 13 September 2009.

13. "Taliban Chief Threatens to Dispatch Militants to Fight India," *The Times of India*, 15 October 2009.

14. "Taliban Pose Danger to US, Pak & India, Admits Zardari," *Indian Express*, 20 February 2009.

15. "Al Qaeda Vows more Attacks across India," http://www.zeenews.com/news604454.html.

16. "Taliban Force Sikh Exodus," *The Telegraph*, 3 May 2009.

17. *The News International*, 1 May 2009.

18. *Dawn*, 30 April 2009.

19. "CIA: US does not know location of all Pakistan's nuclear weapons," http://www.telegraph.co.uk/news/worldnews/northamerica/usa/5348930/CIA-US-does-not-know-location-of-all-Pakistans-nuclear-weapons.html.

20. *The Hindu*, 21 May 2009.

6

Troubled South Asia

South Asia's volatility has probably never come to sharp focus as in the recent past as almost all countries in the region, perhaps with the sole exception of India, underwent tumultuous phases. The terror attack in Mumbai though impacted India; it outgrew its immediate impact with far reaching implications for the neighbourhood and the wider region. The region also witnessed dramatic upheavals owing to diverse factors such as the legitimacy crisis, incongruity between ethnic aspirations and national sovereignty, nation building travails and religious fundamentalism and terrorism. Sri Lanka remained in light for the violent war at home which came to an end in 2009 with the apparent end of LTTE and its leader though the post-LTTE scenario posed challenges before the Sri Lankan state in addressing the issues of rehabilitation, reconciliation and reintegration.

The apprehension that the re-elected President will dither in addressing the issue in right earnest still persists among the minority Tamils as they fear the president may be swayed by the military victory over the rebel group only to further bolster the Sinhalese nationalist agenda. In Nepal the resignation of the Maoist government in 2009 further polarized the divisions in the Nepalese polity with the Maoist threat looming large in derailing the difficult peace process. The coalition government post-Maoist resignation phase too sailed through troubled waters as it became difficult on its part to evolve a national agenda incorporating diverse demands including that of the Maoists. The mutiny in Bangladesh in 2009 brought forth political fissures and fragility of civilian authorities in Bangladesh with potentials to destabilize democratically elected government.

The Hasina government which is perceived friendly to

India may have to confront such challenges in the country infested by extremist elements in connivance with some of the opposition parties. Afghanistan's predicament in tackling the Taliban, prospects of a stable and transparent order and its geo-strategic importance too emerged prominently in recent years. The controversial elections in the war torn state in 2009 indicated the fragile nature of Afghan politics. Equally importantly, the churning process within Pakistan in tackling the Taliban further complicated by the supposed link of the radical elements with sections of policy establishment appears unending as the developments on the ground indicate. The South Asian region will likely remain unstable unless a broader paradigm, which includes diverse voices in a wider democratic format, is evolved within and among the nations of the region.

Failed States?

If one sifts through the findings of the study [1] conducted by the noted organization Fund for Peace (FfP) and the Foreign Policy journal (FP) in 2008, it is not difficult to find how far the diverse indices have brought to the focus the state of the affairs in the world. There may be arguments as to the accuracy or efficacy of the report or its findings, but it can not be ignored that the finding has put to test the system of governance in many countries. The joint exercise has also taken into account the national as well as international environment in a broader context in order to see the relative stability or instability of nations, their domestic environment and their ramifications for the world order. It is a crucial theme on which the FfP and FP have conducted joint research and gradually they have increased the nature and scope of the study. The number of states studied increased from 75 in 2005 to 148 in 2006 and from 2007 onwards the number of states studied increased to 177.

In the 2008 study they took into account 12 indicators of state cohesion and performance to find out the relative state coherence and stability of the states. The 12 indicators included: Demographic Pressures, Refugees and Internally Displaced Persons, Group Grievance, Human Flight, Uneven Development, Economic Decline, Delegitimization of the State, Public Services, Human Rights, Security Apparatus, Factionalized Elites, and External Intervention. The Failed States Index mainly focused on prospects of state vulnerability or risk of violence for one time period each year by analyzing the data collected from May to December of the preceding year. The joint study analyzed more than 30,000 publicly available sources and then ranked the states in order from most to least at risk of failure.

One of the crucial issues that can be observed from the findings is the rising menace of terrorism and religious fundamentalism. It is Somalia in which radicalism coupled with poor infrastructure, excessive violence and criminality and lack of basic services have made it the number one failed state. The state has witnessed failure of state mechanisms as since 1991 it failed to witness a stable government, further compounded by the fighting between the radical forces like Al Shabaab with the government, and other factors such as poverty. The study has cited the case of Yemen as 'the next Afghanistan: a global problem wrapped in a failed state,' due to rising menace of Al Qaeda. Some of the most troubled regions of the world such as Afghanistan (number 6) have been ranked high as the risk of state failure has increased. Interestingly, the fragile situation in South Asia has been well reflected in the findings. The situation in South Asia vis-à-vis India portrays a different picture. The report admits the conditions of India have become better. India ranked 87.

India's stable democracy; stable politics, economic development, lack of communal riots in recent years, and its role in global affairs have probably led it to secure a low rank in the list. Except India all countries are in difficult situations. Pakistan ranked 10, Bangladesh was at 19th position, Sri Lanka at 22nd and Nepal at 25th.The mutiny in Bangladesh, and the lack of stringent action on part of the government to tackle these forces; the political instability in Nepal; and the recent conclusion of conflict in Sri Lanka thus raising the post-war ordeals, have worsened the situation in South Asia. As the study argues while there are weak governments which propel instability, there are also authoritarian governments as in Myanmar which obstructs the rise of democratic forces. In the case of Pakistan the findings suggest that the country is undergoing a troubled phase despite its risk of failure has gone down by one rank.   Its fighting with as one Pakistani commentator writes 'the rabidly savage and murderous Taliban insurgents' [2] in its north west has cost too heavy for the fragile state.

The fighting between Pakistan's security forces and Taliban has led to the increase in the number of internally displaced more than one million. The Swat deal imposing Sharia, its later break down, the further Taliban encroachment and the Pak manoeuvre to fight the Taliban elements have made the situation troublesome. Though it is a matter of debate as to who actually controls the affairs in Pakistan, undoubtedly the lead of civilian government at least on surface indeed is something which can be called an achievement in the midst of chaos and instability. It may be debatable as to the validity of such an exercise about states, despite its stated adherence to the principles of objective research. It may be questioned who is actually to be blamed for the worsening situation in the volatile regions or how far the global financial crisis does play a role in worsening the situation in countries particularly in Africa and in some countries in Eastern Europe, or the world? However, it may not be a good idea to out rightly reject the findings of the report. Rather, it makes sense for states including the states of South Asia to interpret and ponder over its findings since the ranking of the South Asian states did not improve in 2009.

Emerging Trends

One can have a glimpse over the developments in South

Asia in the first week of April 2009 to gauge how fragile the system of state is in some of the countries of the region. Within a period of one week, Pakistan witnessed three terror attacks in Lahore, Islamabad and Peshawar. The more terrifying was the video footage broadcast in media on 3 April 2009 of flogging of seventeen-year-old girl Chand Bibi in public in Swat valley. On 6 April India witnessed four bomb blasts in Assam province in its north east on the eve of its prime minister's visit. The Sri Lankan government on 6 April 2009 stated it has defeated the LTTE in its northeast while encircling the rebel's last strong hold in Puthukkudiyiruppu area and cornering its leader V. Prabhakaran. The violent conflict in this island nation has led to loss of thousands of lives. Similarly, the situation in Nepal became more precarious as the Maoists did not give up guns and its cadres continued to rule interior areas with unbridled power. In Bangladesh the failed mutiny revealed deep cracks in the establishment.

The developments in South Asia broadly indicate three trends. First, it is the tussle between the forces of democracy and the forces of extremism and other forms of violence. Second, it is the competitive ambition and rivalry between the forces of federalism and separatism. Third, it is the tussle between the values of egalitarianism and fundamentalism. The noted Pakistani Human Rights Activist Asma Jehangir, aftermath of the public flogging of Chand Bibi in Swat, argued "Under the peace deal (by the Pak government with the Taliban in February 2009), the government has put the lives of the people in Swat in the hands of the Taliban. The administration says there is peace there. I challenge them to take their family there for a picnic."

Perhaps while arguing in this manner she was representing the moderate voice of Pakistan and expressing their concerns. Pakistan that is fighting the war against terrorism and fundamentalism in its soil has witnessed mushrooming of terrorist organizations like LeT, JeM, HM and Taliban. Besides Pakistan, in Bangladesh also there is mushroom growth of terrorist organizations. Its Chittagong hill tracts are occupied by the deadly terrorist organizations like HUJI. On 6 April 2009, Bangladesh police arrested one Faisal Mustafa who headed the Green Crescent, a UK based charity for allegedly running a terror network in Bangladesh soil.

One of the worrying factors in the context of Pakistan is the likely increase of tussle between civil society and the forces of terrorism and fundamentalism. The Supreme Court of Pakistan took suo moto cognizance of the Swat incident and asked the government to take action. Similarly, the Zardari government ordered the NWFP government in which Swat is located to take stringent action against the perpetrators. On the contrary, the Pakistani Taliban organized demonstrations justifying public flogging of the girl. It can be mentioned here under a deal between the Zardari government and Pakistan Taliban in February 2009, the region was to run under strict Islamic law. The problem is the weakness of civil society to confront the rising menace of violence in the region. It was clearly evident when aftermath of the flogging incident the members of civil society came to streets with placards which read, among others, 'army save your citizens,' 'army eliminate Taliban.' The appeal to army, not to civilian government, makes it clear the power the army wields in Pakistan in contrast to the civilian government. After a gap of eight years, Pakistan witnessed a democratic government in 2008.

Perhaps in its history, the democratic government in Pakistan has never faced the tussle between the forces of democracy and terrorism so acutely. In India the twin forces of terrorism and religious fundamentalism have attempted in weakening its democratic structure but lack of official patronage and lack of support from civil society to these elements have deprived them any stronghold in India. The rise of Indian Mujahideen, ULFA, the Maoists have posed challenges to Indian state in recent years. The terror events in India's northeast have revealed the complicity between ULFA and HUJI in perpetrating terrorist violence. The Maoists have reportedly built a corridor in forest and hilly areas from Nepal in the north to India's south and perpetrated violent activities targeting public officials and killing innocent people. According to a report India from the year 2004 to 2007 has lost more people to terrorism than any other country in the world. [3] The ULFA and Indian Mujahideen with networks across border have challenged the Indian state and its integrity. Sri Lanka, until recently, was fighting the LTTE considered the most powerful terrorist organization in the world with missiles and aeroplanes. The developments in Nepal indicate the fragility of the state as there are no apparent signs of sustaining and strengthening of the nascent democracy in the country.

There is also tussle between federalism and separatism. Almost all countries of South Asia experience doses of separatism in varying degrees and with varied underlying reasons. In India, the forces of separatism are in the regions of the northeast and Kashmir, in Pakistan these are in Balochistan and in other regions, and in Sri Lanka separatist forces played havoc in Tamil dominated north-eastern region. All these countries confront separatism, which has challenged the spirit of national integrity. The striking case of fragility comes to picture further when these forces of separatism use the method of violence to further their agenda. The third trend appears to be most dangerous in comparison to the first two as it feeds them and in turn gets further strengthened. It works in a more subtle manner, targeting the cultural ethos prevalent in a society. The Swat deal in NWFP is the most recent example in this context. The deal gave Pakistan Taliban unencumbered right to impose fundamentalist rule in the region. Perhaps South Asia has never passed through such a violent phase. Its descent into instability has been precarious due to triple forces of terrorism, separatism and religious fundamentalism.

Taliban in Pakistan
That a war against the Taliban is waged by Pakistan army in its territory does not come as a surprise as the army has

engaged the Taliban earlier but without much success. Hence, the element of surprise will come only after the conclusive defeat of the extremists, who have wielded the method of terror to establish an orthodox society in Pakistan. Pakistan Prime Minister Yusuf Raza Gilani's statement in the parliament on 11 May 2009 regarding Taliban that, "The very existence of the country was at stake. We were left with no option" (but to eliminate the extremists) [4] reflects the concern of the Pak government at the proliferation of the radical elements in Pakistan especially in its border areas. However, the Pak actions against the Taliban need to be watched carefully as to how far these actions are successful in taming the violent extremists.

The global significance of this war against the Taliban is manifold pending on the degree of success of the Pak army in containing the menace. As the noted Pakistani diplomat, Hussain Haqqani, argued in his book *Pakistan: Between Mosque and Military*, [5] the Pakistani establishment has used the Taliban and Islam as arsenals in its strategies against India and Afghanistan, and as strategic levers. This strategy will likely get a set back with the defeat of the Taliban. Hence, it needs to be seen whether the Pak army mounts a sudden attack with all hype, as in 2006 in Swat valley, and then retreats, and let the Taliban return back with vengeance. The peace deal of February 2009 provided room for Taliban manoeuvre in terms of spreading their influence in the region as they ran their own system of governance. The global implications of the rise of the Taliban will depend on how the Pak army deals with the extremist forces with which it has close links. The defeat of the Taliban will not only weaken the global network of terror and break the link between the Taliban and Al Qaeda but also rescue Pakistan from radicalization of its polity and society.

It may be futile, in contrary to views aired in some quarters, talking to Taliban to lay down arms and take part in peace talks. Some analysts have argued that a distinction needs to be made between 'hardline' and 'moderate' Taliban, so that peace talks can be initiated with the moderate forces. However, the situation on the ground speaks otherwise. The command of the Afghanistan Taliban and the Pakistan Taliban lies in the hands of the extremists, who openly preach violence, and oppose peace efforts. Three Taliban leaders Baitullah Mehsud (killed in a US drone attack), Hafiz Gul Bahudar and Maulvi came together to form *The Council of United Holy Warriors* to fight against the Pakistan government. [6]

In this context the spectre of violence that now has gripped Pakistan can be linked to the peace deal the NWFP signed with the Taliban in Swat in February 2009. The whole episode led to the atmosphere in which the government succumbed to the extremist demands and let them grow large and ferocious in their ambitions and actions. The failure of the Swat deal is a testimony how the Taliban has never understood the language of peace. In all likelihood there may be a clash of interests between the civilian government on which pressure is mounted from the civil society to counter these forces, and the army which is interested in retaining the Taliban as a strategic lever. Hence comes to picture the testability of Obama's AfPak strategy, which some strategists term PakAf strategy, as the Pak border areas have become more violent than the regions of Afghanistan. It is well known that the Afghan Taliban leader Mullah Omar has shifted his base to Quetta in Pakistan. The important point that needs to be remembered is though the NATO forces in Afghanistan has been partly able to checkmate the Taliban in Afghanistan, it has failed to rein in these radical forces in AfPak border areas. In fact after the NATO onslaught against the Taliban in Afghanistan these radical forces have made deep inroads into border areas of Pakistan with impunity. Probably, anti-Americanism with the queer combination of radical Islam has further emboldened the Taliban spirit and helped growth of their ranks. The danger of Pak nukes falling into their hands too has been a matter of concern.

There has been an understanding between Pak army and the US to use the US drones under Pak guidance in targeting the Taliban. Earlier the Pak officials had expressed dissatisfaction against the US drones targeting the extremists within the Pak territory without permission from the government. The Biden-Lugar bill which enhanced the aid to Pakistan to the tune of US$ 15 billion, and tripled the civilian aid, has faced opposition by some US senators on the ground that the earlier US$ 12 billion aid has not produced expected results.

The Obama-Zardari-Karzai meeting in Washington on 6 May 2009 dwelt upon the Taliban menace and the strategy to tackle it. Promising that "Pakistan's democracy will deliver," [7] President Asif Zardari reiterated the Pak resolve to eliminate the Taliban. In a surprise to many Indo-Pak relations watchers Zardari told to PBS News Channel in Washington on 9 May 2009, "I have never considered India as a threat", and Pakistan is facing danger from the terrorists inside the country. This unusual statement by the highest civilian leader of the country might have rattled the Pak army which has argued India as a factor in not withdrawing forces from the eastern border and deploying them in the north west to fight the Taliban. It is the unity of purpose between the civilian government and the army that can lead to defeat of the Taliban. The differences between the two will provide room to Taliban to manoeuvre. Hence, it is the balance or imbalance of interests between the civilian government and the army on which will depend the defeat of the Taliban, or their temporary hibernation or further resurgence.

The developments in Pakistan in October 2009 show how it is grappling with extreme terrorist violence within its own territory. The attack on the army head quarters in Rawalapindi on 10 October 2009 apart, the five attacks in Lahore, Peshawar and northwest town of Kohat on 15 October 2009 confirm not only the sophistication of the attacks, and the terrorists' superior plans and designs, but also the penetration of the extremist elements as well as inefficiency of the administration to contain the violence. As the battle between Pak army and the Taliban goes on, it is the civilians who have suffered the most. According to Pak army spokesperson, General Athar Abbas 1.3 million people have been internally displaced since August 2008 when the Taliban implemented archaic laws in Swat.

The UN Office for the Coordination of Humanitarian Affairs has estimated that more than 3,60,000 displaced people have registered after escaping the worst-affected districts of Buner, Lower Dir and Swat. The Taliban forces have killed at least 1800 civilians across Pakistan in less than two years. The slain Taliban leader, Hakimullah Mehsud had openly threatened Pakistan of more attacks unless it stops its planned operation in South Waziristan. To add to the malaise further the Taliban with having dominant base in Waziristan forged alignments with banned outfits like JeM, Lashkar-e-Janghvi in Punjab the heartland of Pakistan. The Lahore attacks of 15 October have been claimed by one Amjad Farooqi, who belonged to Punjabi Taliban. This brings twist to the Pakistan's plan in fighting terrorism as the Taliban menace has further penetrated and supported by the terror groups from other parts of Pakistan. In this background it can be dangerous if the nuclear-weaponed Pakistan slides down into the morass of instability and crisis.

Delving deep into the history in brief, Pakistan it appears has suffered from two incongruities which it has made for itself: first, its policy of supporting the Mujahideen against the Soviet forces in the 1980s; and second, its dual strategy in tackling these extremist elements. These two points need further elaboration to put the current scenario in Pakistan in proper perspective. During the height of the cold war when the Soviet forces were in Afghanistan, it was Pakistan, which provided support and the extremist ideology and jihadist slogan to rally the extremist elements to fight the Soviet forces. In fact the Al Qaeda leader, Osama bin Laden is a creation of this era and also the Taliban. The issue that emerged after the withdrawal of the Soviet forces was possible diversion of these forces towards other targets. Besides making Afghanistan a battleground between various radical forces, Kashmir was also an option, which after the Operation Topaz was made a flash point.

However, it could not be sustained long due to India's strong resistance, and also due to the very nature of Taliban to spread its extremist ideology within Pakistan. Pakistan's support to the Kashmir option and opposition to the Taliban agenda within that took a gigantic shape after the 9/11 brought forth the Pak dilemma in confronting Taliban. To fight these forces, which it had sheltered so long, was a difficult option before Pakistan. This brings forth the second point – the dichotomy that has cost heavily to Pakistan. The strategy to use the Taliban and extremist methods whenever it suited the army dominated policy boomeranged Pakistan itself. It was a strategy that could not sustain for long, as the Taliban has in its agenda to radicalize the whole of Pakistan, which has been strongly resisted by the civil society.

Interestingly, the Taliban leader, Hakimullah in a televised broadcast after the attacks in Lahore and Peshawar had declared its objective to radicalize Pakistan and then proceed towards India. Hence, it was a kind of reversal of the Pak policy which wanted to use extremist elements like Taliban, but now it appears Taliban is using the gaffe in the Pak policy. The signing of the US aid to Pakistan bill with stipulations has been further interpreted by the extremist elements including sections of civilian leadership as surrender of Pak sovereignty to the US. This interpretation has also provided the extremists rationale to step up their attacks.

Pakistan army which has played a dominant role (in fact it ruled most of the time in Pakistan's history) has its own version of the game, while the civilian leadership has its own version. Some analysts would say it is the lack of effective control of civilian government, or the lack of vibrant democratic culture, that has provided fertile ground to Taliban to grow stronger and make alignments with other groups in Punjab to target the government structures and common people. In fact among the five attacks on 15 October 2009, the four were on government establishments, Federal Investigation Agency office, Elite force headquarters and a police training Centre (both in Lahore), and a police station at Kohat in northwest. The army head quarter was made target on 10 October 2009 due to its plan to launch offensive against the Taliban in South Waziristan. Pakistan's Interior Minister, Rehman Malik admitted the inefficiency of the administration to contain these sophisticated attacks.

Pakistan is planning to strengthen its security forces by importing Chinese-made scanners and bullet proof jackets to counter these attacks. From a broader perspective, Pakistan's prospects of descent into chaos will be in nobody's interest. An important strategically located Islamic country, with nuclear weapons, with stakes in development and stability in South Asia is currently under ferment. Though the task is uphill the crisis in Pakistan needs to be contained. It is Pakistan which knows the nerves of these hard line elements can act effectively to neutralize them and woo them to the civilian fold or to eliminate them.

Turmoil in Afghanistan and Regional Dynamics

The Afghanistan presidential elections in August 2009 transcended the politics of government formation in the troubled country. The crisis of legitimacy, fear of the Taliban rising aftermath of the much controversial elections (36 candidates were in the fray) and their further entrenchment in the AfPak area with renewed strength and the chances of chaos and instability in fact far outweighed the immediate results of the elections. The much contested elections further revealed fragile process of democracy building in Afghanistan with wider ramifications. There were allegations of massive fraud, vote tampering and intimidations in the election marked by low voter turn out.

The Electoral Complaints Commission received more than 230 complaints of electoral malpractices. The two main contenders in this election were the incumbent President Hamid Kazai, having a strong base among ethnic Pashtuns and Abdullah Abdullah, the former Foreign Minister, having a strong base among the ethnic Tajiks. None of them could secure required 50 percent vote, thus opening the prospects for second elections in October. Since 2001 the war-ravaged country, infested by the fundamentalist politics, the ethnic turbulence, the new great game politics and the drug menace, has taken steps towards democracy under the Western patronage. The process for a transition to democracy has not been smooth. The elections added to uncertainty to the democratic process in the country.

This emerging scenario in Afghanistan will affect the AfPak strategy in which Pakistan is crucial. In this strategy Pakistan is both a player as well as a playground particularly in the context of extremism and terrorism. Pakistan's proximity in terms of geography as well as strategies has endeared it to the US. Being an important crucible in AfPak strategy and an important partner of the US to play a crucial role to fight Islamic extremism and terrorism, Pakistan can play an important role in Afghanistan. It is Pakistan's border areas with Afghanistan, particularly its North West and tribal areas in which the Pak-Taliban pursues a common agenda with their Afghan brethren. Pakistan still enjoys a strong influence over the Taliban (in fact the origin of the Taliban owes in part to the support of Pakistan. It was Islamabad which had recognized the Taliban government in Kabul in the 1990s).

Whether during the Zia regime to fight the Soviet forces or in recent years to fight the forces that had aided the Soviet withdrawal from Afghanistan, Pakistan's role in the region is indispensable. Pakistan's foreign office spokesperson Abdul Basit said on 20 August 2009, "The fates of the two countries were intertwined." Pakistan preferred Karzai in place of

Abdullah in the elections though it expressed dissatisfaction at his closeness with India. Pakistan perceives Abdullah as 'a much greater evil for Pakistan' as he is more pro-Indian than Karzai. Pakistan, it is well known, has been more allergic to India's involvement in the region as it sees India's involvement detrimental to its national interest. The visit of Obama's special envoy Richard Holbrooke in the event of elections to Pakistan and Afghanistan appeared crucial, as the US perceived that the success of the AfPak strategy is predicated on the success of the Afghanistan elections and the emergence of a legitimate, acceptable leader. The US has made huge investments in the region and is interested to have a hold in this strategic region. In a broader context the Afghan turmoil adds to the politics of the new great game in the wider Central Eurasian region.

Failure of the democratic process in Afghanistan will bolster the Taliban spirit. The Taliban is a force to be reckoned with, whether one agrees to deal with it or not. The Taliban and its spread from Afghanistan to Pakistan will be strengthened due to instability in the region. Some analysts opine the post-Mehsud period will likely help further inroads of Afghan-Taliban to Pakistan and influence the domestic politics. It will likely help further rise in instability, corruption and further Talibanization. Or it may happen otherwise or both ways. The Pakistan-Taliban may cross over the border to join Afghanistan-Taliban and Al Qaeda to fight the NATO forces. The Afghan-Taliban leaders like Gulbuddin Hekmetyar, based in North Waziristan will increase their strength from further weakening of the democratic process. They have carried out suicide bombings in Kabul and other parts of Afghanistan during the elections. The instability may seriously jeopardize the prospects of reconciliation among various competing forces. It will provide occasion to the Taliban to capture power in Kabul and rule the reign of fundamentalism and terror. The international community watched the horrors of the Taliban regime in Afghanistan about a decade ago.

The return of Taliban and its consequences will be more dangerous as their come back will have two-fold implications. First, it is the failure of democratic process in the trouble torn country. Second, the Taliban has emerged more powerful than the combined forces in Afghanistan raised to contain it. The new great game of which a major centre is Afghanistan may witness another bout of crisis. The troubled region perhaps has to go through phases of turbulence to achieve stability. The international community have to play a major role for peace, stability and development of Afghanistan as the descent of the country into chaos will be dangerous not only for the country but for the world.

A New Dimension to Indo-Pak Conflict
The opinion polls in Afghanistan conducted in December 2009 and revealed in January 2010 have shown India as the most favourable country among the people particularly in aspects of development measures. Pakistan's policy of keeping India out of the solution format of the Afghan turmoil and its discomfiture particularly at Pakistan-US deliberations about India's influence in its neighbourhood is well known. The reiteration of Pakistan of 'thousand years of war' with India in Pak controlled Kashmir too has brought to the forefront the deep tensions in India-Pakistan relations. The Afghan scenario after the likely withdrawal of NATO forces in 2012 and the strategies of various players in the region have further complicated the geopolitical matrix of the region.

The series of attacks in Kabul on 18 January 2010 while President Hamid Karzai was administering oath to 14 ministers in the presidential palace reflected the open discontent of groups against the elected Karzai government. The attacks were aimed at displaying the militant groups' discomfiture, among others, at the government's getting close to New Delhi. As per a poll conducted by the Afghan Centre for Socio Economic and Opinion Research 71 percent of 1534 respondents in 43 Afghan locations overwhelmingly welcomed

India's role in developmental activities in Afghanistan. [8]

India has already committed US\$ 1.2 billion in Afghanistan in terms of building bridges, roads, and schools and other developmental activities and also in training Afghan police. India is the largest regional donor in Afghanistan. The Indian activities have been viewed with suspicion by Pakistan. The poll registered support of only 2 percent in the context of Pakistan's supportive role in Afghanistan. Surprisingly the Taliban secured 3 percent of votes, one percent higher than Pakistan. The Gallup poll with regard to reconstruction of the war-torn country, conducted in November 2009, too overwhelmingly indicated this scenario. But, Pakistan has openly declared its reservation over India's activities in Afghanistan and viewed Hamid Karzai's friendly gesture towards India with suspicion.

According to Pak analyst Rasul Bakhsh Rais, "There is a degree of disappointment with him (Karzai), in particular over the way he has provided Afghanistan as a playing field for India." Another development that further added, or at least helped maintain the tense relation was the speech of Pakistan President Asif Ali Zardari in Pak controlled Kashmir. Addressing a joint session of its assembly and the Kashmir Council, Zardari almost reiterated Zulfikar Ali Bhutto's theory that Pakistan will wedge thousand years war with India in Kashmir. He attempted to moderate it by saying the war will be on the level of ideas. Describing Kashmir as the jugular vein of Pakistan, he said, "Soon the time will come when the world will take important decisions regarding Kashmir." [9]

However, the statement did unnerve New Delhi which has repeatedly complained against Pakistan's inaction against terrorist elements in its controlled Kashmir and other parts of Pakistan. India has argued that these groups have a determined policy to destabilize India. Pakistan has also long suspected India's hand in playing havoc in Balochistan. The inclusion of Balochistan word in the joint statement of India and Pakistan in Sharm el Sheikh in Egypt in July 2009 has provided

Pakistan ammunition to accuse Indian agencies for playing devious role in Pakistan's troubled region. The statement by Indian Army Chief in December 2009 that India is ready to fight a two-front war simultaneously against Pakistan and China has further ruffled the feathers of Pakistan as to the intentions of India. The volatile situation in Pakistan, the surge in terror activities, the rising imbalance in policy approaches of army and civilian government exacerbate this vulnerability factor in Pakistan, which has already fought three full fledged wars and one limited war with India.

In the context of Afghanistan the withdrawal of US led NATO forces will create a vacuum to be contested by various powers to fill in. Pakistan apprehends India getting an upper hand in this game, which may likely motivate it to follow a more complicated policy in terms of using elements under its control against India and Afghanistan. It is true that Afghanistan has miles to go to have semblance of stability, and a transparent and effective governance system but the already set pace for a democratic governance in the trouble-torn region can be considered a good start. In this background it appears more an imperative for the regional powers like India and Pakistan to coordinate their policies to stabilize the region. The fact remains unless there is peace between India and Pakistan, and unless there is evolution of a common approach on the sensitive issues, the region will likely remain unstable and violent.

The terrorist organizations like LeT have not hidden their agenda to trigger a conflict between India and Pakistan by using devious means. In this critical juncture it appears imminent that India and Pakistan must shun suspicions and resolve or at least moderate contentious issues. It is undoubtedly a long and arduous process, but it must begin without loss of precious time. Besides India and Pakistan, other players like US, Russia, Iran and China will be crucial players in any conflict resolution process in Afghanistan. One of the ideas that makes round is to return Afghanistan to its traditional policy of neutrality. [10] Another idea is to make a de facto partition of Afghanistan into Taliban infested south and relatively stable north. Whatever may be resolution process, the gap in relations between these two nuclear weapon states created by mistrust and suspicion will provide the terrorist organizations and other similar elements occasion to further realize their agenda and take the South Asian players into ride with serious implications for the region.

Mutiny in Bangladesh

Bangladesh, a small country in South Asia, surrounded by India and Bay of Bengal, witnessed a chaotic situation when the country's premier paramilitary force, Bangladesh Rifles engaged in a two-day mutiny, killing about a hundred in its headquarters in capital Dhaka in February 2009. The country emerging out of turmoil with December 2008 elections with the election of Awami League leader, Sheikh Hasina as Prime Minister, after almost a two-year spell of army rule suddenly found itself in the vortex of instability with thousands of BDR personnel raising the banner of revolt not only in the capital but in other parts of the country.

The reasons behind the mutiny are not amply clear though there are two theories in circulation. First, it was a reflection of grievances of the neglected BDR personnel, or second, it was a plot to dethrone the elected democratic government by a well calibrated strategy by the opponents. The grievances of the paramilitary force included the following: First, its members, engaged in protecting border and other tasks such as counter-terrorism activities, were paid less than their counterparts in the army. Second, it was always a bone of contention as BDR was led by army officers, while its cadres insisted their officers should be from their own ranks. Third, its personnel were less privileged than the army in terms of subsidies, pay hikes, and related benefits. Fourth, while the army personnel were sent to the UN Peace Keeping Operations, the BDR personnel were denied any such opportunities.

The immediate trigger behind the mutiny was the supposed rejection of the pay hike demand. The poor economy of the country further affected by the global financial crisis might have impoverished the border force, thus compelling its ranks to take such a radical step. But, the frustration factor might not provide enough rationale for such a massive attack. There are instances not only in Bangladesh but in other countries when a disgruntled soldier shoots his officer. But organization of such a mutiny indicates a conspiracy angle behind it. There are reports the opposition hatched the conspiracy to create a violent friction between army and BDR, thus leading to chaos with the ultimate dethroning of Hasina government. With its cosy relations with radical parties like Jamaat-e-Islami and its soft stand on terrorist organizations like HUJI, the opposition Bangladesh Nationalist Party does not appreciate the moderate policies of Hasina. The father of Hasina, Sheikh Mujibur Rehman, had led the freedom struggle of Bangladesh under the banner of Mukti Bahini (freedom force) with support from India. He was killed by the radical elements due to his moderate policies.

The action of Hasina government to control the mutiny was commendable. On a nation wide broadcast on the second day of the mutiny, Hasina told the mutineers to calm down and surrender otherwise she would be compelled to apply force. She sent her home minister to negotiate with BDR. On 1 March 2009 she declared constitution of a special tribunal to try the culprits of the mutiny. The mayhem that started on 25 February ended the next day with the arrival of Rapid Action Battalion and army tankers which surrounded the headquarters. The mutineers besides murdering the army officers including its head Major General Shakil Ahmed, also killed family members of army personnel residing in the complex and dumped their bodies in mass graves, sewers and manholes. The crisis was not indicative of only law and order problem rather it reflected the very weakness of the system that was unable to control or to weed out such kind of undemocratic, barbaric incidents.

Though the crisis is apparently over, Bangladesh's future may remain uncertain unless Hasina reins in the armed forces and BDR. The small state that emerged in 1971 is replete with episodes of dictatorship by army (for instance from 1982 to 1990 and from 2007-2008 it was ruled by army). The mass poverty in the country provided space to radical elements to consolidate their position in political affairs by recruiting the poor to their ranks. The coming years may pose more challenges to the Hasina government in tackling huge problems of poverty, illiteracy, terrorism and Islamic fundamentalism.

India maintained silence over the issue with the viewpoint that it is an internal affair of the neighbour. Probably, India did not want to feed the opposition forces to Hasina government by criticizing the incident and the mutineers, as it could be construed as interference by an external power. India shares a border of about four thousand kilometres with Bangladesh which is not fully secure. There are millions of illegal Bangladeshis residing in India and with the rising menace of terrorism India has suspected the HUJI hand in some of terror activities in India. In the past years, there were also scuffles between BDR and Indian forces at borders.

Any instability in Bangladesh will not only impact India but also South Asia. The last months of 2008 and early months of 2009 witnessed South Asia passing through a phase of turmoil with 26/11 terror attacks in Mumbai, Sri Lanka government's offensive against the LTTE, turmoil in Swat valley in Pakistan and the Bangladesh mutiny. The rise of terrorism with its bases in some of the countries of the region has posed challenges to peace of the region and the world. The Bangladesh episode does not portend well for the future of the country and its neighbours. This development coupled with other tumultuous developments in South Asia necessitate a comprehensive approach on part of the countries of the region to fight the problems in a broader consensual framework.

Democracy in Nepal

In the fast stream of changing events in Nepal, one thing has become certain that the country has spiralled downwards towards a crisis. The peace deal of 2006, after a decade long spell of violence killing about 13,000 people, has appeared to be in a quandary since the Maoist led coalition government locked in a conflict with the president over the issue of dismissal of army chief. The prime minister dismissed the army chief on 3 May 2009 on the pretext that he does not abide by government orders and appointed a new army chief. The move was disapproved by the president as unconstitutional. Amidst the accusations of violation of constitution, two coalition partners Communist Party of Nepal-Unified Marxist Leninist and Sadbhavana party withdrew from the government accusing it of taking unilateral decision to dismiss the army chief without taking into confidence the coalition partners. As the developments took place rapidly, the Prime Minister Pushp Kumar Dahal (nom de guerre Prachanda, literally meaning ferocious) resigned on 4 May 2009 in a televised address to the nation. A new coalition government was formed after his resignation. The new government was headed by the Unified Communist Party of Nepal-Maoist. But the dramatic developments did not end there and continued to persist in 2010. This uncertain atmosphere has led to the fear of a revival of Maoist violence.

The roots of the crisis must be sought into the very nature of the Maoist party and the functioning of the government it led. Nepal, a tiny Himalayan republic, surrounded by India on three sides and by China on the north, had witnessed monarchy for a long time. In 1990, the then monarch, Birendra declared constitutional monarchy and from 1990-2002 there was a period of democracy under the guidance of the monarchy. The Maoists as a force emerged in 1996. Poverty, underdevelopment and feudalistic social order widened their base. The Maoist promise of a classless society and economic prosperity motivated its cadres to indulge in violent activities and target public officials and properties. It was the royal palace massacre of 2001 and the imposition of the emergency rule by the new king since 2002 provided much needed fodder to the Maoist struggle and brought forth the situation to their advantage. The year 2006 brought relief to the troubled nation as the Maoists agreed to give up arms and joined the interim government. In April 2008 constituent assembly elections the Maoists became the largest party with 238 seats in the 601 member parliament. In the same year the Himalayan nation abolished 240 year old monarchy and declared it a republic.

After coming to power the coalition government under the leadership of Prachanda failed to keep the promises. The Maoists rebels refused to give up arms. They used the government machinery as a tool to further their agenda. The government labelled the media which exposed government malpractices as foreign stooges. As per a report by Reporters Sans Frontiers, within 2008-2009, there were 214 attacks on media. No actions were taken against the alleged Maoist culprits. In November 2008 the National Council meeting of the Maoists in Kharipati on the outskirts of Kathmandu accused the army and the judiciary as prime obstacles against implementation of their policies.

The crucial issue was the prospect of integration of Maoist rebels into the army. The Maoist government argued for their induction into the army while army argued that only those cadres who meet the requirements of the Nepalese army will be inducted into the cadre. Then Army Chief, General Rookmangud Katawal strongly opposed the idea of inducting all Maoist cadres. There is a significant section in the army afraid of the Maoist cadres as they are politically indoctrinated. This issue had become a bone of contention between the President, Ram Baran Yadav, who is also commander in chief of the army, and Prachanda. The constitution did not clearly elucidate the powers of the constitutional authorities and particularly in the case of appointment of army chief it was silent. Earlier in March 2009 the Supreme Court of Nepal had reversed the decision of the Maoist government to retire 8 generals, thus earning the Maoist anger, calling the Supreme Court as an obstacle to democracy.

The Maoist government was selective in targeting the opponents in the name of democracy and freedom. The atmosphere of uncertainty too took its toll on the Nepalese economy. It discouraged the foreign investors to invest in the troubled region. Nepal's tourist industry which is one of the biggest foreign exchange earners for the country suffered due to this uncertain atmosphere. The democratic crisis brings into picture the fragile nation building process in the tiny Himalayan country. It also brings into focus the lack of collaborative approach on part of political parties to meet issues of national importance. Unless the political parties irrespective of ideologies come together on a common platform on an urgent basis, Nepal may witness its sliding into the pit of chaos and instability.

Sri Lankan Turmoil

The crisis in the island nation characterized in some quarters as one of the 'world's most politically unstable countries' spiralled beyond control as the fighting between the army and the most dreaded secessionist organization LTTE since August 2006 led to loss of thousands of lives and displacement of millions with disastrous humanitarian consequences. With the determined army onslaught the LTTE had been trounced from its stronghold in north-eastern Sri Lanka. Sri Lanka, tear drop shaped, beautiful, Indian Ocean island nation, full of natural bounties is only about 19.3 miles south off Indian coast, separated from India by Gulf of Mannar and Palk Strait. Known as gateway between South East Asia and the West Asia the unitary, multiethnic and pluralistic state, as per the 2001 census, is inhabited by 20 million people. The Sinhalese, who practice Buddhism, comprise about 75 percent of population and the Hindu Tamils confined mainly to the north east of the country comprise about 12 percent of the population. While Buddhism entered the country around the 3rd century BC with the propagation of Buddhism by the Magadhan emperor Ashoka, the Tamils both native and transported from India by the British profess Hinduism.

Besides, there is minority population comprising Muslims, Christians and of other faiths. With the country gaining independence from the British in 1948, the post-colonial Sri Lanka has never been free from political turmoil. The Tamils have alleged discrimination by the Sinhalese dominated administration. With the rise of the secessionist organization LTTE in 1983, the discontent took a violent turn with suicide attacks, guerrilla warfare, and use of child soldiers. The LTTE orchestrated the killing of many mainstream Sri Lankan leaders. It was also involved in the killing of India's former Prime Minister, Rajiv Gandhi, in a bid to avenge his government's decision under a joint agreement with Sri Lanka to send Indian Peace Keeping Force to suppress the rebels in 1987. The banned organization acquired modern sophisticated weapons and its air raids on the Sri Lankan military bases in 2008 reflected its military prowess. Peace talks, some of them brokered by Norway, failed due to the LTTE intransigence and its insistence on complete independence, and also due to the Sri Lankan government's failure to grant internal autonomy to the Tamils within the larger framework of Sri Lankan state.

The UN criticized the Sri Lankan government for restricting the visit of journalists to the war torn area. Many nations of the world too expressed concerns against human rights violations by the army. The killing of Lasantha Wickramatunga, the editor of *The Sunday Leader* in January 2009 brought to the international light the harassment and torture meted out to journalists. The UN too castigated the Sri Lankan government for the deplorable humanitarian conditions within its controlled camps, and urged it to provide basic amenities to the displaced. India officially took the stand that the issue is an internal affair of Sri Lanka, which should be resolved internally though the implications for India of the Sri

Lankan developments are varied not only due to India's traditional link with Sri Lanka but also due to presence of significant Tamil population in south India.

As Sri Lanka's immediate neighbour, India expressed concern at the humanitarian as well as political situation after the wiping out of the LTTE. On 18 May 2009 the Sri Lanka President called then Indian External Affairs Minister, Pranab Mukherjee to inform the current situation. India has adopted a balanced approach by recognizing Sri Lanka as a sovereign state, but at the same time it has expressed concern at the deplorable situation of the Tamils. There are more Tamils in India than in Sri Lanka. This demographic dynamics affects Indian electoral and national politics as well. Besides, thousands of Tamil refugees have reached the shores of India due to war and their return needs to be facilitated. The regional parties in south India have expressed concern at India's studied silence over the turmoil.

The DMK, the ruling party in the south Indian state of Tamil Nadu, threatened to withdraw its support from the government at New Delhi if it does not pressure Sri Lanka to stop the attacks. But the consequences of 1987 episode have been a lesson for India. India also took into account that the major arms supplier to Sri Lanka, China and Pakistan, may take leverage over the issue if it adopts a policy which goes against Colombo. Besides, official condemnation of Sri Lankan government might encourage separatists in parts of India including in Kashmir to push their demand for independence. The larger point the current situation has brought forth for regional as well as international politics is the tussle between state sovereignty and secessionism. The basic question that needs to be addressed: whether diverse aspirations of the constituent elements in a multiethnic, pluralistic state can be accommodated in a consociational model, or is it imperative to grant every separatist claim for independence to have their way?

The conflict resolution process in Sri Lanka will likely be

further complicated after the routing of the LTTE. The Sri Lankan crisis may be over, at least for now, with superior military power of Colombo over the rebel groups. However, any popular discontent can not be suppressed by mere gunpoint. It may surface again. The real test for the Colombo aftermath of the war will be how far in the post-LTTE phase it accommodates the interests of Tamils in a broader agreeable framework. The time, hence, appears ripe for Colombo to initiate post-conflict reconciliation measures by accommodating diverse aspirations.

Post-LTTE Scenario

The challenges before Sri Lanka aftermath the routing of the LTTE are manifold, which include the issues of post-war rehabilitation, reconciliation and reintegration. The killing of the LTTE leader Vellupillai Prabhakaran and his top aides including his son, Charles Anthony has in no way ended the conflict in Sri Lanka. The most gruelling task before Sri Lanka in the post-LTTE scenario is primarily three fold. First, it is the protection of the internally displaced persons in the government managed camps. Second, it is the issue of their rehabilitation. Third, and most important from a long term perspective, bringing back to the minority Tamils the sense of dignity and unity with Sinhalese dominated Sri Lankan nation state. As per the data available in 2009, about 2,00,000 people have been languishing in the government managed camps. There is urgent need for food, shelter and medicine all of which are in short supply.

The government itself has admitted that the camps are overcrowded, and in the last days of the war, the UN has estimated further 40,000-60,000 IDPs were huddled into these camps, particularly in the camp at Manik Farm in Vavuniya. The more pressing concern for the government must be the rehabilitation of the IDPs. This is no doubt a mammoth task which the Sri Lankan government must undertake. The government stated 80 percent of the IDPs will return to their homes by the end 2009. An ambitious target set by the government but which has not been implemented properly so far. The homes of the displaced have been completely devastated by the war. For many people particularly the women and children the trauma is much deeper as they have lost their sole bread earner to the bullets of either the LTTE or the army. Among the IDPs living in the camps, there are about 55,000 children below the age of 18, many of whom are malnourished. They are also traumatized by the horrors of war and many of them who fought forcibly under the banner of LTTE suffer psychological trauma. The UN apprehends the volatile situation may turn to a human catastrophe unless Colombo addresses the humanitarian issues swiftly.

The other crucial issue is that of harmony and reintegration of the Tamils into the Sri Lankan society. There had been violent incidents breaking out between the diaspora Tamils and Sinhalese in different parts of the world. The government of Sri Lanka must take immediate steps to heal the pangs of the suffering Tamils. Though it is understandable that the Sri Lankan media terms the defeat of LTTE and killing of its leader Prabhakaran a victory of Sri Lanka and has showered praise on Rajapaksa as his cut-outs were displayed throughout the nation with enthusiastic supporters displaying national flag, in the post-LTTE phase it appears a national challenge before the government as to how it addresses the concerns of the minority Tamils. The routing of the LTTE which at a time controlled about 15,000 square kilometre in the north east of the island nation, and which was at war with the government for about 26 years, could be cherished as one of the historic triumph for the Rajapaksa government. The post-LTTE phase will test the acumen and efficiency of the government in establishing rapport with all the minorities including Tamils to build a strong, united and prosperous Sri Lanka. The displaced who witnessed the horrors of war from close not only need rehabilitation and resettlement but also reintegration in the framework of the wider, inclusive nation state.

While speaking before the parliament on 19 May 2009 the beaming President Rajapaksa declared victory over LTTE. He also admitted the uphill task to accommodate diverse aspirations including the Tamil aspirations. While speaking part of speech in Tamil language the President tried to assuage the Tamil sentiment by invoking national unity. He further stated the defeat of LTTE no way entails the defeat of Tamils in Sri Lanka. These high spirited words need to be carefully weighed against their practice on the ground. It needs to be seen how far the government concedes political space to the Tamils in the overall ambit of the unitary Sri Lankan state. In this context, the Amendment 13 of 1987 to the constitution that provided Tamil a national language status towards addressing the Tamil concerns could be studied and utilized. Similarly, the Norwegian brokered peace deal which talked about internal autonomy to the Tamils within the Sri Lankan state could be considered. Beyond the past agreements and resolutions, the government can also meet the moderate Tamil leaders to devise novel mechanisms to address the minority concerns.

Any failure on part of the government to address the concerns might witness the emergence of LTTE like organizations with more vengeance. There are fears expressed in some quarters that the scattered LTTE might resort to suicide and guerrilla attacks unless the issue of Tamils is not addressed with due urgency. The most urgent issue before the Sri Lankan government at present, hence, is to address the issue of the displaced and then gradually move towards the political sphere to accommodate the minority concerns within the framework of unitary sovereign state. The government needs to display the political will which it displayed in destroying the LTTE to address the concerns of all its citizens including the minorities.

Post-Electoral Tensions
The presidential elections in Sri Lanka on 26 January 2010

and the results declared the day after created tensions in the island nation. The election results showed the fractured verdict again on ethnic lines. Though some analysts argued that the election results reflected participation of all communities disregard of ethnic diversities, the fact remained that the re-election of incumbent President, Mahinda Rajapaksa was mainly based on the support of Sinhalese dominated southern parts of the country. This support base of the President is likely to demean the importance of minorities like Tamils, and further jeopardize their future already devastated by the bloody war in the north eastern parts of the country in 2009. Both Rajapaksa and the former Army Chief and opposition candidate Sarath Fonseka emerged war heroes after the army trounced the Tamil tigers and killed their leader. Rajapaksa for the first time got elected in 2005 on a promise that he will end the Tamil insurgency and bring the country to the path of peace and development under the framework of united Sri Lanka.

It was under his presidency that the Sri Lankan army led by Fonseka waged the violent war that reached its peak in early months of 2009 ending in the defeat of the LTTE. The international attention on Sri Lanka remained high not only because of the war itself, but because of the consequences of the war that befell on the civilians. After the victory of Sri Lankan army over the rebels, the government was in a mood to capitalize on the gains of the war. The government of Rajapaksa promised to address the sufferings of the ethnic minorities. Rajapaksa's 14-point 2010 manifesto emphasized on a modern, developed and peaceful Sri Lanka in the line of Singapore. He envisaged to make Sri Lanka a kind of bridge between east and west, and to make it a beautiful island nation which can do business with the world. The President declared his intention to have national elections before the completion of his term as he was sure that the huge upsurge in Sinhalese nationalism will lead him to victory.

Sarath Fonseka emerged as a challenge to President

Rajapaksa primarily owing to two reasons. Besides his Sinhalese origin, he was also considered a war hero as under his leadership the Sri Lankan army defeated the rebels and ended the 26 year insurgency. He was supported by many opposition parties including the party of former president, Chandrika Kumartunga, and a Tamil group called Tamil National Alliance. The rainbow coalition was keen to cut into size the influence of Rajapaksa by supporting Fonseka. After the war, Rajapaksa was immensely popular among the majority Sinhalese, though Fonseka too was popular, he did not have the mass base as a political leader like that of Rajapaksa. On 27 January 2010 the day the election results were declared there was wide media coverage that the disputed results may likely whet up violence in the island nation. There were reports that the armed troops surrounded the hotel Cinnamon Lake in Colombo where Fonseka was staying, though later the forces were withdrawn.

As per the data revealed by the Election Commission, Rajapaksa's Sri Lanka Freedom Party secured about 5.5 million votes while Fonseka's New Democratic Front secured 3.9 million votes. In percentage terms, Rajapaksa won about 58 percent of the votes, much higher than 50 percent of votes he secured in 2005. Fonseka secured 40 percent of votes. In north and east Fonseka secured more votes than Rajapaksa as he was supported by the pro-government Eelam People's Democratic Party in the north and Tamil National Alliance in the east. However, the Sinhalese-Buddhist dominated south overwhelmingly voted in favour of Rajapaksa. Fonseka wrote to the Election Commissioner alleging irregularities and use of government machineries by Rajapaksa to ensure his victory. Amidst massive celebrations in the southern Sri Lanka, the Tamils and Muslims in north east apprehended that the victory of Rajapaksa, for whom they did not vote, may likely further affect the reconciliation and development process in their regions.

Rajapaksa emerged the most powerful leader in the island

nation after the elections. The apparent peace which his government could secure after the defeat of the LTTE may fizzle out unless he reaches out to the disenchanted minorities in the north east with some kind of accommodation that is acceptable to all. It may be easy to conclude that the Tamil tigers are wiped out, hence there is no obstacle to peace, but it may not take much time the alienation of the minorities and their likely negligence in future may give birth to new insurgent movements. As President Rajapaksa promised to address all these issues during elections, it is likely that he will not be arrogating himself as the only representative of the majority after his massive victory but also as the leader of the whole Sri Lanka and initiate policies for an all inclusive development of all communities in an equitable framework.

Third Party in Indo-Pak Conflict

The joint US-China statement on the eve of US President Barack Obama's visit to China in November 2009 sparked a fierce debate in South Asia. The statement called for joint endeavour on part of both the countries to step up measures for peace and development in South Asia. It read that both the countries would 'work together to promote peace, stability and development in the region (South Asia).' [11] While Pakistan welcomed the statement, India following its official policy rejected the overtures as detrimental to spirit of bilateralism, as the problems pertaining to the region including Kashmir could be solved only by bilateral means. Further adding to the complex nature, a Chinese organization invited one of separatist leaders in Kashmir, Mirwaiz Umar Farooq to visit China.

Earlier, about twelve years ago both the countries came together in issuing a joint statement condemning the nuclear tests by India and Pakistan. But this time, the situation was different. What prompted the US and China to include South Asia in their joint statement particularly India and Pakistan is unclear. In fact there are diverse interpretations as to this development. One shred of argument is that it is because of the US' dependence on China for its economic recovery it induced China to play a role in the South Asian conflict. The US needs China to boost its economy. According to one report Chinese exports to the US rose from US$ 100 billion in 2000 to US$ 296 billion in 2009, while imports rose from US$ 16 billion to US$ 70 billion. [12]

Another shred of argument goes like this. China was irked at India's policies particularly its granting permission to Tibetan leader Dalai Lama to visit Arunachal Pradesh in India, which China claims to be its territory. Both the countries went to war in 1962 due to contested claims on the unsettled border. One more contentious issue is India's sheltering the government in exile of Tibetan spiritual leader. It is the Dalai Lama's visit that might be the immediate trigger and have prompted China to factor the India-Pakistan relations in joint statement. In the context of Kashmir, the invitation of China to the separatist leader Mirwaiz was the first of its kind. Kashmir dispute is one of the longest running disputes in South Asia, in which India and Pakistan have fought three major wars, a limited war and many border skirmishes. The princely state of Jammu and Kashmir, has been currently spread into three countries—India, Pakistan and China. [13] India raised objections to the Pakistan-China agreement in 1963 in which Pakistan ceded more than 5000 square kilometres of its controlled territory to China. The separatist leader Mirwaiz's statement that China has a stake in Kashmir conflict has further complicated the matter.

The situation took a turn with US developing cold feet over the joint statement in China. William J. Burns, the US Under Secretary for Political Affairs, while speaking at the Carnegie Endowment for International Peace in Washington on 18 November 2009 observed, "The pace, scope, and content of the peace process is for Indian and Pakistan leaders to decide." Indian foreign ministry has strongly rejected any possibility of third party mediation in Kashmir. India's Prime

Minister, Manmohan Singh became the first state guest of the US after Obama coming to power. In a move to display India's rising prowess, within a week he visited Russia in December 2009. The overall sum of the argument is that the US cannot ignore India's interests while pushing for its own national interests. The US is interested to explore India's civilian nuclear technology market, its arms market as well as its need for technology. The supposed boost of bilateral relations will likely get dampened unless the US takes into account India's interest in the overall ambit of security challenges in South Asia, including Afghanistan which has now become a member of SAARC. Unless there is a multi-pronged approach involving regional and other powers including India, Russia, China, Central Asian countries as well as Iran, its AfPak strategy will have to go through rough weathers. A disturbed South Asia is for nobody's advantage, not even for India and Pakistan. But the question then follows what are the basic parameters that will govern the peace and security framework in the region? In this contest, there seems to be a paradoxical position between India and Pakistan. The joint statement of the US-China may not salvage much the current turmoil in the region, unless the parties India and Pakistan come together, build trust, and agree on a common framework to move forward.

Can Tashkent Repeat?

The meeting of Indian prime minister with his Pak counterpart at the sidelines of SCO summit at the Russian city of Yekaterinburg on 16 June 2009 evoked the historic event of Tashkent in 1966 when the Soviet Union brokered peace between the embattled South Asian neighbours. The reference to the Tashkent meeting assumed double significance as the Yekaterinburg meeting was the first between India and Pakistan at the top level after the Mumbai terror attack in November 2008. It was for the first time after the 26/11 that Indian Prime Minister Manmohan Singh agreed to 'come more than half way' and meet the Pak President Asif Ali Zardari at the sidelines of the SCO summit. Singh in his speech in the upper house of the Indian parliament on 9 June 2009 reiterated his commitment to 'pursue the path of dialogue' as there is no other alternative in this changing world order. Both India and Pakistan along with Iran and Mongolia are observers in the SCO comprising Russia, China and four Central Asian states.

Though the Indian officials remained tight lipped over the outcome of the meeting, it was no doubt the breaking of the seven month old logjam led to optimism in circles that probably things will move forward after the meeting. Also the meeting outside the respective countries provided flexibility to leadership of both the counties particularly to the leadership of Pakistan to do some good exercise in dialogue and deliberation. Though events of the Indo-Pak war of 1965 and the 26/11 Mumbai terror attack vary in their scope and significance, their similarities particularly in the context of the post- event peace process could not be overlooked. The 1965 war was not 26/11, but the latter's significance both for national and international politics is undoubtedly manifold.

More than forty years ago the Soviet Premier, Alexei Kosygin, was called a good friend by both India and Pakistan for his role in facilitating peace between the two by offering the Soviet good offices at Tashkent. The Tashkent summit could break the deadlock after the 1965 Indo-Pak war and emphasized on peace and dialogue between India and Pakistan. The statement of Kosygin at the opening of the summit on 4 January 1966 indicated the Soviet desire to promote peace in South Asia. The Soviet Premier had stated, "in proposing this meeting, the government of the Soviet Union was guided by the feelings of the friendship towards the people of Pakistan and India, by a desire to help them find a way to peace and to prevent sacrifices and hardships brought by the disaster of war." [14] Then Indian Prime Minister, Lal Bahadur Shastri, while thanking his Soviet counterpart for the 'great and noble role,' [15] praised the Soviet leader for facilitating the talks.

The probability of Russia playing a similar role in the present context is, however, a subject of conjecture in a changing world order. But, the event provided the venue for the leaders of India and Pakistan to meet and deliberate on various issues. However symbolic their meeting was, its significance after the diplomatic rupture of seven months was far reaching. The meeting at the sidelines of the SCO becomes doubly significant as the grouping has, among other things, on its agenda tackling terror menace. Pakistan which has witnessed mushrooming of terror groups in its territory must root out terrorism to herald a new age of peace and security in South Asia. The meeting would likely goad the Pak leadership to take concrete steps to tackle the terror menace to bring to justice the culprits of Mumbai terror attack and to move forward towards a new beginning of trust and friendship in the Indian subcontinent.

Manmohan Singh's exhortation to Pakistan to show 'courage, determination and statesmanship to act against terror' is matched by his forthrightness 'I assure them we will meet them more than halfway.' In fact the developments aftermath of the 26/11 have caused enough embarrassment to Indian leadership as the assurances given by Pakistan to bring to justice the culprits of the terror still remain unfulfilled and with the release of the LeT Chief, Hafiz Saeed India's suspicion over Pak earnestness has grown further. Needless to add the LeT played a major role in masterminding the attack. Among much glitter and pomp of the SCO summit in Yekaterinburg, it was not inconsequential that the leaders of India and Pakistan met for the first time in Russia after the Mumbai terror attack but possibility of repetition of Tashkent in terms of bringing peace in the region remained a non-reality though it led to cooling off tense Indo-Pak relations.

Saudi Arabia as Interlocutor?

Since the inception of India-Pakistan bilateral animosities

playing the role of mediator becomes a prize catch in international politics. In the list of players the name that has emerged recently is that of Saudi Arabia. Indian Prime Minster visited Saudi Arabia on 27 February 2010 on a three day state visit. The visit at the highest level that took place after 28 years evoked optimism in bilateral relations, but at the same time it raised apprehensions as the discussions during the visit brought to the fore. The last time any Indian Prime Minister visited the most powerful country in the Gulf was in 1982 when Indira Gandhi made an official trip. India signed about ten bilateral agreements with Saudi Arabia during the visit of Indian Prime Minister Manmohan Singh. During the visit of Singh, many agreements in the fields of regional security, terrorism and money laundering were signed. A prominent agreement was the signing of the extradition treaty between the two countries.

The spirit of the Delhi Declaration signed during the visit of the King Abdullah to Delhi in January 2006 was further bolstered with the signing of the Riyadh Declaration during the visit of Singh. The visit and its outcome were virtually overshadowed by a controversial statement by then Indian Minister of State of External Affairs, Shashi Tharoor, who was also part of the delegation led by the Prime Minister. Tharoor to a question from media said that Saudi Arabia could play the role of a 'valuable interlocutor' [16] between India and Pakistan to ease tensions in bilateral relations. It remained unclear whether the utterances by the Indian Minister were gaffe or part of a deliberate strategy but the opposition in India took umbrage at the Minister's statement.

Many Indian political parties expressed reservation against the idea of South Asian amity at the behest of Saudi Arabia. Bhartiya Janata Party, the main opposition party in the Indian parliament called the statement 'utterly irresponsible.' The Left parties criticized the statement on similar grounds. Almost all opposition parties urged the Prime Minister to clarify in the Indian parliament on his return the true nature and spirit of the statement of his minister. There were also references to the foreign secretary level talks held in New Delhi on 25 February 2010, which concluded without any tangible result. Pakistan during the talks termed Indian dossier on Hafeez Saeed, the master mind behind 26/11 Mumbai attack, 'literature,' not evidence. The acrimonious tone in bilateral relations got further highlighted when the bilateral talks ended without any joint statement.

Undoubtedly Saudi Arabia is a major player in the regional politics. The United Nations' special envoy had met the leaders of moderate Taliban in Dubai in January 2010 to broker peace in the trouble-torn Afghanistan. [17] Saudi Arabia, which enjoys special relations with Pakistan, has enough clout in ruling establishment in Islamabad. Its influence on Pakistan in terms of economic, religious and cultural influence is enormous. Pakistan's civilian rulers and army, both enjoy special rapport with the ruling establishment in Saudi Arabia. The two major religious places in Islam- Mecca and Medina- are situated in Saudi Arabia.

However, there is also a point of view that the powerful Gulf country has used its influences to spread radical Sunni Islam in Pakistan and surrounding regions. It is argued that the Taliban in Pakistan and Afghanistan and other radical organizations draw inspiration heavily from the Gulf country. Credence to these arguments also stemmed from the fact that Saudi Arabia recognized Pakistan-supported Taliban regime in Afghanistan that emerged in the mid 1990s with its radical agenda. The Pakistan press immediately pointed out the minister's statement as Indian keenness to involve Saudi Arabia in the peace negotiations between the two countries. Indian official position since long, particularly after the 1972 Shimla Accord between the two South Asian neighbours, has been that all bilateral and contentious issues between India and Pakistan must be resolved through peaceful bilateral dialogue without any third party role. As already mentioned, the only successful initiative by any third party in moderating tense relations between the two countries took place in 1965-1966 when then Soviet Premier Alexi Kosygin took the initiative to call the leaders of both countries to the dialogue table in Tashkent in the wake of a full fledged war between India and Pakistan.

The potential of Saudi Arabia as a player in India-Pakistan dialogue can be a matter of debate. However, the Saudi royal kingdom can use its levers in Pakistan to tame the radical elements. How far that is possible will depend on the policies of the Saudi establishment, as well as the will of the Pakistan establishment to curb these elements. Besides India, Pakistan of late is also bearing the brunt of terrorism and religious fundamentalism that it has fuelled. In this background, the best case scenario for India, Pakistan as well as Saudi Arabia will be that the Saudi establishment pulls the right strings in Pakistan in right direction so that the violent, radical elements can be curbed. In that way Saudi Arabia can serve the best for peace and amity in South Asia. This is what Indian Prime Minister Singh intended while saying that he asked the Saudi King Abdullah 'to use his good offices' to persuade Pakistan to desist from the path of terror. [18]

References

1. For a detailed Failed States Index 2009 see, http://www.fundforpeace.org/web/index.php?option=com_conte nt&task=view&id=99&Itemid=140.
2. Salman Tarik Kureshi, "A State of Failure...Again?," *Daily Times*, 4 July 2009.
3. Madhur Singh, "Will Terror Threaten India's Economy?," http://www.time.com/time/world/article/0,8599,1656500,00.htm l.
4. http://www.dawn.com/wps/wcm/connect/dawn-content-library/dawn/news/pakistan/07-gilani-calls-donors-conference-for-idp-funding-01.
5. Hussain Haqqani, *Pakistan: Between Mosque and Military* (Washington: Carnegie Endowment for International Peace, 2005).

6. Imran Khan, "Talking to the Taliban,"
    http://english.aljazeera.net/focus/2009/03/200939102529353355
    html.
7. Quoted in Pamela Constable, "Pakistan Announces Army
    Offensive Against Taliban," *Washington Post*, 8 May 2009.
8. For detail findings of the report see,
    http://news.bbc.co.uk/2/shared/bsp/hi/pdfs/11_01_10_afghanpoll
    .   pdf.
9. *The Times of India*, 7 January 2010.
10. Karl F. Inderfurth and Chinmay R. Gharekhan, "Afghanistan
    Needs a Surge of Diplomacy," *The New York Times*, 20 January
    2010.
11. Quoted in Lydia Polgreen, "China Gains in U.S. Eyes, and India
    Feels Slights," *The New York Times*, 23 November 2009.
12. Eswar Prasad, "The U.S.-China Economic Relationship: Shifts
    and Twists in the Balance of Power,"
    http://www.brookings.edu/testimony/2010/0225_us_china_debt_
    prasad.aspx.
13. For the division of Kashmir between the three countries and its
    implications, see Debidatta Aurobinda Mahapatra and Seema
    Shekhawat, *Kashmir Across LOC* (New Delhi: Gyan Publishing
    House, 2008).
14. *Hindustan Times*, 5 January 1966.
15. *The Times of India*, 11 January 1966.
16. *The Times of India*, 28 February 2010.
17. Julian Borger, "UN in Secret Peace Talks with Taliban,"
    http://www.guardian.co.uk/world/2010/jan/28/taliban-united-
    nations-afghanistan.
18. "Persuade Pakistan to Stop Terrorism, PM Urges Saudi," *The
    Times of India*, 1 March 2010.

7

India's Foreign Policy and Relations

India's emergence as a significant player in global scheme of things and its display of indigenous prowess came to evident picture and recognition in the last decade. The developments that added substance to India's rise included the clinching of the civilian nuclear deal with the US, assertion of India on issues of global importance, display of technological prowess such as building of nuclear submarine and its economic growth. India confronted challenges both within and outside. However, the post-Mumbai attack deadlock in India-Pakistan relations affected its foreign policy postures as the prospects of cordial relations suffered a set back in the region with wider implications. The revival of relations appeared in sight at Sharm el Sheikh in 2009 but got dampened sooner to be revived again with the meeting of foreign secretaries of both the countries in February 2010. India's clinching of the nuclear deal with the US displayed mutual understanding and cooperation between the two vibrant democracies and with its traditional friend Russia, as reflected in Putin's New Delhi visit in March 2010 which witnessed the break of logjam over the Admiral Gorshkov aircraft carrier, India could sustain the bonhomie despite differences. With China India could devise a cautious approach without affecting the pace of relations while devising policies to secure national interests.

One of the crucial transformations in India's foreign policy in recent years is the multitasking of its diplomacy. India in the post-cold war world has not been restricted to the barriers or confines of the past as it has followed a multi-vector policy while keeping its national interests on the top of agenda. The tensions on the border in the north east added challenges to Indian diplomacy in handling the developments in a manner not jeopardizing India's relationship with neighbours, but at the same time not sacrificing India's national interests. While balancing its relations on the face of contrary demands or pronouncing its aspiration to play a global role, India has displayed enough acumen and confidence in facing the emerging challenges. Though India has a disturbed neighbourhood, its leadership has displayed enough statesmanship to devise policies towards stability in the region.

Independent Foreign Policy

On 15 August 2009 Indian government while celebrating 63rd Independence Day with fanfare at Red Fort of New Delhi made policy outlines for home and for abroad. Besides the customary exhortations to security, unity and integrity of the nation, democracy and the virtues of peace and non-violence, the foreign policy projections of India on the occasion marked a continuity of its non-antagonistic approach to inter-state relations but tailored in a manner to suit the interests of a rising India. As outlined in Prime Minister Manmohan Singh's speech to mark the occasion, the foreign policy projections of India need to be looked carefully as they reflect India's aspirations to play an important role in the post-cold war changing world. The prime minister talked about India's emergence in a world which is 'becoming smaller' in many respects. He stated, "Whether it is the international economic crisis or terrorism or climate change - what happens in one part of the world has an effect on other parts also." [1]

In the world of technologies and interdependence it is but a truism that what happens in one part of the world has its vibrations in other parts. In the era of globalization, further fostered by technologies particularly the communications technology, the world has become a 'global village.' In this changing world India's robust economic growth, its huge human capital and emerging technology prowess stand her in good stead to play a major role in international affairs. In the 21st century, also predicted the Asian Century, India is going to be a major driver in international politics.

India through its peaceful and non-antagonistic diplomacy has the potential to develop the array of inter-connectedness between the nations towards a peaceful, vibrant and prosperous world. India's emphasis on multilateralism also got renewed emphasis on the Independence Day. In this context the issue of relevance of multilateral bodies like the UN, WB and IMF has to be seen with reference to their effectiveness, adaptability and dynamism. These bodies have not been effective enough to fulfil the objectives for which they were established. In the language of jurisprudence they have failed to bring justice to the needy. There has been a raging debate over the reform of the UN. India has staked claim to permanent membership of UNSC in order to make the decision making process democratic. The claim has been supported by many international powers.

Hence, the exhortation as to effectiveness of multilateral bodies will assume a newer dimension in the coming years. India has emphasised on regional organizations to broad base its reach and to widen cooperation through groupings such as BRIC, NAM, SAARC, ASEAN-India (ASEAN+1) and G-20. India also expressed concerns against terrorism on the occasion. It has become a victim of the menace. The attack in Mumbai in November 2008, in which people from different nations got killed by the terrorists, stands important not as a case in isolation as it provides the international community the occasion to comprehend the nefarious designs of the radical elements, which have strong bases in different countries with huge men and material support. The prime minister mentioned that the terrorism scourge will not be tolerated as 'there is no place for violence in our nation.' He reiterated, it is the strength of Indian democracy coupled with the strength of its conscientious citizens that will challenge and defeat the menace of terrorism. India has proposed for an international convention against terrorism. Its concern to fight the terror menace and to forge an international network in this direction was amply emphasized on the occasion.

India expressed concerns for peace and stability in the South Asia. To quote the prime minister, "As far our neighbours are concerned we want to live with them in peace and harmony. We will make every possible effort to create an environment conducive to the social and economic development of the whole of South Asia." As already mentioned, the year 2009 proved troublesome for the region. Whether it was mutiny in Bangladesh, or war and post-war rehabilitation scenario in Sri Lanka or weakening of the democratic process in Nepal, or the violence in Pakistan, India expressed concerns over these incidents. India on the occasion reiterated its resolve to play an important role to work with the neighbours towards peace, stability and development in the region. Equally importantly, India on the occasion expressed its willingness to develop closer relations with all the major powers. India has developed closer relations with major powers without antagonising any of these powers. It has moved closer to other important regions such as South East Asia and West Asia.

While it has made significant inroads into Africa, it has yet to cement strong relationship with countries of other regions likes Latin America. India's policy since independence has been marked by a format of relationship characterised by friendship, equality and mutual benefit. Here, the statement of the prime minister reflects the non-antagonistic approach of India's foreign policy. To quote him at length, "We have good relations with the United States, Russia, China, Japan and Europe. There is a tremendous amount of goodwill for India and its people in the countries of South East Asia, Central Asia, West Asia and the Gulf. We have further strengthened our traditional ties with Africa. We are looking for new opportunities in Latin America."

In the context of India-Pakistan relations, the Independence Day declaration was a departure from the earlier such occasions. The prime minister's speech did not mention Pakistan. This was construed as India's intention to come out of its Pak centric policy and widen its policy agenda to develop good neighbourly relations not only with Pakistan but also with other neighbours and countries of the world. It is a fact that much animosity has been generated between the two neighbours in the past sixty years. The prime minister's exhortation to develop friendly relations with all neighbours including Pakistan appears sensible enough in a nuclear weapon age where war would bring nothing but utter destruction. India's Independence Day pronouncements provided sufficient indication of its aspiration to emerge a new leader of the world. The emerging India's aspirations to play an important role will depend how far its leadership ensures fair democracy, robust economic growth and an equitable society and also how far it is able to make a difference at international level. The prime minister's speech while outlining India's foreign policy projection had taken into cognizance the concomitant relationship between a strong and secure India and a peaceful and stable multipolar world. Undoubtedly, India's growing muscles and multi-pronged policy in building and strengthening relations with apparent rivals have shown maturity in a fast changing world.

Launching of Arihant
India launched its first indigenously developed nuclear submarine named INS Arihant at Bay of Bengal coast dockyard of Vishakhapatnam on 26 July 2009. On that Sunday morning Indian prime minister's wife cracked coconut on the hull of the submarine to the chants of Sanskrit hymns from Atharva Veda to observe the Indian tradition of inaugurating a new naval product by a lady. With the launch of the submarine named after Sanskrit term Arihant (meaning destroyer of enemies) India shot to prominence by becoming a member of a small group in developing indigenous nuclear submarine. While declaring the objective of the submarine to protect India's interests without posing threat to others, Prime Minister Manmohan Singh congratulated Indian scientists on

the occasion of completion of the project that was initiated in 1980s by then Indian Prime Minister Indira Gandhi.

The nuclear submarine Arihant will likely provide the requisite thrust to India's nuclear capability. Besides adding to India's nuclear triad, the submarine will enable India to strike after surviving any possible first nuclear attack. Arihant will ensure India's capability due to its stealth capability as it can hide under sea for months unlike the earlier diesel powered submarines which need to appear on surface for air. The submarine powered by 80MW nuclear reactor will enable it to remain under sea for a long time without any need to appear on the surface. Hence, the argument that the nuclear submarine will enable India to recognize and respect its no first use principle has appeared cogent and provides the Indian officials much needed ground to support the principle.

The 6000-ton submarine is 112-metre long with 11-metre diameter at maximum. It can accommodate about 100 crew members. In the beginning the submarine will be armed with 700-km range two-stage K-15 SLBMs (submarine-launched ballistic missiles). It will take some psychological exercises for the crew to adjust with the kind of claustrophobic situation inside the submarine. The crew will undergo tests with the Russian Akula-II class submarine. Russia played a key role in the miniaturisation of the submarine's nuclear reactor. Indian prime minister, defence minister and advanced technology vessel project head were in full appreciation of 'consistent and invaluable cooperation' by Russia in building the submarine.

The occasion to launch the missile has raised speculations in many circles. Should India launch the submarine at a time when the atmosphere in the region is tense with the terror cloud hovering in its north and west and when there is poverty and underdevelopment in the country? As per estimates China has a fleet of 62 submarines, out of which at least 10 of them are nuclear-powered. While China has extended range K-5 missile with a 3,500-km strike range or even more, it is building its strike capability of over 7,200-km. [2] India undoubtedly lies far behind China in terms of its defence preparedness. Manmohan Singh while speaking at the launch of the submarine stated, "We do not have any aggressive designs, nor do we seek to threaten anyone. We seek an external environment in our region and beyond that which is conducive to our peaceful development and the protection of our value systems." [3]

Further he added, "it is incumbent upon us to take all measures necessary to safeguard our country and to keep pace with technological developments worldwide." He articulated India's non-antagonistic foreign policy which aims at maximizing India's national interests without harming interests of other powers. But at the time, as the prime minister stated, India will take all necessary measures to safeguard its interests. It appears India downplayed the importance of the submarine. It probably did not want to disturb the present international nuclear regime when it enjoys nuclear rapport with countries like US, Russia, France and other powers. Though the induction of the submarine into the navy may take two years after the sea trials, it may send signals to India's neighbours to factor this development in their foreign policy.

Though Prime Minister Singh's statement can be reassuring in terms of peaceful objectives of the launch of the submarine, the launch will likely impact the geopolitical balance of the Indian Ocean region. The launch and its further success, in fact the overall success of India's AVM project will help it rise as a responsible power in the Indian Ocean, Bay of Bengal, Arabian Sea and farther to protect its interests and contribute to international peace. It may further add to India's responsibility to protect sea routes for smooth international trade and commerce. However, it will depend on varied equations in the region and how India's emerging clout is viewed and reviewed in different quarters.

Lunar Aspirations

22 October 2008 will remain a crucial date for India as

India on that day found included in the special club of space research. Besides, Indian scientific achievement did not signify achievement of mere a show of scientific prowess but enormous business potentials. While critics called the moon mission wastage of public money of a developing economy, the advocates supported it as a feat for India's Diwali celebrations as no country could wait for the status of developed and then involve in scientific explorations. The Chandrayaan-I mission, projected for two years, put the space vehicle into five-and-a-half day geotransfer orbit. The cube shaped space craft had a length of 1.5 meters on each side with a total mass of 1,050 kilograms. Its design was based on ISRO's Kalpansat meteorological satellite, launched in 2002. It carried a 30-kilogram probe designed to penetrate the lunar surface. A bipropellant engine was employed to enter orbit and to maintain the spacecraft's orbit at the Moon. The total mission cost at INR 3.8 billion was at a considerable less cost than China's and Japan's moon missions in 2007. [4]

With Chandrayaan-I India for the first time sent its indigenous space craft to the moon. As per the ISRO calculations India will be able to send astronaut into space by 2012 and a manned mission to the moon by 2020. The United States-India Business Council in its statement observed that India's success at space will open multiple vistas for space business at comparatively cheap prices. The Indian space vehicle used Raytheon Technology supported by the NASA of the US. Section of Indian establishment expressed optimism that Helium 3 and minerals available plenty in moon could be made available to meet energy crunch in India. The Indian public expressed jubilation at the success of the launch and Indian media appeared quite confident, however symbolic it meant.

Despite the financial crisis characterized by global market slow down and recession the surge towards science and technology assumed newer dimensions. Then ISRO Chairman, Madhavan Nair observed, "We have launched almost 16 satellites for other countries. It (Chandrayaan-I) will show the reliability and confidence of PSLV system. I am sure more and more opportunities will come in the near future." [5] This may sound ambitious, keeping in mind India's problems such as huge population, poverty, poor infrastructure, but the fact remains that India's stride towards development has never been so visible earlier. India's growth trajectory has an unsung side attached to it that in spite of myriad problems India's growth has been smooth. India's Prime Minister who was on a visit to Japan and China congratulated ISRO community for the successful launch of the space satellite. It may be a just coincidence that the prime minister's visit to both Asian powers coincided with the launch of the space vehicle.

In last few years China and Japan had launched their moon missions. The three events may be disparate without any connections, but it symbolizes the rise of Asia. At the same time it symbolizes the likely balance of power in Asia in which the three powers will engage each other in a paradigm of competition and cooperation. Though some analysts have predicted competition of India with China, the Indian policy makers have never pronounced any such ambitions and both the countries appear to have engaged each other in a non-confrontational manner, primarily in the field of economic cooperation.

How far the Indian success in space will impact the international manoeuvres in space? India's democratic credentials, its non-imperialistic ambitions, its non-hegemonic designs will likely vault it into a place where it can use its scientific achievements for welfare of human beings. There are reports that India will likely sign agreements with both Russia and the US to explore space on a different format. India probably is a power which has maintained good working relations with both Russia as well as the US. That is what explains India's agreement with the US to use NASA technology in Chandrayaan-I and with Russia to develop Chandrayaan-II.

India's endeavour in lunar exploration no doubt was a moment of pride for Indian scientific community. Though the space vehicle could not last in space more than a year after its launch as it lost radio contact with the mission control following a technical glitch, the space mission undoubtedly added to India's scientific research and capabilities.

Nuclear Odyssey

The debates both at home and abroad on the Indo-US civilian nuclear deal brought into focus India's nuclear policy and its various dimensions since it emerged an independent country in 1947. An understanding of India's nuclear journey from the very beginning will put the debate on the deal in perspective and enable one to see merits and demerits of various arguments both in support and against it and weigh those in the light of India's core foreign policy objectives. India's freedom struggle was mainly based on the Gandhian principle of truth and non-violence, and it was this principle that the first Prime Minister of India, Jawaharlal Nehru reinforced in interstate relations. It was reflected in the Panchsheel Agreement (also called principles of peaceful coexistence) signed between India and China in 1954. Nehru upheld these principles in the height of the cold war and adopted along with developing countries the policy of non-alignment.

At the dawn of India's independence Mahatma Gandhi at the Inter-Asian Relations Conference in New Delhi in March 1947 had called for an Asian way to confront international issues and criticized the making of atom bombs as dangerous to world peace. When India's nuclear programme started under Homi Jehangir Bhabha, the architect of India's nuclear programme, Nehru declared that India has the capacity to build nuclear reactors for peaceful use of nuclear power and after Apsara and Circus programmes, Nehru made it clear that India is now capable of making nuclear weapons. It was the 1962 Chinese aggression that shook the Indian principles of peace and non-violence. Under the leadership of Indira Gandhi the nuclear policy remained ambiguous. Despite the nuclear explosion under the code name Smiling Buddha in 1974, enabling to build nuclear weapons India called it Peaceful Nuclear Explosion.

Though India crossed the threshold, it did not declare itself a nuclear weapon state despite sanctions from various powers. Perhaps Indian leadership was under the impression that there would be global nuclear disarmament. It objected to Non Proliferation Treaty (NPT) and later to Comprehensive Test Ban Treaty (CTBT) which, it argued, would perpetuate the discriminatory P-5 nuclear regime. The international leaders poured criticism at India's ambiguity, and it appeared India was suffering from a paradox: advocating global disarmament but not signing CTBT; and keeping its nuclear options open.

In 1995, Narasimha Rao government attempted to test nuclear device in Rajasthan deserts but got noticed by the satellites and stopped by the US. The NDA government under the leadership of A.B. Vajpayee tested nuclear device in 1998. It was for the first time India declared itself a nuclear weapon state amidst international sanctions and criticisms. It declared self moratorium and no first use principle. Pakistan later tested nuclear device ostensibly with the help of China. Its nuclear establishment has remained under scanner and shrouded by controversies, and the father of Pakistan's atom bomb, A. Q. Khan has been many times put in awkward situations due to alleged Pak complicity with Iran and North Korea in developing nuclear weapons programme. There are also fears of sensitive nuclear material and technology falling in the hands of terrorist elements. India has, on the other hand, emerged as a responsible global power with a robust economy. This probably influenced the international nuclear regime, and the US under its Republican government recognized this imperative, resulting in the Indo-US civilian nuclear deal.

The supporters of the Indo-US nuclear deal put forward the following arguments. First, the deal will enable India to build nuclear reactors with access to nuclear technology and uranium from 45-member NSG. The Manmohan visit to Moscow in 2007 could not witness the signing of the proposed nuclear deal with Russia ostensibly due to the NSG restrictions. Other countries like France and Australia too refused nuclear cooperation with India unless it gets the NSG approval. Second, related to the first, India's energy security can not depend solely on imports. By 2030 India will be importing about 90 percent of its energy needs. [6]

Hence, the need for exploring safe, clean nuclear energy. In fact developed countries like France and South Korea generate significant percentage of energy from nuclear resources. India's noted scientist and former President, A.P.J. Abdul Kalam, and a host others put forward this reason to clinch the deal with the US. To quote him, "We need the uranium supply and definitely the pact is important if we want to meet the target of nuclear energy's contribution in the total energy production." [7] Third, the signing of the deal will make the implicit knowledge of India's capacity as a nuclear weapon state to an explicit recognition of its nuclear status. Fourth, India can continue its nuclear programmes as there are separation of reactors which can be accessed by the IAEA and which can not. The deal does not incapacitate India's nuclear programmes.

Regarding nuclear testing, the advocates say India can go for computer simulation tests, and if the need arises it can break the deal as there is no binding clause, and go for testing, while facing the sanctions, as it did after the 1998 tests, and withdrawal of nuclear material by the supplier country. The opponents of the deal kept forth the following arguments. First, the signing of the deal means bowing before the US and surrendering national sovereignty. This argument was vigorously put forth by the Left parties, who withdrew support from the government on 8 July 2008. Second, it will cap India's nuclear capabilities. Third, the use of nuclear energy is not cheap as its costs are heavy with long gestation period.

India's foreign policy never witnessed such a fragmentation in its approach as the row over the nuclear deal reflected. Despite political differences at home, earlier almost all the parties posed a similar front regarding foreign policy issues. It is difficult to comprehend how the deal could amount to surrendering to the US imperialism and to George W. Bush, as later the Democratic leader, Barack Obama also expressed his support to the deal. Regarding huge expenditure, it is true that the initial costs will be heavy but the long term advantages overshadow the short term costs.

Prime Minister Manmohan Singh put a brave face in challenging the Left's dictates by going ahead with the deal. The question that haunted India's foreign policy discourse is whether India can still rejoice as a leader of non-alignment, and rest in peace as an upholder of an 'independent foreign policy,' which is steeped in cold war calculations. Prime Minister Singh seems to have realized the emerging imperatives of the world order in which independence does not imply isolation but interdependence for mutual benefit.

A New Nuclear International Order

It appeared a paradox to analysts who hold a statist approach to international politics that the NSG, founded in 1975 in the wake of India's nuclear test a year earlier to control nuclear material supplies, made a special waiver for India on 6 September 2008. India's political establishment hailed the waiver as a grand achievement for India in international nuclear architecture. Despite oppositions to the nuclear deal, its implications far out reach India's immediate concerns and will likely impact international developments in coming years. China's attitude towards the waiver came as a surprise to India. India's National Security Advisor expressed disappointment at the China's approach during deliberations in Vienna. India on the 6 September sent a demarche to China protesting its approach in the NSG meeting in Vienna from 3-6 September 2008.

During the final rounds of discussion Chinese representative threatened to leave the meeting. Despite traditional rivalries especially on the border and on issues like Tibet and Pakistan, the Chinese leadership had promised the Indian prime minister, during the G-8 Summit at Hokkaido in Japan in the first week of July 2008 that China will not hamper India's nuclear aspirations. But, China finds it difficult in supporting India's ambitions. It is common knowledge that Pakistan's much of the strategic nuclear programme is supported by China. Hence, it may be difficult on part of China to appreciate India's smooth rise as a nuclear power, and as a member of prestigious nuclear club, which it has so long desisted due to peculiar rivalries between the two rising Asian nations.

In contrast to China, Russia despite its differences with the US on many crucial issues coordinated with it to moderate the opposition from NSG members such as Austria, Ireland and New Zealand against the special waiver. Russia's cooperation in building India's nuclear capabilities is well known, and its special assistance in times of desperate need as in 2006 when Tarapur nuclear plant suffered fuel shortage is well appreciated in India. [8] The victory at NSG in Vienna had both symbolic and substantive values for India. Symbolically, India enjoys special status in NSG, and now it faces no constraints in dealing with all NSG members. It could have been impossible for India to achieve this status a decade ago. Indian policy makers know the difficult time India passed through post-Pokharan II after 1998. Then Indian prime minister declared India's unilateral moratorium, no first use principle, even had shown willingness to sign CTBT, but India had to face the sanctions. Contrast to that situation, India is no more afraid of being nuclear weapon state; it is no more a nuclear pariah state.

Almost all major NSG countries have expressed interest for nuclear cooperation with India. In a sense, India's special status at NSG has led to the development of a new international nuclear structure, which will likely remould the non-proliferation discourse. From a substantive point of view India will gain from the special waiver at NSG. India as a growing market and consumer economy is an energy hungry country. It imports more than seventy percent of its energy needs, which will further grow in coming years. Nuclear energy can be an alternative source of energy. It may be irrelevant at present to argue about future nuclear testing and consequent repercussions when the advantages of nuclear technology can be immense for India.

Balancing Relations and National Interests

Developments in April 2008 witnessed a kind of diplomatic muscle flexing involving India, the US and Iran. The US sent message to India on the eve of the visit of Iranian President Mahmoud Ahmadinejad to the effect of pressuring the West Asian country to abandon its uranium enrichment programme. India reacted sharply cautioning the US not to teach it lessons in foreign policy. Indian government's strong reactions, arguably influenced by the Leftist parties who were part of then coalition government in New Delhi, received comments from intellectual and political circles from within and outside India. The common agreement that emerged is that the national interest of India necessitates a multitasking of diplomacy in which relations can be managed with both the US and Iran without hampering India's national interests.

On 21 April 2008 the US State Department Deputy Spokesman Tom Casey stated "India should tell Ahmadinejad to suspend Iran's uranium enrichment program, end its interference in Iraq and stop supporting terrorist organizations such as Hamas and Hezbollah." [9] The US also expressed concern that Iran might use revenue from gas sales to India (through Iran-Pakistan-India gas pipeline) to finance its nuclear programme. It instead advocated for a gas pipeline from Turkmenistan to India via Afghanistan. On 22 April 2008 Indian Ministry of External Affairs issued a statement, "It is important that the genius of each nation living in a particular region is respected and allowed to flower to meet the expectations of enriching relations with neighbours." It further stated, "India and Iran are ancient civilizations whose relations span centuries...Both nations are perfectly capable of managing all aspects of their relationship." [10] The foreign policy watchers were surprised at the reaction by the Indian external affairs ministry. Though the message was clear the language appeared harsh, which did not form part of India's foreign policy culture.

In international politics relations among nations are governed by a realistic assessment of actions and reactions which would likely affect national interest. In fact, India's relations with either country can not be seen as a zero-sum game as India has stakes in both the countries. The US is one of the largest trading partners of India. Indian skilled labourers work in the US in the fields of science and technology including IT. Outsourcing from the US has played a role in boosting Indian economy. Though the US has been recently called a 'diminished giant,' [11] it is still the most powerful country with leverage in international decision-making process. There can be no denying the fact that India needs the US support to get recognition as a global power as well as access to nuclear technology.

Regarding Indo-Iran relations following factors count for India's interests. First, Iran is a regional player in West Asia with huge resources of natural gas. It has the world's second largest known gas reserves after Russia. India that imports almost 70 percent of its energy needs can rely on Iran to meet its needs. There have been talks on the US$ 7.5 billion project to transport Iranian gas to India via Pakistan. The project was first mooted in 1994 but stalled by disagreement over prices and transit fees. The visit of Iranian President was mainly aimed at giving a final shape to the pipeline by removing the hurdles delaying the 2,600-kilometre project. India in 2005 signed another deal with Iran for the supply of five million tonnes of gas per year for 25 years. There are also prospects of participation of India's ONGC Videsh Ltd and Hinduja Group in the South Pars Phase 12 in Iran, which would help set up downstream petrochemical projects in both countries. There are also prospects of joint participation in the development of the Azadegan oil field.

Second, Iran has a standing among Muslim nations. Iran in many instances has blocked Pakistani manoeuvres to introduce the issue of Kashmir in OIC, the leading organization of Muslim countries. The statement of Iranian Vice President on 30 April 2008 that the Kashmir issue should be resolved between India and Pakistan through dialogue and terrorism cannot bring peace in the region can not be underestimated. Third, India has the second largest Shia population in the world. Hence, happenings in Iran impact the Shia people in India, thus indirectly affecting Indian policymaking. In this background India cannot afford to neglect its relations with Iran. Though India has voted against Iran at IAEA deliberations, but as Ahmadinejad stated during the recent visit, it has not dampened the bilateral relations.

Ignoring a global power may not serve India's interests, but also for the very interests India cannot afford to ignore regional powers like Iran. An independent foreign policy is of utmost importance for any sovereign country but that in no way hinders development of cordial relations with diverse nations to pursue national interests in the post-cold war deideologized world. Indian diplomacy has to brace up to meet such complicated challenges the coming years will likely pose as India is increasingly poised to play a greater role in international affairs.

Indo-US Relations
During the cold war period India-US relations were influenced by the bloc politics and super power rivalry. After the emergence of India and Pakistan as independent countries with the end of the British rule, Pakistan moved closer to the

US as reflected in SEATO in 1954 and the Baghdad Pact in 1955 which offered Pakistan the US military support. In the initial period India maintained under the leadership of Nehru equidistance from both the super powers, but later tilted towards the Soviet Union. Some of the prominent issues that further sharpened the contours of India-US relations included the issue of Kashmir and its ramifications at international bodies like the United Nations, in which the Soviet Union almost took unequivocal pro-India stand, while the US tilted in favour of Pakistan. Similarly on issues like defence cooperation, cooperation in the field of heavy industries, the Soviet Union clearly had an upper edge over the US in the context of bilateral relations with India, which followed a kind of quasi-socialist model for development. The postures of the super powers as displayed during the Indo-Pak wars in 1965 and 1971 further drew India to the Soviet orbit. Despite the US Presidents Dwight Eisenhower and Jimmy Carter visits to India in 1959 and 1978 respectively the relations remained low during the cold war period.

After the end of the cold war the relations took a positive turn but in a slow manner. India in the post-cold war world adopted capitalist model for development and liberalized its economy. Despite initial hurdles in many areas such as nuclear disarmament, human rights, intellectual property rights and the issue of Kashmir the relations during the period of Bill Clinton could be called positive particularly in the late 1990s before India tested nuclear device in 1998. Indian Prime Minister visited the US in 1994 which marked a positive turn in bilateral relations. A record of 15 agreements was signed between the two countries on 13 July 1994 to boost bilateral ties. Pokharan-II and later sanctions temporarily dampened the relations. The 14 round Strobe-Jaswant talks within a span of two years could help shun much of the bilateral mistrust. The role of the US during the Kargil crisis of 1999 in reining Pakistan to withdraw its forces from across the LOC was appreciated by significant section of policy makers in India. As a sign of emerging relationship the US President Bill Clinton visited India in March 2000. The relations marked an upward trend with a burgeoning bilateral relationship.

The Republican government in Washington under the leadership of George W. Bush took initiative to strengthen relationship between the two countries. Before coming to power, Bush during his presidential campaign stressed the importance of rising India, with which the US must develop closer ties to contain other powers which are opposed to norms of democracy. His speech at Reagan Library on 19 November 1999 further corroborated the Republican approach to give emphasis to the rising India in the global scheme of things. The year 2001, when Bush came to power, witnessed the withdrawal of sanctions by the US administration. The 9/11 attack further brought the policy perspectives of both powers closer in fighting the menace of terrorism and religious fundamentalism. Despite the US engagement in Afghanistan in terms of Operation Enduring Freedom and aftermath, the Bush administration never lost sight of the rising India.

On the issue of terrorism in Kashmir, unlike its predecessor, the Bush administration clearly emphasized that Pakistan must stop patronizing terrorist activities in India. Bush and Indian Prime Minister A.B. Vajpayee announced the Next Step in Strategic Partnership in 2004. The visit of President Bush in 2006 further strengthened the relations, as both the countries signed agreements spanning from space cooperation to cooperation in the field of nuclear technology. Bush's Asia policy never lost sight of India as he strongly believed the partnership between the democracies could play an important role in the evolving world order. Bush's policies towards India in according it the status of a nuclear power through special waiver at the NSG could be called one of the most significant achievements in bilateral relations.

Though the deal has been subject to fierce debates and competing viewpoints in India, US and in other parts of the world, the fact remains that the US played the crucial role for inclusion of India into the nuclear power club though the same kind of provision to Pakistan was denied. Besides the democratic set up in both the countries there are many other common factors that bring India and US closer. Both the countries strongly oppose the menace of terrorism and religious fundamentalism. In 2000, both the countries established the joint working group on counterterrorism. However, some sections of Indian policy making share the view that the US adopts a kind of apathetic attitude towards the terror situation in India. In the global war against terrorism Pakistan emerged as a special ally of the US, thus influencing the US' postures towards India particularly on the issue of terrorism. The argument has been that the US needs Pakistan more than India in its fight against the Al Qaeda and the Taliban, thus letting it developing a soft attitude towards terrorism in India. However, the common ethos of democracy, free market economy and also the role of more than 2 million Indian diaspora in the US play a crucial role in cementing the relationship between the two countries.

India-US relations in the later years of the Bush Administration were conducted under the rubric of three major 'dialogue' areas: strategic (including global issues and defence), economic (including trade, finance, commerce, and environment), and energy. The US is India's largest partner in trade, investment and technology. The bilateral trade in 2007-08 stood at US$ 42 billion. A report by Confederation of Indian Industries has predicted that the bilateral trade will likely reach US$ 320billion in 2018. Some of the areas for further cooperation include arms and armaments, civil nuclear cooperation, and retailing sector and education. Besides emphasizing on the prospects of cooperation in the field of civilian nuclear cooperation, the report argued for expanding partnership in the sectors such as agriculture, science and technology, intellectual property rights, cyber security and higher education. [12]

After Barack Obama's coming to power, there is a sense

prevailing in a section of policy establishment in India that Obama administration is not according due importance to India as was given by its predecessor. Obama's comparison of Bangalore with Buffalo in the context of business process outsourcing became a crucial point of consternation between the two countries, as it gave way the apprehension that the US is going to strengthen protectionist policies. Besides, there are differences on the issues of climate change, nuclear disarmament and the policies in the region of Af-Pak. The US has adopted a kind of apathetic attitude towards India's reconstruction activities in Afghanistan. These are some of the developments which are interpreted in some sections that the US is probably indecisive as to which role India can play in the South Asian as well as global politics. To quote one of India's strategic analyst, C. Uday Bhaskar, "Be it Iran, Pakistan, terrorism or nuclear issues, Washington had still not been able to figure out if India was part of the problem or solution." [13]

It is also apprehended that the US has emphasized its relations with China in Asia at the cost of India. The Sino-US joint statement in China in November 2009 that emphasized on the role of China to bring stability in South Asia under its aegis peeved the Indian leadership. However, it will be premature to conclude that Indo-US relations have reached its nadir and Obama is going to reverse the initiatives his predecessor undertook. Manmohan Singh in November 2009 was the first dignitary to be the state guest of Obama administration. The strategic dialogue between the two countries in the first week of June 2010 has reduced gap in bilateral relations. Obama will be visiting India in later part of 2010. The visit will likely put to rest the apprehension that the US is neglecting India.

Partnership with Russia

India and Russia celebrated the 60th year of establishment of their diplomatic relations in 2007. Broadly, Indo-Russian (Soviet) relations can be divided into four phases since its establishment in 1947: the Stalinist phase (1947-1953); the phase of friendship and assistance (1954-1991); the phase of uncertainty (1991-1992); and the revival of friendship (1993-till date). After the independence of India the Stalinist regime in the Soviet Union (SU) looked at the emerging country disparagingly. Guided by Andrei Zhdanov's thesis that there are only two camps in the world: socialist and the capitalist, the regime viewed the emergence of India as an offshoot of capitalism. But the situation changed dramatically afterwards. The impulses of the cold war helped shaping the relations. Following factors in this contest need special mention.

First, the growing US-Pak axis motivated the SU to look for a partner in South Asia, and they readily found it in India. Second, India's role in the non-aligned movement motivated the Soviet leaders to see India not as an attaché to the capitalist west but as an independent sovereign nation. [14] India's role in mitigating the Korean crisis and Nehru's principle of peaceful coexistence generated respect, preparing the base for diplomatic relations between the two countries. The visit of Soviet leaders Khrushchev and Bulganin to India in 1955 was noteworthy. From this year onwards till the breakdown of the SU, the relations never looked backward. Whether it was the signing of the Indo-Soviet friendship treaty in 1971 or the SU's policy during the Sino-Indian war in 1962 or the Indo-Pak War in 1971, the Indo-Soviet relations were cordial. The establishment of heavy industries in Bokaro, Bhillai and Durgapur, the establishment of the system of planning, and development of defence sector, in all these areas the contribution of the SU was clearly visible. This positive trend in the relations continued almost unbroken till the collapse of the huge socialist edifice in December 1991.

The disintegration of the SU had its manifold impact on the bilateral relations. Russia (the successor of the SU) no more remained a superpower. The economy, polity and the system of governance remained fragile during the initial years after the systemic collapse. Some experts comment that the Russian leaders did not even have a clear idea about the border of Russia after the collapse. Also both India and Russia adopted the capitalist model of growth during the same year-1991. Hence, it was on the expected lines that in the era of market economy and globalization when there is no ideological factor governing relations, the relations would take a new turn. The relations were jeopardized due to rupee-rouble controversy, the cryogenic deal controversy, and due to Russia's stand on Kashmir. In December 1991, Russian Vice President Alexander Rutskoi visited Pakistan. For the first time, in the history of bilateral relations, the Russian leader declared that the Kashmir issue must be resolved as per international agreements. [15] Secondly, he supported the Pakistani idea to convert South Asia a nuclear-weapon free zone which India opposed.

The year 1993 witnessed revival of bilateral relations with the visit of President Yeltsin to India. While during the cold war bloc politics and other dynamics shaped the relations, in the post-cold war era the major factors were: concerns about the rise of unipolarism and the establishment of a multipolar-cooperative security order, rise of religious extremism and fundamentalism (whether in Chechnya or in Kashmir) [16], and cooperation in the fields of defence and economy. In June 1994, during the visit of Narasimha Rao to Moscow, both the countries signed the Moscow Declaration on the protection of sovereignty and integrity of multi-ethnic and pluralistic countries like India and Russia. It is important here to mention that both the countries as the declaration reflected were afraid of the rising forces of religious fundamentalism and extremism.

The year 2000 marked a high watershed in bilateral relations. In this year, during the visit of Russian President Vladimir Putin, both the countries signed the document of strategic partnership, under which both the countries agreed to work together towards the emergence of a multipolar world. Both the countries agreed to develop common positions on the issues of UN, Iraq crisis, and West Asian crisis. In 2001, both the countries signed the Moscow declaration against terrorism. In 2002, they established joint working group on terrorism. In the field of economic cooperation, both the countries in the same year established Integrated Long Term Programme and Intergovernmental Commission on Trade, Economic, Scientific, Technological and Cultural Cooperation. India has invested to the tune of US$ 2.7 billion in the Russian far eastern island of Sakhalin. The Russian agreement to explore Bay of Bengal and its involvement in Tehri, Barh and Obra power plant projects indicated improvement in bilateral economic relations. Russian gas giant Gazprom and some of its affiliates such as Stroytransgaz are already working in India, though synergy needs to be infused in such ventures.

Rupee-Reactor Syndrome
    The usual summary of Indo-Russian relations is: both the countries enjoy bonhomie in strategic and political relations but lack needed synergy in economic relations. Indian Prime Minister Manmohan Singh's statement in Moscow during the 8th annual summit with then Russian President Vladimir Putin on 12 November 2007 further corroborated this point of view when he juxtaposed bilateral trade of Russia with China and the European Union with that of India which languished then at the level of about US$ 4 billion. [17] Indo-Russian trade topped US$ 2.1 billion in the first half of 2007, up 38 percent compared with the same period of 2006, when the annual figure was US$ 3.9 billion. Russia's trade with China is US$ 35 billion and with the European Union it is more than 200 billion euros.
    Since 1991, both India and Russia launched market reforms. The Indian economy recorded an impressive average annual growth at a rate of about 7 percent. Similarly, the Russian economy especially after 1998 registered tremendous growth mainly due to high energy prices. As per one estimate, the rate of annual GDP growth of Russia was 6.4 percent in 1999, 10.0 percent in 2000, 5.1 in 2001, 4.7 in 2002, 7.3 in

2003 and 6.6 in 2004. The high natural resource prices especially of the petroleum products sailed Russia through the difficult phase of its transformation from a sagging economy to a vibrant one.

However, in spite of tremendous boost in economy of both the countries and in spite of having huge potentials of economic cooperation, the relation did not witness any substantial achievement on economic front. While the post-cold war witnessed a shift in the geo-strategic balance from the West to the East, it too marked a transformation of international political scenario from the military-centric approach in foreign policy to economic diplomacy. While the countries flourish around the world and forge economic ties to boost their relations, the Indo-Russian journey in this context remained dismal. The rupee-reactor syndrome proved to be a major factor behind this sluggish performance. The syndrome denotes in a broad sense the lack of diversification of economic cooperation and its confinement to only few sectors. Indo-Russian economic cooperation is mainly confined to three sectors: arms and armaments including arms transfer, joint development and design; space; and nuclear energy. More than 50 percent of Indian defence structure and its new counterparts are from Russia or dependent on it.

The recent years have witnessed signing of big deals in the arms sector. Brahmos missile was the first attempt in the direction of joint development and design of arms and armaments. Similarly, under a US$ 1.8 billion contract for a 10-year lease of two nuclear submarines Russia has resumed the construction of the vessels, which were frozen in the 1990s. Russia has also offered MIG-35 to India. Each of the fighter planes that Indian Air Force will likely buy costs anywhere between INR 1500 million to INR 2000 million, while the total contract will well be over INR 25,00,00 million. The aircrafts are an improved version of the MIG-29s with capabilities. A Russian firm, Beriev, is building three A-50 AWACS (Airborne Warning and Control Systems) called A-

50Ehl. The surveillance aircraft will be the first of its kind to be built in Russia, and combines a variety of systems from Israel, India and Russia. The narrow range of traded commodities and high share of raw materials has become another major obstacle against widening the scope of economic cooperation.

Besides the arms and armaments, about 60 percent of Russia's exports to India fall in four main commodity groups: raw materials, ferrous and non-ferrous metals, fertilizer and news print. There are also problems in the way of expanding the potential of trade in the pharmaceutical sector, which has huge potentials. Registration of products takes up to 2-3 years. By the time registration has been completed, the market scenario changes and producers have to file for new products. There is also a need to improve and diversify the range of commodities. There are opportunities for cooperation in the fields of electronics, biotechnology, diamond-cutting, communications, infrastructure development including construction of highways, ports, airports and metro, extraction and transportation of hydrocarbons, pipe line laying, ferrous and non-ferrous metallurgy and automobile industry.

One major factor that plagues bilateral economic relations is the lack of information between the two countries regarding business prospects. The contentious issue is related to the signing of a visa re-admission treaty. India demands that if there is an invitation then the visa to Indian businessmen to attend business fairs should be immediate and automatic. Russia has been demanding that India sign the re-admission treaty with it in order to minimize illegal immigrants to Russia via third countries. The Russian and Indian leaders while looking at economic cooperation must respect each other's national interest, and must come out of the old cold war environment and thinking which largely shaped the bilateral economic relations, mainly confined to arms and armaments. The psychological barriers need to be crossed over and this may be redressed to a great extent with the easing of visa restrictions, so that more interactions can take place between the people of both the countries.

The deficient infrastructure, both geographical and organizational, makes the trade relations time-consuming and cumbersome. The proposed north-south international transport corridor is yet to be realized. It represents the shortest route to Europe and Russia. When weapons are left out of the equation, bilateral trade actually fall to a very low level. The 'rupee-reactor' syndrome has to be overcome and transformed into multifarious economic activities in India-Russia relations to add substantive content to their strategic partnership.

Gorshkov Controversy

It is the defence cooperation that has been the crowning glory of bilateral relations; hence any dithering in its pace will further dampen relations. The Gorshkov controversy is an interesting case in this context. Admiral Gorshkov is a Soviet era aircraft carrier built in Ukraine in 1980s and decommissioned after the collapse of the Soviet Union ostensibly due to its expensive maintenance cost. The negotiation between India and Russia regarding the carrier started in 1997 but concluded in January 2004 in New Delhi at the presence of defence ministers of both the countries at a cost of about US$ 1.5 billion. The carrier was a necessity for the Indian navy as the only ageing aircraft carrier INS Viraat was already in a fragile shape. The Gorshkov was supposed to be delivered in 2008 in order to fill the critical gap in the Indian navy. Viktor Zubkov, then Prime Minister of Russia, made a two-day official visit to India from 12 February 2008. The main purpose of the visit was to inaugurate Russian Year in India, besides presiding over the second joint forum for trade and investment. The visit acquired significance due to the differences over the air craft carrier and nuclear cooperation in the overall ambit of bilateral economic and defence ties.

Despite long drawn debates and discussions about the defence ties recent developments indicate that both the countries, taking into account the changing imperatives of the world order, muster enough political acumen to give final shape to the Gorshkov deal. In this context, it may not be an exaggeration to consider the Gorshkov controversy as a real test of partnership between India and Russia. Russia announced in November 2007 that the aircraft carrier will require further US$ 1.2 billion (almost double the cost agreed on in 2004) for its delivery in 2012, instead of 2008. The sceptics in bilateral relations preferred to call it a day. In fact, the deal was signed hastily without studying the details. As one Indian defence official admitted, 'the original contract was sketchy.' [18]

For instance, the recabling of the carrier at the time of signing of the agreement was estimated to be that of 700 km, but later it was discovered to be about 2400 km. Similarly, the ship requires more sea trials than envisaged earlier. Other technical issues such as converting the ship surface into flattop were earlier under evaluated. Russia took steps in persecuting the officials of the Sevmash for the gaffe. India too agreed to pay about half of the hiked cost. In a sense, it is good that the Admiral Gorshkov controversy cropped up. It might serve a forewarning for things to be tackled in advance while negotiating deals in future. Indo-Russian defence cooperation is remarkable and no two countries share such close defence ties which extend to joint research, design and production of weapons. Controversy involving Admiral Gorshkov could be considered a real test of partnership, which both the countries with the record of friendship and cooperation must tackle without entangling themselves in short-term calculations.

Reinventing Ties

The summit level meeting between India and Russia marked a decade in 2009 with the three-day visit of Indian Prime Minister Manmohan Singh to Russia beginning on 6 December 2009. The warmth of relationship remained high despite the global economic slow down and other changes in international political equations. Describing bilateral relations 'factor of peace and stability,' Singh in his pre-departure speech observed 'no other relationship which is of greater importance to India than the relationship with your (addressing President Dmitry Medvedev) great country.' [19] Both the countries while realizing the roadblocks in the smooth conduct of economic cooperation, nevertheless could foresee a good future ahead in bilateral equations. As the joint statement on 7 December made clear, both the countries enjoy special relationship and in this competitive world scenario the problem of terrorism, the changing dynamics in the AfPak region, energy and other areas of economic cooperation are some of the important areas of common interest.

The global issues like terrorism, particularly the terror menace in Afghanistan and Pakistan, global climate change, drug trafficking, global economic slow down can not be confronted by any particular global power as these problems need a coherent global approach. India and Russia have strongly argued for an equitable global order in which all the members of the comity of nations can have fair play. For this to achieve it is necessary to reform the international bodies like the UN. It is comforting for the Indian policy makers that Russian President Dmitry Medvedev assured Indian leadership of Russia's support for India's claim for the permanent membership of the UNSC.

India and Russia are among the victims of terrorism in their regions. Both the countries have formed joint working groups and declared their common resolve to fight the menace. While the terror attack in Mumbai in 2008 brought Indian terror situation to the global attention, Russia's confrontation with terror problem in its south is well known. Regarding Afghanistan, Prime Minister Singh argued, "Both India and Russia have an interest in a stable, prosperous and moderate Afghanistan, and we have agreed to regularly consult each other on the important issue." The joint statement expressed the explicit Russian solidarity with India in its fight against terrorism. It read, "Russia expressed solidarity and support to the government and people of India in connection with terrorist attacks in Mumbai on 26-29 November 2008 and both sides underscore the need to bring the perpetrators of the attack to justice." Both the countries also strongly advocated for the implementation of various UN resolutions to fight the menace of terrorism.

On the issue of nuclear proliferation India and Russia shared the viewpoint that further nuclear weaponization of states is a dangerous sign for global peace and development. Both the countries voted in favour of IAEA's inspection of Iran's nuclear sites particularly at Qom, which is allegedly developing nuclear technology with possible aim of building nuclear weapons. While India and Russia enjoy traditionally good relations with Iran, both also equally realize the dangers of proliferation of nuclear weapons.

The visit of Indian Prime Minister to Russia witnessed many concrete agreements. Russia agreed to supply nuclear material to India. In the field of nuclear cooperation India enjoys a special relationship with Russia in comparison to other countries. While the Indo-US nuclear agreement puts many restrictions on India, Russia's cooperation with India does not put any restriction on its nuclear capabilities and growth. For instance as per the Indo-US agreement, the US can withdraw its nuclear supplies on certain circumstances, the Russian cooperation does not put any such restriction. Russia is establishing four more nuclear reactors in the Indian state of Tamil Nadu. Indo-Russian CEOs' Council set up in 2009 is indeed a good sign for strengthening of bilateral economic cooperation.

The council co-chaired by India's Reliance Group Chairman Mukesh Ambani and Russia's Sistema Corporation Chief Vladimir Evtushenkov is comprised of a powerful group of industrialists. The council has met to deliberate on the issues related to economic cooperation. During the Manmohan visit, both the countries signed an agreement regarding after-sales support of Russian military systems in India. Both the sides also agreed on a formula extending a credit line of US$ 100 million by the Export-Import Bank of India to a Russian bank for the purchase of certain equipments. In a measure to boost economic cooperation both the countries have decided to take bilateral trade to US$ 20 billion by 2015. The bilateral military-technical cooperation slated till 2010 is extended for another decade to 2020. The transformation of the relationship laden with good political content but less economic content to a full-fledged substantive relationship can take place in coming years with strong resolve of leadership from both the sides.

Engaging China

The Tibetan issue has its bearing on India-China relations. On 21 March 2008 the Chinese government summoned the Indian Ambassador in Beijing in the late hours of night to convey the Chinese discomfiture at the crossing of the Tibetans over the Chinese embassy wall in New Delhi. It raised apprehensions over the security of the Olympic torch that had to pass through India from 17 April 2008. China's insistence led to cancellation of the proposed meeting of Dalai Lama with the Indian Vice President, M. H. Ansari, scheduled earlier. Indian government reacted by cancelling the proposed visit of Indian Commerce Minister, Kamal Nath to Beijing for trade talks. During his visit to the US, then Indian Foreign Minister, Pranab Mukherjee along with his US counterpart, Condoleezza Rice, called the Chinese government to come to negotiating table with the Tibetans.

The Chinese annoyance with the Indian government is mainly centred on three factors. First, the seat of Dalai Lama in India has provided much room for provocation to China to suspect India's hand in fomenting the crisis. India providing asylum to the Tibetan leader since 1959 has not been erased from the Chinese memory. Second, the recent security lapse in the Chinese embassy and swelling of numbers of the Tibetan protestors might have strengthened a sense of Indian complicity. The protests in India could not have been possible without tacit Indian government's consent, it was apprehended by China. Third, the joint statement by India and the US in Washington in March 2008 urging for Chinese restraint might have provided the ground to China to smell Indo-US collusion against its interests.

India too has its basket of concerns. The cultural relations of India and Tibet date back to centuries. Strong cultural bonds are reflected in the Buddhist monasteries in the Ladakh region of India. The author's visit to Ladakh and survey of monasteries such as one at Lamayuru in May-June 2007 illustrate the influence of great Buddhist monks like Milarepa on Ladakh. Second, India as a matter of traditional policy, also reflected in Panchsheel Agreement, has always advocated for a peaceful resolution of conflicts. In the wave of Cultural Revolution in China many Tibetan dissidents were eliminated, and some of them like Dalai Lama crossed over to India and granted asylum.

The Tibetan cause is well articulated by Dalai Lama. In a NDTV (one of Indian News channels) programme on 28 March 2008, the Tibetan leader pointed out that his followers do not want complete independence, but genuine autonomy. Narrating his tragic experience while crossing over to India in the garb of a soldier on a horse back, he mentioned how there were amity between the Tibetan and the Chinese shopkeepers and merchants at Lhasa. It was only during the 1960s, and afterwards, when the Chinese leader Mao launched Cultural Revolution, the Tibetan dissidence was suppressed. He expressed anguish over the recent vilification campaign by the Chinese authorities, accusing 'Dalai clique' behind the protests. China has made inroads into the Tibetan Buddhist religion in order to influence the protests in its favour. Many Chinese soldiers, Dalai Lama alleged, wore monks' garb and infiltrated into the ranks of Buddhist monks in Tibet. A Tibetan monk in Lhasa displayed sword, which in fact, was not that of Tibet but that of China. In the volley of allegations and counter allegations it is the Tibetans who suffer endlessly. Dalai Lama expressed dismay at the Chinese ignorance of him and its reluctance to invite him for talks despite repeated pleadings. [20] China instead has called Dalai Lama the main instigator of violence.

One of the ways for reconciliation for both Chinese authority and the Tibetans in the present circumstance can be accommodating Tibetan interests within the Chinese territorial integrity framework. Granting independence to Tibetans may have wider repercussions for other Chinese regions such as Xinjiang in which the Uighur Muslims are at odds with Chinese authorities. The Chinese reluctance for dialogue may prolong the unrest and lead to wider violence. The resort to repression may likely suppress the current violence, but it will unlikely put the unrest to end conclusively.

Indian political elites are not unanimous on the Tibetan issue. Though almost all political parties in India sympathize with the Tibetan cause, the Left parties have expressed dissatisfaction at the Dalai Lama's actions, especially his interactions with the Speaker of the US House of Representatives on 21 March 2008. The leader of Communist Party of India, A.B. Bardhan, cautioned Dalai Lama 'to behave himself' and not to be cosy with the US'. The Left's vitriolic dislike and oversensitive caution against the US, and its serenading with China is well known. Though many political parties do not share the Leftist viewpoint; the Leftist influence on the UPA-I government (as they supported the coalition government at the Centre) understandably impacted India's approach to the crisis. The Tibetan issue will likely impact India-China relations unless China addresses it while taking into account the Tibetan grievances, in which India can cooperate as it has a significant Tibetan population and their government in exile in its territory.

The Finger Point
Finger Point is a location in the north-eastern part of

Indian state of Sikkim bordering China. The area came to focus after China insisted on demolishing stonewalls from the area built by Indian forces in 2009. Both India and China had territorial disputes over the state but during the NDA rule in New Delhi the Chinese government had given up its claim on the territory, and accordingly the Chinese official map showed the area as part of Indian territory. In May 2008, China conveyed its intention on demolishing the walls in this strategically important area, about 2.1 sq km, arguing that the stone wall threatens its security. India protested and called the move a surprise amidst growing friendly relations between the two countries. Two things come out clearly in the context of the Finger Point crisis. First, China displayed its prowess in the region. China earlier defeated India in 1962 war and afterwards successfully built up its army with modern weapons, while India lagged behind.

Second, the Chinese muscle flexing might be a foreign policy tactic to undermine India, which is widening its cooperation with diverse international powers. China suffered a huge loss due to the earthquake that killed thousands of people and displaced millions in its Sichuan province. India as a humanitarian gesture sent US$ 5 million as aid and dispatched two aircrafts carrying tents, blankets and other relief materials. But matters of politics transcend other matters, as the Finger Point crisis reflected. The Chinese action at the border might be characterized by the motive to show the world that the catastrophe did not affect its national power portrayal. Earlier, China expressed dissatisfaction at the visit of Indian Prime Minister to Indian state of Arunachal Pradesh, which it claimed to be disputed.

Sliding back to the history of India-China relations, both the countries enjoy centuries old relations. In fact, Buddhism travelled from India to China, and the great Chinese scholars like Huen Tsang and Fahien had studied in India. In 20th century, especially after the Second World War it was the relationship between the communist China and democratic

India that took a different shape. The Chinese bid to have a permanent seat at UNSC had been supported by India. Similarly, during the Tibetan crisis of 1949 and afterwards, India and China signed the Principles of Peaceful Coexistence in 1954 to have friendly relations. The relations got bitter over territorial disputes which led to the 1962 war. The relations remained a non-starter till then Indian Prime Minister Rajiv Gandhi took the initiative. He visited China in 1988 and met its leader Deng Xiaoping.

The credit also goes to the former Indian Prime Minister, A.B. Vajpayee who visited China in late 1970s as India's Foreign Minister. China introduced state controlled privatization in late 1970s. India's entry into market reforms and globalization in 1991 furthered the prospects of bilateral cooperation. The bilateral economic relations are now at all time high. The projected target of bilateral trade of US$ 40 billion by 2010 was surpassed in 2009. The economic relations between India and China are noteworthy but the political relations suffer from rigid posturing and inflexible attitudes. Though at multilateral level both the countries appear to share common perceptions about world affairs as the BRIC meetings or the BASIC approach at Copenhagen displayed, but poor management of political relations will likely affect prospects of cooperation in other areas. Commitment to multipolar global structure and objective to tackle terrorism might not be enough binding factors to avoid hostilities between the two countries.

The Finger Point crisis might lead to further entanglement of both the neighbours at the border. India reopened the airstrip at Ladakh region overlooking China and Karakoram Range after 43 years. In case of military confrontation India could target the Karakoram highway range. M.M. Pallam Raju, the Indian Minister of State for Defence stated, "The country will not accept any Chinese claim over Sikkim and Arunachal Pradesh and Indian army will continue to build-up forces in Sikkim areas till this threat perception is obliterated." The

Indian army decided to raise two new mountain divisions of around 15,000 troops each, for deployment along the 4,05 km of disputed border in that region. However, it will be premature to perceive any kind of military confrontation in near future. Indian leader Pranab Mukherjee visited China from 4 June 2008. The visit could not break much of the logjam in bilateral relations, though it undoubtedly moderated the rigid positions of respective countries. The realization on part of India and China that mutually beneficial relations could not be made hostage to border issues is indeed an important realization among the two neighbours.

Despite robust economic relations between India and China, both the countries lack the collaborative spirit to resolve contentious issues. There appears to be an inverse relationship between the political equations and the economic equations between the two countries. India sees China-Pakistan relations with apprehensions as China supplies arms and weapons to Pakistan. In fact Pakistan's nuclear programme could not have been successful without assistance from China. Besides, China has declined to call terrorism in Kashmir by name, and agrees with Pakistan it is a genuine freedom struggle. That has further soured the relations between India and China. India argues how terrorism in Kashmir and terrorism in Xinjiang can be viewed differently while the source and design in both the cases remain similar.

Since the India-China war of 1962, the border remained unsettled with differing interpretations about its clear demarcation. China has declined to accept the Mac Mohan line drawn in 1914 between India and China as a just line of division. From April 2009 onwards there are about 400 violations of the border. An article in a semi-official Chinese website predicting the division of India into 15-20 sovereign states has not been received well by the Indian establishment. Despite the joint mechanism between the two countries to deliberate on the border issue, and despite several meetings, the issue remains unresolved with rising uncertainty. Two former Indian foreign secretaries, Shyam Saran and Shiv Shankar Menon have advocated that India and China should collaborate along with other stakeholders in shaping the security architecture in the Indian Ocean region. Though officially India has not stated this idea of collaboration, it remains to be seen how India and China can cooperate amidst the deficit in mutual trust.

The String and Pearls

One of the noted Indian national dailies in its editorial on 22 May 2009, while outlining the possible policy options before the newly formed Indian government, articulated the concerns of a section of Indian policy makers about the rising clout of China in India's neighbourhood and surroundings. [21] While pointing out Chinese initiated string of pearls strategy, the editorial observed that from a medium to long-term perspective the China question is likely to be an important part of the government's action plan.

The Chinese string of pearls strategy is the latest in a series of strategies China initiated in the post-cold war world to build its international stature. In 2002, China started developing Gwader port of Pakistan and established a naval base there. It invested four times more than Pakistan in developing this port. Chinese premier Wen Jiabao visited Pakistan in August 2005 to commemorate the completion of first phase of the port, not far from the straits of Hormuz at the throat of the Persian Gulf. In the Indian Ocean it is developing the Hambantota port. During the war between Tamil Tigers and the Sri Lankan army in 2008-2009, the weapons from countries like China helped Sri Lanka win over the tigers. India's refusal to give weapons to Sri Lanka had moved the beleaguered nation to opt for China and Pakistan, which were eager to offer arms. The increasing relationship earned China the opportunity to develop the southern Sri Lankan port of Hambantota.

The Chinese President Hu Jintao made a whirlwind tour to Saudi Arabia and four African states Mali, Senegal, Tanzania and Mauritius in February 2009 to boost relations. With the Indian Ocean state of Mauritius he signed deals worth more than US$ 270 million to fund infrastructure projects. In the Bay of Bengal China developed a container shipping facility at Chittagong port in Bangladesh. It also developed a deep water port at Sittwe of Myanmar and established a base in Coco Island (not far from the Indian island of Andaman and Nicobar). It upgraded an airstrip at Woody Island off the coast of Vietnam at 300 nautical miles and established a submarine base in Hainan Island in South China Sea. Connecting all these points or the 'pearls' is the string that the Chinese policy makers have in mind which can enhance its interests in the region.

The concept 'string of pearls' first found mention in a report titled 'Energy Futures in Asia' commissioned by the US Department of Defence in 2005. This strategy of string of pearls China has pursued vigorously. The question arises–what does exactly explain the Chinese vigour in pursuing a strategy which would enable it to stretch its bases from the South China Sea through Malacca straits to Bay of Bengal, thence further through the Indian Ocean towards Arabian Sea towards West Asia and Africa? Three factors explain this policy of China. First, China is interested to ensure energy security. China one of the fastest growing economies is going to be the highest consumer of energy in coming years. To meet the growing demands, it needs to have secure routes in blue waters to enhance its oil accessibility in the countries in Arab and in Africa. Second, it is more of strategic and geopolitical interests. In the emerging world order, China intends to rise as a super power, to have its policies as guiding principles in international politics for which it needs to have control over major sea routes and presence in far off places. Third, and related, China has been apprehensive of threats to its territorial sovereignty and integrity. Whether it is the issue of Taiwan, or Xinjiang or Tibet, China has made it clear that it will not tolerate any move which threatens its territorial integrity and sovereignty.

The vigorous pursuit of string of pearls strategy has no doubt increased China's clout in international affairs, at which various powers have expressed concerns. The US policy makers have taken this development into account while making policy postures towards Asia. Australia in its white paper released in May 2009 has expressed concern at the military programmes of China. However, the string theory may be taken as a policy measure which is non-antagonistic in its ambitions so far China, as Hu Jintao stated, pursues policies of 'harmonious seas'. India's troubled relationship with China and divergence of their interests in the countries of South and Southeast Asia, and China's friendly relations with Pakistan and its building of Karakoram highway in the Kashmir region to Gwader port have shaped the relations and raised apprehensions in policy quarters of India. Some sections in Indian strategic thinking believe that the string of pearls theory is a means adopted by China to encircle India by controlling the levers of powers in surrounding seas and Indian Ocean.

Whatever may be the implications of string of pearls theory, China like other powers has the right to adopt policies to secure energy, thwart attempts which threaten its integrity and protect and enhance its national interests. It has already stated on many occasions that its moves aimed at peaceful realization of its interests.

In April 2009 while speaking before the delegations from the naval fleets of 14 nations at the Chinese port of Qingdao, Hu Jintao assured China 'would never seek hegemony, nor would it turn to arms races with other nations.' [22] India can do well to reenergize its strategy in the surrounding seas and ocean to protect and promote its national interests. It is on the balance or imbalance of diverse national interests in the blue waters of Asia the future of the string of pearls theory as well as the future course of international politics and India-China relations will depend a lot.

India-Pakistan Relations

The debates over prospects of dialogue between India and Pakistan acquired a key stage in Indian policy discourse since the bilateral peace process got stalled when Pak based terrorists attacked India's commercial capital Mumbai in November 2008. The 26/11 attack spiralled down the bilateral relations to a new low. At least a revival in a year's span was far from sight. The joint statement on 16 July 2009 at Sharm el Sheikh not only revived the prospects of bilateral dialogue, but also brought to surface the common ground of both the countries on issues of terrorism with Pakistan's promise to do 'everything in its power' to bring the perpetrators of the Mumbai attacks to justice. The dialogue as envisaged in the joint statement at Sharm el Sheikh might have earned applause for the leaders of India and Pakistan in international media, but drew flak from significant section of Indian analysts. Perhaps it was the first time that any joint statement between India and Pakistan was subject to fierce debates and criticism. The prime minister of India's vision of promoting bilateral relations with Pakistan became subject to interrogation not only from the opposition parties but also from his own political party with the argument that he conceded too much ground to Pakistan without getting anything in return.

The joint statement appeared tilted in favour of Pakistan position that composite dialogue needs to be started between the neighbours despite the ongoing deadlock on the issue of terrorism. Earlier, India insisted unless Pakistan takes credible action against the culprits of Mumbai attack there is no possibility of dialogue. This is what the Indian Prime Minister Manmohan Singh exactly conveyed to the Pak President, Asif Ali Zardari in June 2009 at Yekaterinburg at the sidelines of the SCO summit. But in contrast to this, the joint statement signed by prime ministers of India and Pakistan on 16 July 2009, at the sidelines of the 15th NAM summit, read, "Action on terrorism should not be linked to the Composite Dialogue process and these should not be bracketed." [23]

Apparently, it favoured Pakistan's position which accused India for the stalled peace process after the terror attack. However, the above interpretation of the statement may not be absolute. The contrary may be true that terrorism and composite dialogue can not be linked together, i.e. it is not imperative that actions against terror elements can not be taken unless there is composite dialogue. But, then arises the question: which comes first—whether Pakistan's credible actions against terror elements or the composite dialogue. It will ostensibly depend on the kind of interpretation one makes. The prime minister of India emphatically stated in the Indian parliament on 17 July 2009 that Pakistan cannot be given a blank cheque to perpetrate, or to give patronage to terrorist elements to play havoc in India, and expect India at the same time to shake hands with it. In a move, either calibrated or coincidental, one of the main accused behind the Mumbai attack, the LeT Chief, Hafeez Saeed was released by Pakistan from arrest just before few days of the meeting of the prime ministers at the Egyptian Red Sea resort.

The significant sections of Indian establishment found it difficult to reason the inclusion of the word Balochistan in the joint statement. It is for the first time the word entered into any joint statement between India and Pakistan. The prime minister of India argued that India's policy to Pak troubles is an open book, there is nothing to hide. Hence, if Pakistan wants to include the term then India has no problem. The joint statement read, "Pakistan has some information on threats in Balochistan and other areas." The question is what was the urgency to include the term in the joint statement? It is true that there is problem in Balochistan since the creation of Pakistan. There are grievances of the people since the instrument of accession was signed in 1948 by the Khan of Kalat with Pakistan under duress. India has stated as a matter of policy it has kept its hands off from the internal affairs of Pakistan. But, Pakistan as a matter of policy has often accused India of fomenting violent activities in Balochistan.

Hence, it is no surprise that Pakistan's prime minister, Yusuf Raza Gilani after returning home told Pak media about India's implicit admission of involvement in its internal affairs. The Pak media as well as public rejoiced at the success of the Pak diplomacy. Probably, the Indian prime minister had a different objective, vision in his mind while allowing the word to slip in the bilateral document, but the hard diplomacy goes beyond idealistic thinking, and Pakistan got a brownie point to score over India and raise the Baloch problem as India's making. From Indian policy view point, the non-inclusion of K (signifying Kashmir) word might be comforting though its implicit admission was there in the bilateral document. Both the countries agreed to resolve 'all the outstanding issues,' which also included the issue of Kashmir.

Perhaps, it is the implicit admission on part of both the countries that terrorism other than Kashmir has become the biggest curse to the subcontinent. Interestingly in 2006 India conceded that Pakistan is also a victim of terrorism and a joint anti-terror mechanism was constituted aftermath of the Havana NAM summit in 2006. The mechanism has almost reached a dead end without yielding any result. What was crucial from the relations view point was besides terrorism, both the countries recognized the challenges of poverty and underdevelopment afflicting the subcontinent and resolved to eliminate the factors which prevent "our countries from realizing their full potential." The joint statement also noted "India's interest in a stable, democratic Islamic Republic of Pakistan." But, how far both the countries will work together for a better future of the subcontinent is yet to be seen. The mutual suspicion is quite deep; both sides find it difficult to erase the old sheltered menace of distrust. The contrasting interpretations of the joint statement fortify to this fragile nature of bilateral relations.

However, an infinite distrust or hatred is neither sustainable nor practicable between the two neighbours. It is in this context, the meeting of foreign secretaries of India and

Pakistan on 25 February 2010 in Hyderabad House in New Delhi far outweighed its immediate outcome primarily owing to two reasons. First, though the meeting did not produce any tangible result both the parties agreed on the importance of dialogue. Second, aftermath of the Mumbai terror attack, it was the first bilateral official interaction. Equally importantly, the meeting brought to realization that the tenuous process of peace in South Asia can not be dramatic and the complex situation demands small and significant steps.

For most of the history of independent India and Pakistan, the relations have never been smooth. Both the countries view their past, present and future differently at times bordering contradiction and antagonism. The issue of Kashmir, which cropped up at the time of independence of the Indian subcontinent and which coloured most of the bilateral relations is a prominent crucible of these differences. Kashmir has always been a bone of contention between the two neighbours. Some of the recent developments in the undivided Kashmir bring to fore the uneasy nature of regional dynamics in the Indian subcontinent. Pakistan-China agreement to develop hydroelectric project at Bunji in the Kashmir currently under the control of Pakistan and India's objection to Pakistan's granting of an ambiguous autonomous status to Gilgit-Baltistan areas of Kashmir indicate the troubled nature of politics in the region.

The agreement to build the dam was reached during Pakistan President Asif Ali Zardari's visit to China from 21-24 August 2009. As per the agreement both the countries will develop the hydroelectric project in the region of Astore district to generate about 7000 MW of electricity. On 11 September 2009 India officially lodged a protest by summoning the Deputy High Commissioner of Pakistan and also ordered its embassy in Islamabad to protest against the deal. India's argument against the deal is mainly two-fold. First, the region is legally not part of Pakistan. Even if Pakistan rejects India's claim that it is not part of territory of

India, the UN has labelled the territory disputed. Can then China and Pakistan build the dam in a disputed area? Second, it is a matter which concerns not only Pakistan but also India. Pakistan rejects India's protests on the ground that India has no *locus standi* on the matter, and it is going ahead to build the dam. In an agreement in 1963 Pakistan ceded more than 5000 sq km of area of Kashmir to China.

India has also strongly objected Pakistan's Gilgit-Baltistan Empowerment and Self-Governance Order 2009 which provides autonomy to Gilgit-Baltistan areas of Kashmir. India has called the move a sham made to avoid the real issue and lodged official protests. Pakistan has reiterated the same argument that India has no *locus standi* on this matter. The regional dynamics of South Asia too have a role to play in shaping India-Pakistan relations. Afghanistan has emerged a crucial factor in regional rivalry. Its re-emergence in international scene after the 9/11 has sharpened the contours of rivalry. Pakistan sees the region north-west to its territory as its natural zone of influence in which its rival India has little or no role, while India perceives the developments in the region through the prism of its national interests and aims at playing an important role in its reconstruction. The attack on Safi Landmark hotel in Afghanistan leading to death of nine Indians on the very next day of the meeting of the foreign secretaries in February 2010 indicates that there are elements which are not happy at the idea of revival of dialogue between India and Pakistan.

As soon as the meeting was scheduled the difference over the agenda came to forefront. The Indian argument that Pakistan must do more to bring the culprits of Mumbai attack to justice was matched by Pakistan insistence that Kashmir must be discussed in the meeting. The divergent positions have surfaced several times with Indian official position being Pakistan must first curb terrorism targeted towards India from its soil, stop infiltration in the Indian side of Kashmir, before other issues can surface in the dialogue framework. Pakistan has argued that India must discuss the issue of Kashmir, the most contentious one, and other issues like water and Sir Creek need to be resolved before dialogue in other areas. The rigid positions make the rules of the game almost ineffectual. The press conferences aftermath of the meeting brought the acute differences in open. Indian foreign secretary claimed that the talks primarily focused on curbing terrorism from Pak soil. India also gave Pakistan three dossiers for taking action against Hafeez Saeed and others like Illyas Kashmiri, and two serving Pak army officers; all having role in 26/11 Mumbai attack. Pakistan foreign secretary on the other hand claimed that Kashmir was discussed at length in the meeting.

Pakistan also rejected the dossiers and stated these are not evidence but 'literature.' Pakistan foreign secretary during interaction with media also declared Pak policy, 'we do not like being sermoned on terrorism.' Attempts at scoring brownie points over each other, rather than looking at broader objectives of peace, stability and development of the region as a whole, have certainly emerged as the roadblock in the achievement of peace between the two neighbours.

The composite dialogue process that commenced between the two countries in 2004 and was then called 'irreversible' due to its potential became 'non existent' after the Mumbai attack. Since February 2010 when direct official talks started between India and Pakistan after a gap of about one and a half year, hopes have gathered momentum among the civil society members who love peace and stability that something positive will come out gradually. The meeting of prime ministers of both the countries in the Bhutanese capital Thimpu in April 2010 further increased the peace constituency and raised the hopes. Both the prime ministers emphasized on the initiatives to bridge 'trust deficit' between the two countries. Prime Minister Singh of India, known for his peace overtures to Pakistan despite criticism from sections at home, promised to 'walk extra mile' to promote friendly relations with Pakistan. The Indian leadership too is optimistic that peace and dialogue is the only way forward to resolve the contentious issues. The point that needs emphasis is: how far the dialogue will continue without any substantive outcome?

Mere exercise in dialogue without breaking the trust deficit will lead nowhere but ensconce the radical spirit that all these exercises are niceties in vain and these are ploys to divert attention from core issues, and the only way to solve the issues is war and violence. Besides, the patience of the civil society in both the countries may wear thin in passing days, which may give rise to pessimism that nothing positive will happen in bilateral relations and the political leaders are at best can fix dates for dialogue, but without any substantial result. Such a development will be precarious as it will put the framework and the spirit behind the composite dialogue into jeopardy, and goad extremist elements into action.

The meetings at their face value may be called a 'disappointment,' 'meaningless' or 'old story,' but certainly they put the radical constituents in discomfiture. These elements feed on tensions and violence. Instead of hoping for miracles, India and Pakistan need to continuously take these small but significant steps, towards alienating the radical constituents and building peace in the region. Lack of progress in bringing to book the culprits of the Mumbai attack orchestrated from the Pak soil has significantly contributed to the tense nature of the relations. To add spice to these developments, former Pak President Pervez Musharraf in an interview on 14 September 2009 admitted Pakistan has diverted aid meant for fighting terrorism and for socio-economic development to building weapons to fight adversaries, including India. [24] India has strongly protested against this diversion and appealed to the US to rethink about its strategy of providing aid to Pakistan.

India has engaged Pakistan after the Mumbai attack in contrast to the majority of public opinion disfavouring it, but as the foreign policy makers in New Delhi understand there is no alternative to constructive engagement to resolve the contentious issues. Finding a middle ground in which both the parties can engage with confidence, trust, and bargain with a political will to look for practical compromises may appear difficult but attainable. The case of India-Pakistan relations is complicated despite both countries sharing many commonalities. It is impossible to change neighbours and also it is almost impossible to resolve the issues by military means in the post-cold war world order. Hence, the best way to resolve contentious issues is dialogue and deliberation.

Transcending Conflict in Kashmir

Barack Obama as President-elect in his first interview on 4 November 2008 envisaged Kashmir issue as one of his policy initiatives in South Asia. He envisaged of sending a special envoy to South Asia to foster resolve the Kashmir issue. His post-electoral statement to the effect that the US will be interested in resolving the Kashmir issue raised apprehension about US intervention in Kashmir. Obama's argument in bringing the Kashmir issue to the forefront appears two fold. For India he would say, "You guys are on the brink of being an economic superpower, why do you want to keep on messing with this?" For Pakistan he would suggest, "Look at India and what they are doing, why do you want to keep being bogged down with this particularly at a time where the biggest threat now is coming from the Afghan border?" [25] A fine argument it seems, but the complexities seem too stringent.

In the Indian state of Jammu and Kashmir (J&K) some separatists with their base confined only to the Kashmir valley welcomed the Obama plan with open arms. They also expressed strong desire for the reopening of the possibility of the UN mediation on the issue. Indian position being no third party mediation on the Kashmir issue, understandably there was uproar against Obama's statement. What needs emphasis is the long pending issue of Kashmir need serious attempts for resolution. Kashmir needs an early solution for more than one reason. The conflict has caused heavy damage to the common people in both material and moral terms, and spilled innocent blood. Its costs on public exchequer of both India and Pakistan are too high. As per a study made by *Strategic Foresight Group* in 2006, from 1989 to 2002, over 1,151 government buildings, 643 educational buildings, 11 hospitals, 337 bridges, 10729 private houses and 1,953 shops have been gutted in some 5,268 attacks on infrastructure in J&K. [26]

The enormity of economic damage caused due to devastation of such magnitude can be gauged by the fact that the damage till December 1996 cost approximately INR 4 billion. The Census of India 2001 put forward that the rate of employment has decreased in J&K after the violence became a norm of everyday life in late 1980s. One of the reasons terrorist organizations such as HM, LeT and JeM have been able to recruit large numbers despite popular disillusionment with violence is that they offer the opportunity to earn living. The local authorities claim 'young impressionable local boys are being lured by militants for money'. The people of the region long for peace. Since India is set to play an effective role outside the South Asian region, the conflict should not be an obstacle against its rise as a global power.

The scepticism regarding the solution of the Kashmir issue gets heightened due to the following factors. First, though violence has gone down in the region, it has not totally died down. Second, the intransigence on part of both the countries still remains unchanged. India holds that the whole undivided Kashmir is its integral part and Pakistan supports the ideology of 'Kashmir *banega* Pakistan'. Third, the anti-terrorism meetings between the two countries brought no meaningful results. But, it would be both unwise to say Indo-Pak relations are a non-starter. Since 2003, there is a sea change on this issue. Whether it is the opening of the LOC or allowing the local people to meet their relatives on either side, or mooting of the ideas of demilitarization, these are definite indicators that peace process is moving in a steady manner, though slow. The peace process till the Mumbai terror attack of November

2008 could achieve tangible results, thus earning the tag 'irreversible.'

Taking into account the complexities involved, it is natural that the process towards the resolution of the vexed issue will take some time. But, the common realization in the recent years that violence cannot bring any solution to the issue is no doubt a grand achievement in itself. In this context, the speech of Pervez Musharraf at Rawalpindi is noteworthy. During the press conference on 3 February 2007, General Musharraf categorically decried violent elements as a major obstacle in the peace process. To quote him, "We cannot take people on board who believe in confrontation and who think that only militancy solves the problem." [27] The General's statement reflected the change in the mood in Pakistan's politicians. However, as the later developments indicate it is naïve to expect that violence will end soon, and all the violent organizations in Pakistan and its controlled territories will close their shops at least in near future. There are complexities involved in the issue and politicking makes the issue further complex. The former of Chief Justice of 'Azad Kashmir', a part of Pakistan controlled Kashmir, Abdul Majeed Mallick told the author that the vested interests, which he derisively called mafia, have vested interest in the continuation of the conflict and are actually spoiling the genuine interests of the Kashmiri people. [28]

Both the countries need to bring genuine democracy in their parts of Kashmir. The incidents of fake encounters show the human rights situation in Indian part of Kashmir in a poor light. The situation is far worse in Pakistan controlled Kashmir. Terrorist violence must end because only in an atmosphere of peace the *vox populi* can find its utterance. The environment of peace must be further strengthened by adopting substantial measures. There is enormous scope for cooperation in the region. All Intra-Kashmir routes need to be opened.

Other options such as troop reduction, joint management

(to begin with it can be applied to tourism and environment) can be tried. India can take initiatives towards this direction in order to rise beyond the conflict with Pakistan and play a dynamic role in the global stage. Whether it is Indian side or Pakistan side of Kashmir, the people must be given right to raise their voices without any hindrance. It is the people who can better decide their future. For India, engaging people of J&K on the one hand and Islamabad on the other hand is crucial for a durable peace in the region. Of late India has realized that involving people is crucial and a series of steps have been taken by the Indian government in this context.

Involving People

India convened a meeting of the people of J&K on 24 April 2007 to have dialogue in what is famously called round table conference. It was the third such conference. The main agenda of the conference was to discuss the reports presented by the four working groups established in the last RTC in Srinagar in May 2006. While the first working group focused on Confidence Building Measures, the second one focused on strengthening relations across LOC, the third group dealt with economic development of the state, the fourth working group aimed at providing good governance to people. The fifth working group on centre-state relations had not submitted its report till then. The recommendations made by the four working groups came up for discussions during the third round table. The RTC gave in principle endorsement to the approach suggested by the working group on CBMs across segments in J&K: strengthening human rights protection and improving relief and rehabilitation of widows, orphans and other victims of violence.

The roundtable also endorsed the recommendation of group two to further promote people-to-people contacts and trade and commerce across LOC and streamline these processes. It also decided to expand these measures in tourism and other spheres of life. The roundtable approved the suggestions of the group three on balanced economic development of different regions of J&K and asked the central and state governments to take steps to carry them forward. It also backed the recommendations of the group four on good governance and asked the state government to bring greater transparency, efficiency and accountability in the process of governance.

The Indian prime minister addressed the meeting and called for the establishment of *naya* (new) Jammu, Kashmir and Ladakh (these three entities represent three distinct regions of Jammu and Kashmir). He announced setting up of a standing committee and a monitoring mechanism to ensure speedy implementation of decisions for benefit of the state. Seeking to reach out to the 'hearts and minds' of the people of the state, the prime minister expressed concern over human rights violations and promised to take steps to minimize these violations. India asked the security forces to carry out their 'difficult tasks in a humane manner.' It appeared New Delhi increasingly realized the need to apply a 'soothing balm' on the scars left by violence to make a new beginning. One of the important messages in the Prime Ministers' speech was related to violence in the state.

His speech could be termed a reply to the ongoing debate on demilitarization of the state. The Indian leader emphasized that army is required in case of emergency situation. He emphasized that development and welfare of the people can be achieved faster in a peaceful environment. Singh revealed during address to the conference his vision for India and South Asia that is linked to 'reconciliation with Pakistan'. Noting two dimensions to the problems of J&K- internal and external- the latter involving Indo-Pak relations, Manmohan Singh said "it is our intention and sincere desire to advance on both fronts towards resolving problems through a process of dialogue." [29] The prime minister expressed concern that "these efforts will not be fruitful unless a peaceful environment is created through honouring of commitments made, in letter and spirit, to curb terrorist activities," apparently referring to Pakistan's promise in this regard made in 2004. The RTC emerged one of most viable forum for intra-J&K dialogue as well as that between Srinagar and New Delhi. The governments have, especially after 2003, taken a people-centric approach to the resolution of the Kashmir issue.

The opening of the routes across LOC is a case in point. However, it must be admitted that such exercises are profitable in long-term, though in short-term they may seem confusing. It may be prudent in the current scenario to achieve peace in pieces rather than expecting miracles to bring permanent peace to the troubled region.

Elections in J&K

The seven-phase elections to 87-seated J&K assembly starting on 17 November 2008 and ending on 24 December 2008 marked a tectonic shift on conflict and peace discourse in South Asia owing primarily to three factors. The separatists lost much of their sheen as the voters despite the poll boycott calls broke the past record of participation as the voter participation percentage at 63 percent surpassed the previous records for two decades. Second, the voters were not subdued by grandiose calls for 'azadi' (freedom) or 'right to self-determination' but were concerned with the issues of common concern such as road, electricity and water. Third, the elections took place amidst the heightened Indo-Pak tensions aftermath the Mumbai terror attack in November 2008. The uncertain atmosphere did not deter the spirit of the people of Kashmir to show impressive sign of activism in participating in the elections enthusiastically. The election conduct as well as massive participation came as a surprise not only to the separatists but also to New Delhi.

Nobody envisaged a peaceful election in J&K, especially after the Amarnath Shrine Board controversy which erupted in July 2008 and engulfed the whole state, leading to death of about 50 people. This controversy had further ensconced the secessionist sentiment in the valley, spearheaded by the Hurriyat leaders with active support from across the border. Some analysts might argue the huge presence of army and security forces and house arrest of some of the prominent separatist leaders led to smooth conduct of elections. But this argument does not bear much weight in view of the fact that despite the same arrangements the voter participation in 2002 elections was much lower particularly in the Kashmir valley, the centre for violence. This time over 13,00,000 more electors voted as compared to 2002 polls. In Srinagar, considered to be stronghold of separatists, 1,11,456 votes were polled in all eight segments which is 400 percent higher than 30,647 votes registered in 2002.

The reason behind the massive electoral participation must be searched elsewhere. The people are fed up with 'azadi' slogans which are much of rhetoric value and less of substance. Besides, the separatist promises for the last two decades have not brought any economic development, but only penury, death and destruction. The people too are fed up with the separatist approach towards conflict resolution which is dominated by political overtones. Another factor that has enforced the voter sentiment in democratic process is that the last five years has almost been peaceful in J&K due to Indo-Pak dialogue. The CBMs in terms of opening intra-Kashmir Srinagar-Muzaffarabad and Poonch-Rawalakote roads in April 2005 and June 2006 respectively, allowing divided families to meet, and also opening the routes for trade, were sure bulwarks for motivating people to shun violence and adopt the path of peace for resolution of the conflict. The separatist propaganda could have borne much value in the heydays of militancy in late 1980s and early 1990s, but in the era of globalization and diplomacy, it becomes difficult to sustain the secessionist agenda for long. Probably, this explains well the rationale behind the massive participation of people despite the separatist calls for boycott. The separatists are much bemused with the elections and are searching for alternative strategies to highlight their agenda.

It is premature to say that permanent peace has dawned in Kashmir. But surely this is a good beginning towards conflict resolution. Perched between three nuclear powers India, Pakistan and China the Kashmir is really a difficult issue to resolve. The past capital of animosity and hatred may take a longer cue to dissipate. There may be peace within J&K that is in Indian side, but any conflagration at border with Pakistan may reinforce the old agents of religious extremism and terrorism. Hence, the onus lie on the elected government in J&K how to manage the affairs of the public, rein in the secessionist sentiments, and assuage the past suffering of the people. The economic formula laced with humanitarian dimensions need to be applied to J&K. Also, how India and Pakistan deal with each other will have its bearing on Kashmir. It is a known fact that the Kashmir under Pakistan's control has sheltered many radical and terrorist organizations, and the terrorist conglomerate United Jihad Council has its head office in Muzaffarabad, the capital of Kashmir under its control. Any war in and over Kashmir will destroy not only the positive outcomes achieved so far, but will also open up the prospect of nuclear confrontation in South Asia, bringing power rivalry in South Asia, further adding to protracted nature of the conflict with larger implications for the region as well as the world.

References
1. For the text of the Prime Minister's speech see, http://pmindia.nic.in/speech/content.asp?id=808.
2. Rajat Pandit, "N-Submarine to Give India Crucial Third Leg of Nuke Triad," *The Times of India*, 27 July 2009.
3. Ibid.
4. http://news.bbc.co.uk/2/hi/7679818.stm.
5. *The Economic Times*, 24 October 2008.
6. For an analysis on India's energy security see, Debidatta Aurobinda Mahapatra, "India's Energy Security and Russia," *World Focus*, vol. 29, no. 8, August 2008, pp. 307-310.
7. *The Economic Times*, 11 May 2008.
8. "Response of Official Spokesperson of the Ministry of External

Affairs to questions on news report regarding fuel supply to Tarapur nuclear plant by Russia," 14 March 2006, http://www.indianembassy.org/prdetail935/--percent09--response-of-official-spokesperson-of-the-ministry-of-external-affairs-to-questions-on-news-report-regarding-fuel-supply-to-tarapur-nuclear-plant-by-russia.

9. Michael Heath, "India Rejects U.S. 'Guidance' on Visit by Iran's Ahmadinejad," http://www.bloomberg.com/apps/news?pid=newsarchive&sid=a eaD3RxLvlTQ&refer=india.

10. Ibid.

11. The phrase is taken from an article by Jagdish Bhagwati. See Jagdish Bhagwati, "The Diminished Giant Syndrome: How Declinism Drives Trade Policy," *Foreign Affairs*, vol. 72, no. 2, 1993, pp. 22-26.

12. http://smetimes.tradeindia.com/smetimes/news/indian-economy-news/2009/Jun/22/indo-us-trade-can-reach-320-bn-by-2018-cii10025.html.

13. "India, U.S. Seek to Bridge Prickly Gaps in Ties," http://www.reuters.com/article/idUSTRE64U0L920100531?type =politicsNews.

14. Roy Allison, *The Soviet Union and the Strategy of Non-alignment in the Third World* (Cambridge: Cambridge University Press, 1988).

15. For the text of the communiqué see *Mainstream*, vol. 33, no.10, 28 December 1991, p. 31.

16. For a comparison of conflicts in Kashmir and Chechnya see, Debidatta Aurobinda Mahapatra and Seema Shekhawat, *Conflict in Kashmir and Chechnya: Political and Humanitarian Dimensions* (New Delhi: Lancer's Publishers, 2007).

17. *The Financial Express*, 13 November 2007.

18. "Indian Team to Visit Russia to Break Deadlock on Gorshkov," http://indiatoday.intoday.in/site/Story/4165/LATEST percent20HEADLINES/Indian+team+to+visit+Russia+to+break +deadlock+on+Gorshkov.html.

19. Surya Gangadharan, "India to Clinch N-deal with Russia during PM's Trip," http://ibnlive.in.com/news/india-to-clinch-ndeal-with-russia-during-pms-trip/106608-3.html.

20. *Indian Express*, 30 March 2008.

21. "Chinese Checkers," *Times of India*, 22 May 2009.

22. "Hu: China Would Never Seek Hegemony,"
    http://www.bjreview.com.cn/quotes/txt/2009-
    04/23/content_192517.htm.
23. The text of the joint statement is available at
    http://www.hindu.com/nic/indopak.htm.
24. "Musharraf Admits US Aid Diverted,"
    http://news.bbc.co.uk/2/hi/8254360.stm.
25. Bobby Ghosh, "Will Kashmir Be an Obama Foreign Policy
    Focus?,"
    http://www.time.com/time/world/article/0,8599,1874627,00.htm
26. For a detail analysis of costs of the conflict and efforts at
    economic reconstruction see, Debidatta Aurobinda Mahapatra
    and Seema Shekhawat, "The Peace Process and Prospects for
    Economic Reconstruction in Kashmir," *Peace & Conflict
    Review* (United Nations University of Peace, San Jose), vol. 3,
    no. 1, Fall 2008, pp. 1-17.
27. *Daily Excelsior*, 7 February 2004.
28. Personal Interview, 6 August 2005.
29. Quoted in Debidatta Aurobinda Mahapatra and Seema
    Shekhawat, *Kashmir Across LOC* (New Delhi: Gyan Publishing
    House, 2008), p. 224. Chapter 8 of the book titled "Intra-
    Kashmir Dialogue: Problems and Prospects" (pp. 219-242)
    offers a critical analysis of the dialogue process in Kashmir.

8

Conclusion

Any evolving world order must in its core have an eclectic approach governing interstate relations and confronting challenges emerging out of the complex web of these relations, while according states big or small, developed or developing equal voice in the global decision making process. The global problems such as climate change, terrorism and epidemics like swine flu preclude prospects of getting resolved with wherewithal of a particular state. Hence, the emphasis that states must discard narrow confinements of rigid thinking and think global assumes increasing significance in the post-cold war world. The 'postness' of the post-cold war world which is so far devoid of any global architecture to govern the relations among nations has in its core negative obliteration or positive transcendence of the existing mechanisms for world peace and security. The world has become truly global with new means of communication and myriad interactions among the people guiding towards ideal human unity transcending national peculiarities. The two factors, i.e. global imperative towards unity among nations and national assertion at the cost of international peace and security can not run parallel or work simultaneously as they embody contrary forces. They need to be reconciled or transcended in a wider framework of ideal human unity.

The post-cold war developments indicate the current state system and its mechanisms have either failed to live up to the expectations or been outdated to cope with new challenges. International peace and stability can not be achieved by mere mechanical coming together of the states but by understanding and feeling the urge from within for the necessity of a world union. Sri Aurobindo argues that this feeling is inherent in the consciousness of every nation but to identify with this consciousness nations must transcend the confinements of narrow national 'ego' which leads to either aggressive nationalism or expansive imperialism found in varied forms in the conduct of nations. Developments in West Asia or in Afghanistan, or the Iran issue or the North Korean crisis, or the divergence of perceptions in tackling global issues like climate change and terrorism, the indicator nonetheless has been that plurality of the nations have identified their interests with crude realism. The religion of humanity which in its centre cherishes the principles of liberty, equality and fraternity, which nations in their policies at home implement or endeavour to implement, need to be widened to the international sphere and only then complicated issues can be resolved in a non-zero sum framework.

The evolutionary urge in the global scheme of things points towards culmination of state system into ideal human unity. Starting from the very evolution of human society from tribe, clan, village, and further towards state, the evolutionary phenomenon cannot stop at the formulations like state and nation in their present formulations as in their very core, in their very consciousness they indicate a better coming of nations together in the spirit of fraternity. In the Hegelian formulation state may be march of God on earth but the march has not reached its zenith and it is still in a transitory phase, or what Einstein says, in another context, it represents 'transitional system towards the final goal.' Any framework of ideal human unity will neither obliterate nor negate the existing state system; rather it will bring to the fullest the richness of each nation-state in a harmonious framework. But this can be possible in a framework in which three supreme values: liberty, equality and fraternity can coexist in harmony and this can be materialized when the nation-states transcend narrow confinements reflected in aggressive ideologies, policies and practices.

Not that there have not been attempts to bring international order and stability by devising global mechanisms like the

League of Nations and the United Nations. These mechanisms at best represented a large number of nations who came together by the force of the prevailing situation without shedding the cocoon of national ego reflected in frequent violations of principles of these bodies and in infusing in these an element of oligarchy. The urge of the parliament of world religions in 1993 to adopt 'Golden Rule' in its positive and negative dimensions can work as an effective guideline if the nations follow it despite differences. This rule, shared by all great religious traditions, when followed by the states will help in the evolution of a global ethic in the post-cold war multipolar world without compromise of national interests but their elevation to a higher pedestal where peace, development and harmony will be core principles. The ideal human unity among nation-states will bring them on a common platform to confront global challenges.

Turmoil in various trouble spots like the Balkans or the Trans-Caucasus or Afghanistan will then be subject to this Golden Rule, and they will be looked not as disparate events but as issues affecting the scales of balance in international relations that need to be resolved collectively. The conflicts and conflicting interests in various parts of the world appeared more troublesome with the states following not Golden Rule but crude realism inflated by national ego thus dividing the nations of the globe, rather than bringing them together. Though the Berlin wall collapsed and the cold war ended two decades ago leading to end of ideological and super power rivalry, it appeared history did not end nor there was victory of liberal ideas as the challenges confronting the world emerged manifold not comprehended earlier.

The post-cold war world witnessed robust signs towards emergence of multiple aspirations to reinforce the idea 'universe is a pluriverse,' but this emergence is not without its inherent weakness. Unless a larger vision dawns on the nation-states and their leaderships, the developments which at present appear sanguine will degenerate into static chauvinism reflected in aggressive policies thus bringing in their trail a plethora of new problems while leaving the current ones unaddressed. The emergence of BRIC and the rising assertion of G-20 can be seen as sanguine developments as they emphasize on the prospects of accommodation and appreciation between diverse powers, but a closer analysis of their functioning shows these bodies are largely obstructed in their functioning due to contradictory aspirations of the members. Similarly, Barack Obama's call for friendly relations with Muslim nations or his resetting button may be seen in the spirit of ideal human unity, but how far these grand formulations will translate into practice and how far they will be received by other powers in the complex state system will determine the scale of things in international relations. This complexity of working of states is well reflected in the Afghanistan situation in which despite repeated invocation to cooperation among regional and international powers the situation appears grim in the region with the extremist threat looming large.

Multipolarism has become the emerging theme in international politics with its varied hues. The future of the world will be multipolar as the post-cold war world abhors a unipolar structure. It is still unclear what shape the future of the world will exactly take. However, in this evolving order, a new approach bereft of antagonism and violence is the imperative to guide bilateral and multilateral relations. The wider context is not whether the world is 'uni' or 'multi' polar in its evolution after the cold war ended, but the issues and challenges that plagued the world in the past still hunt the prevailing world order. It is true that a global system which accommodates plural centres of power with diverse aspirations can better represent the complex interests of nation-states, but it no way can guarantee world peace and stability. Certainly one power or a group of powers in the style of a hierarchical system which the world has already experienced in varying fashions, and which is definitely worse than multiple centres of powers that can work as balancing factor against each other, but a multipolar system does not guarantee effective dealing with international issues.

The rise of Asia in the 21st century is an inevitability to contend with. How far the rising powers China and India will collaborate or dither in tackling common issues of bilateral as well as global importance will significantly determine the shape of international politics. China's 'peaceful rise' and policies like 'harmonious seas' have been viewed by plurality of states with apprehension. The lack of openness in political system but open economic system has created a kind of imbalance between polity and economy which is apprehended to widen further unless the Chinese leadership take measures to bridge the imbalance between the two. Besides, China's policies towards neighbours and various international issues have given rise to apprehension that the Chinese superpower will likely be an 'irresponsible superpower.'

However, the rise of China with its old civilization, its ethics steeped in tradition and strong centralized political leadership is an inevitability which can not be ignored. India lags far behind China in terms of economic growth, which is further complicated by its political system plagued by myriad incongruities. However, its non-antagonistic postures, democratic polity and decision making process and friendly relations with diverse powers have led to shedding of the 'suspicion factor' which is characteristic in the case of China.

The idealism in India's foreign policy does not shun pragmatism while confronting various issues rather the overarching framework steeped in Indian tradition of non-antagonism and non-violence is predicated on a harmonious blending of the two. India has in its core *vasudhiava kutumbakam* (the world is but one family). This spirit of world unity guided India's foreign policy and concerns while dealing with international issues like nuclear disarmament, climate change or restructuring of world bodies. India's non-antagonistic national aspirations in essence have not negated imperatives of international peace and harmony. However, besides building a strong, vibrant, and inclusive polity and economy at home, India must shed symbolism and widen the circles of its policies by nurturing and galvanizing talent and resources for the task.

The volatility of South Asian region has come to sharp focus in the post-cold war situation. The region passed through dramatic upheavals owing to diverse factors such as the legitimacy crisis, incongruity between ethnic aspirations and national sovereignty, nation building travails and religious fundamentalism and terrorism. The two major players in the region India and Pakistan often perceive each other's interests inimical to each other. As reflected in the post-Mumbai attack discourse the distrust seems to have widened, making prospects of amity and friendship further distant. The exchanges at times land in acrimony, clear markers of national ego and chauvinism. Many of the states in the South Asian region still pass through the nation building process. This weakness enmeshed with an asymmetric congregation of power both hard and soft at times vault these nations to the height of national chauvinism and aggressiveness. The elements of religious fundamentalism and terrorism could not have become so strong and lethal in parts of the region without the collusion of state mechanism. The results are quite perceptible chaos, instability, terrorist violence, wars and proxy wars.

The island state of Sri Lanka passed through violent turmoil in the recent past mainly owing to incongruities between aspirations of the minorities and the unitary state. The apparent end of the Tamil Tigers may have brought succor to the Sinhalese dominated power centre but any sustained negligence of rehabilitation, reconciliation and reintegration issues may rekindle ethnic violence with renewed vigour. Whether the Bangladesh mutiny, the Maoist crisis in Nepal, the rise of Taliban in Afghanistan and Pakistan, in all these scenarios the fragile nation building process has become evident.

Among the global challenges that has come to stark appearance in the past decade aftermath of the 2001 attack in the US is the menace of terrorism. How far does religion play a role to motivate the perpetrators to indulge in violence is a matter of debate, but increasing use of terrorism as a method to redress grievances can never be ignored. Theories are in circulation that it is the clash among values represented by different religious systems or the very rigidity and fundamentalist nature of a particular religion that has led to the emergence of the global terror scare with horrendous consequences. Religion which etymologically means 'to reconnect' implies a kind of binding together or assimilating together with a higher imperative that never leads to violence or destruction but building together or developing together in a spirit of harmony. Religion in its true spirit implies nobler values of human nature and their realization in daily conduct. In the Gandhian aphorism 'all religions are like flowers in a garden.' It is the debasement of religion and its invocation to the followers for narrow interests that put the normal human equations in jeopardy.

The Deobond School in 2008 struck the right chord in issuing a diktat negating all forms of violence and terrorism in the name of religion. The school minced no words in criticizing the perpetrators of violence in the name of religion. Perhaps the role of religious heads has never been felt so acutely as in the post-cold war world to guide the misguided to follow the true spirit of religion. States must too play their part in promoting nobler elements of religion. The subtler dimension of the religion must be complemented by means of development and freedom as poverty and unemployment work as deadly combination to motivate the disgruntled youth to join radical movements. The nation-states must shoulder responsibilities and play their part to provide development and freedom to citizens at home while transcending national egos in the conduct of international relations towards realization of the ideal human unity.

Index

Index

Karakoram Highway, 33,
   199
Kargil, 182
Kashmir, 36, 43, 67, 96,
   136, 181, 208, 216
Kosovo, 21, 28, 65

L
L-20, 12, 13
Lashkar-e-Toiba (LeT), 94,
   117
Liberation Tigers of Tamil
   Elam (LTTE), 154,
   201
Line of Control (LOC),
   115
London Conference, 22, 56
Luguvoi Controversy, 24,
   28, 48

M
Mauritius, 202
Multipolarism, 21, 25
Mumbai, 89, 92, 95, 125,
   160, 193, 204
Myanmar, 128, 202

N
Nadwatul Ulama, 90
Nagorno Karabakh, 42, 43,
   67
Nepal, 125, 127, 146, 226
New Great Game, 22, 50,
   62, 139
Non-aligned Movement
   (NAM), 186

North Caucasus, 27, 95,
   105
North Korea, 24, 46, 61
Nuclear Disarmament, 45,
   175, 182, 225
Nuclear Suppliers Group
   (NSG), 17

O
Office for the Coordination
   of Humanitarian
   Affairs (OCHA), 135
Organization of Petroleum
   Exporting Countries
   (OPEC), 28

P
Pakistan, 33, 38, 50, 55,
   93, 113, 141, 182, 207
Panchsheel Agreement,
   174, 196
Piracy, 73, 74

R
Rupee-Reactor Syndrome,
   188, 189
Russia, 22, 27, 34, 50, 158,
   186

S
Saudi Arabia, 57, 160
Second World War, 5, 9,
   79, 188
Shanghai Cooperation
   Organization   (SCO),
   44